THINKING
ABOUT
TOMORROW

THINKING ABOUT TOMORROW

REINVENTING YOURSELF AT MIDLIFE

by SUSAN CRANDELL

WARNER
WELLNESS

NEW YORK   BOSTON

Warner Wellness
Hachette Book Group USA
1271 Avenue of the Americas
New York, NY 10020

Visit our Web site at www.HachetteBookGroupUSA.com.

Warner Wellness is an imprint of Warner Books, Inc.

Printed in the United States of America

First Edition: January 2007
10 9 8 7 6 5 4 3 2 1

Warner Wellness is a trademark of Time Warner Inc. or an affiliated company.
Used under license by Hachette Book Group USA, which is not affiliated with
Time Warner Inc.

Library of Congress Cataloging-in-Publication Data

Crandell, Susan.
    Thinking about tomorrow : reinventing yourself at midlife / Susan Crandell.
  —1st ed.
        p. cm.
    Includes index.
    Summary: "A book about how yesterday's baby boomers are becoming
today's adventurous midlife pioneers, discovering exciting new
opportunities for growth in work, play, family, and happiness, by a
founding editor of MORE magazine."—Provided by the publisher.
    ISBN-13: 978-0-446-57897-4
    ISBN-10: 0-446-57897-5
    1. Middle age—United States. 2. Middle aged persons—Psychology. 3. Middle
aged persons—Conduct of life. 4. Baby boom generation—Psychology.
    5. Baby boom generation—Conduct of life. 6. Self-realization. I. Title.
    HQ1059.4.C73 2007
    305.244—dc22   2006020851

Book design by Charles Sutherland

For Mom and Dad, who invented me,
Stephan, who always makes my world bigger,
and Brook, who reinvented both our lives

Contents

Good-bye, Perfect Job!
Hello, Perfect Life!

"You have the perfect job." That's what someone says to me on a sunny spring morning in New York's Central Park, where we are about to stage the world's first marathon for women over forty. "It must be so much fun being the editor in chief of a magazine." She's right; it is an amazing job, offering tremendous creative freedom. What my colleague doesn't realize is that just a few weeks earlier I quit my job and am now serving out my final few lame-duck weeks. Having reinvented my life, I am living in the tender, scary limbo land between before and after. Her innocent comment sends a chill through me.

The *More* Magazine Marathon is one of the rich rewards of the job I've just given up. The publishing director and I cooked up the concept over cappuccinos one morning a year ago. Now, on an unseasonably balmy March day, the race is turning out to be a huge success, with more than twenty-six hundred women registered to run. Multiple TV crews are here, pointing their cameras at me. For a second, I think, *What on earth have I done?* I have ditched a glamorous job as top editor of *More*, a magazine edited for women in their forties and fifties, a position that had me chatting with Diane Sawyer on national television, lunching with Jamie Lee Curtis, taking a Learjet cross-country with Meryl Streep, and inventing exciting programs like the marathon.

Here's how glamorous my new life will be: I'll make a rapid descent from the top to the bottom of the food chain. As a freelance writer, plankton of the magazine publishing world, I'll be at the beck and call of the very editors who used to call me "boss." I'll give up my power-suit wardrobe to sit at home in a T-shirt and yoga pants, typing away at my laptop. Replacing the Midtown Manhattan skyscrapers outside my office window will be a view of woodchucks waddling around on our lawn. The only place I'll be seeing Meryl or Jamie is on the screen at the local Cineplex.

Hold on, I think, as the race gets under way. *Is it too late to go to my boss and say, "Only joking"?* My stomach clenches as I wonder if I've made the biggest mistake of my life.

That morning in Central Park was neither the first nor the last time I second-guessed my decision to leave the magazine and retool my career. Thank goodness I managed to ignore the panicked chatter in my head and listen to a deeper voice that told me it was time to go. Bailing out of a standard-issue job turned out to be the best career decision I ever made.

Ironically, the very fact that my job was so great made me able to give it up. It was hard to imagine a more desirable job, but I could certainly imagine a better life. Fixing my life didn't mean finding another position; it meant finding a different way to work. I was exhausted by twenty-five years of three-and-a-half-hour daily commutes from my home in the Hudson Highlands to my office in New York City. Too many nights, I lay awake worrying about whether the high-strung A-list celebrity we'd wooed to appear on our cover would throw a tantrum and storm out of the photo shoot. I yearned to spend more time with Steve, my husband of twenty-six years. He'd beat cancer three times, and I didn't want to wake up one morning and realize I'd squandered precious hours I could have spent with him attending some budget meeting. I wanted to be able to knock off work at three on a sunny summer afternoon and jump on my bike.

Three weeks after the marathon, on an overcast Friday in April 2004, I packed up my Palm Pilot and the wallful of model airplanes Steve had built, hugged everybody in sight, and climbed on the train as a commuter for the very last time. There was a tear in my eye, but a gleam there, too. Where would this adventure lead me?

Reinventing Midlife, One Life at a Time

As the 5:46 whisked me north along the Hudson River toward a future that had yet to unfold, I knew one thing: I was in very good company. By quitting my job and revamping my career at fifty-two, I was joining a mass movement of baby boomers who are refusing to go quietly into middle age. Instead of ceding center stage to our kids and letting our own lives wind down, we are making our forties and fifties the most challenging, rewarding years yet.

Following our hearts and acting alone, one by one, across America, we boomers are creating a social revolution that is utterly transforming the concept of midlife. We are having babies, launching businesses, joining the Peace Corps, going back to school.

Along the way, we are reinventing midlife itself. We have reenergized the very words we use to describe ourselves. We're not *middle-aged,* oh no, not us. We're *midlifers,* a slicker, hipper alternative. There is a dawning recognition among us that these are the wonder years, the time when we can finally seek our heart's desire, move to a backbeat that comes straight from our soul.

Seventy-seven million strong, ours is the biggest, richest generation in history, and many of us have more leisure time than ever before. We have more money and better resources to implement our dreams. Most important of all, we know our own minds. We are happier and more confident than we were in our twenties and thirties. We know what we want and we aren't afraid to go after it.

The Good Stuff Is in the Middle

We may not be young, but we sure aren't old. To our happy surprise, we've found ourselves at this magical place in the center of our life span when we're healthy, wealthy (well, at least richer than we've ever been), and wise. At *More,* which was aimed at women in their forties and fifties, we used the Oreo cookie as a metaphor: The good stuff is in the middle. Yes, one day we will face the ravages of aging. But right now, in our middle years, life is sweet with possibilities: We can fulfill long-held dreams, or conjure up brand-new ones. We can travel, learn amazing things, even run marathons.

We're bullish because while we may be teetering at life's midpoint, we feel younger than our age. Many of us are late-blooming athletes, the fittest we've ever been. Ours is the healthiest generation at midlife ever. Heart disease and cancer deaths are down, and we're getting a better handle on how to treat chronic conditions such as diabetes. A record number of us will live to be centenarians. Boomers are rushing to the gym in unprecedented numbers, and we're flooding hiking paths, ski trails, and biking routes.

Our generation has always known how to dream big. In the

1960s, we climbed on buses and headed south to join the fight for civil rights. In the '70s, we formed consciousness-raising groups and battled for women's rights in the workplace. We registered African American voters. We swarmed the Democratic convention to protest the Vietnam War. We stormed corner offices and persuaded corporate America to make room for women executives. In short, we were on the scene at the great social revolutions of the twentieth century.

A New Generation of Life Entrepreneurs

Today we're fomenting another social revolution, the first of the new millennium. This time, it's a quiet revolution, an underground movement. We're not protesting in Washington or legislating change. This time, our activism comes via private rather than public actions—through the life choices we make. We're taking vibrant new directions that say to the world, *We're having the time of our lives!* Our generation is teeming with people who approach their forties and fifties with creativity and courage. These men and women are shining a true entrepreneurial spirit on their lives.

It's a trickle-up revolution, where as life changes multiply, a new credo is spreading. This is our belief:

> *There are no rules for how we behave at forty-two or fifty-nine. We will decide what is right and appropriate for us. We will take chances, we will seek out or create jobs that fulfill us, volunteer work that sustains us, family and friends who nourish us. We are not marching through prepackaged decades, checking them off on some master life list. We are making it up as we go along. Sometimes we will exhibit the playfulness of a twenty-year-old; sometimes, the wisdom of an octogenarian. If we're lucky, occasionally*

both. We are the CEOs of our own lives, the architects of our
future.

That's the sassy, new sky's-the-limit approach to midlife.
After sitting ringside as editor of *More* for six years, watching
the women in our audience experiment with their lives to great
success, I finally found the courage to shake up my own life.
Part of the charter I set for my new career was to look more
deeply into this amazing phenomenon of reinvention.

I resolved to explore this social revolution more fully. I
knew women were becoming the mothers of reinvention. But
were men writing new scripts for themselves, too? I wanted to
find out. Were they boldly launching new lives? The answer is
a resounding yes.

As I talked to men and women across the United States, a
phrase popped into my mind: *Life Entrepreneur.* That's exactly
what these people are, with their heady idea for a richer, fuller
future, and the ingenuity and smarts to pull it off. Stirring together a recipe that reads one part imagination, one part pluck,
they are entrepreneurs playing on the biggest stage of all: their
lives.

Turning the Midlife Crisis on Its Head

The old model was the midlife crisis. You'd turn fifty and start
to panic that more than half of your life was over, but you
hadn't really lived. You'd try a quick fix like buying a Harley or
having an affair. Eventually, when those things didn't satisfy the
craving you felt, you'd come to terms with the fact that the richest part of your life was finished, and settle into your September years.

This new model turns the midlife crisis on its head. The
boomer generation's Life Entrepreneur sees the yearnings and

dissatisfactions of midlife as a call to action rather than a curse. Midlife crisis becomes midlife opportunity. The trigger may still be a feeling that life hasn't measured up to your expectations. But here's the difference: You feel powerful enough to make change happen, to create the fulfilling life that's been bouncing around the back of your brain.

At *More,* I witnessed such success stories time and again. *More* was launched in 1998 to celebrate the new upbeat attitude we were seeing among women in their forties and fifties. We wrote about the gutsy moves they made at midlife—ditching unsatisfying jobs, starting businesses they'd always wanted to run, booking the African safari they'd dreamed of since they were fourth-graders paging through *National Geographic.* We reflected that attitude in our magazine, and readers ate it up. It gave them the courage to pursue their fantasies, and showed them they weren't alone in dreaming big. By the time I left, the circulation had climbed to one million.

I was humbled by the women we were writing about, who had such courage and heart. I remember one story in particular that I told over and over again when I was presenting the editorial concept to advertisers. A successful forty-year-old surgeon in Louisiana was feeling itchy. Her practice just wasn't doing it for her anymore. Then her marriage broke up, and her sister was diagnosed with ovarian cancer. This middle-aged physician's life could have fallen apart. But it didn't. She took an ice-climbing course and declared a new goal—to climb Mount McKinley, North America's highest peak. For a year she trained, ascending stairs over and over again bearing a backpack weighted with wine bottles. Then she headed to Alaska and gave the mountain her best shot. She didn't make it to the top. Was she discouraged because she hadn't achieved her goal? Yes indeed, but that didn't stop her from hatching a new one. She fell in love with Alaska and decided to move there. She landed a job at a clinic in Anchorage with a week-on, week-off work schedule that left her plenty of time to explore the magnificent landscape. A year after her first attempt, she again tackled McKinley. This time, she made the summit. But standing at the top turned out to be just icing. She'd already triumphed by revamping her life.

The thing that made her story stick with me was that this wasn't a buttery-smooth transition. Hers was a tale of lemons-to-lemonade. There were black moments when it would have been easy to retreat, to sit and lick her wounds. But she didn't. Somehow she found the imagination and resourcefulness to envision a new life and then go get it.

Three years after her story ran, I stood before my wonderful staff, many of whom had been with *More* since the magazine's launch, and said: "After six years of publishing reinvention stories, I am becoming one myself. I am leaving the magazine."

When I quit my job, my chief worry was whether my life would ever be as interesting again. I knew I craved more time with family and friends, but would my work be a pallid version of what I'd done before? As I sit here writing, sixteen months after I last reported to a desk job, my life has zoomed off in directions I could not have imagined. I have just returned from a week in Uganda tracking mountain gorillas for a travel article. In two weeks, I'll be helicopter hiking in the Canadian West for another assignment. My earnings may be a fraction of what they were, but I've got a new motto for success: *One-third the money, three times the fun.*

I've always been too tightly wound, an obsessive organizer, a borderline control freak. Now friends tell me they've never seen me so mellow, so stress-free. I can't say I've never had dark days or second thoughts since making the change. But once the initial worries and doubts settled down, I found a level of calm I didn't know my type-A personality was even capable of.

Life Stories That Inspire

I wasn't a natural Life Entrepreneur. Far from it. Risk-averse when it came to my career, I tended to settle into a job, do the best I could, and hope that diligence would be rewarded. As a reinventer, I was a slow learner, a latecomer to the life makeover party. I needed the encouragement of hearing many other reinvention stories before I was able to take the plunge myself. I wasn't as brave as the women we'd written about. But ultimately, by learning from them, I was able to do what they'd done.

That got me thinking about other people like me, men and women who yearned for a different life but were afraid to act, immobilized by what they'd have to give up to get where they wanted to go. Why couldn't I help them the way my job had helped me? I would write a book filled with reinvention success stories, people who'd faced down fears to craft satisfying new lives.

By profiling people who've hurdled the midlife crisis barrier into a bright new future, I hope this book will offer inspiration and resources to people who feel stuck at the starting gate. I'd like to turn midlife crisis victims into Life Entrepreneurs.

When I began researching this book, I thought I had made a huge life change. It sure felt big to me. But when I talked to other reinventers, I realized what small potatoes my own reinvention was. I had stayed in the same profession, simply shifting my role. Other people were making sweeping changes, like the forty-five-year-old man in Louisiana who quit a successful banking career to buy a small-town zoo. Or the woman who began cave diving at forty-two. Or my friends Tina and Steve, who became first-time parents in their fifties.

What I discovered is that life reinvention is like an operation: There is no such thing as minor surgery when it's happening to you. Making the change can bring on turbulent, emotional times. But if you listen to your heart, you'll stay headed in the right direction, toward a fulfilling second act.

I worried whether I could come up with enough good stories for the book. As I began my research, sending query e-mails to colleagues and friends, I discovered that reinventers are everywhere. It truly is a revolution. Almost everyone I asked was either making a life change or knew somebody else who was. This book tells the stories of forty-five of them. You'll notice that unlike many such books, where interviewees hide behind pseudonyms, these people are using their names. They're proud of their lives, and happy to have their stories told. As Susanna Goulder, who transitioned from set designer on *Sex and the City* to pastoral counselor, told me, "My heart gets big and tears come to my eyes when I think of all the pain and struggles, the disappointments, that really were preparing the way for who I am today. I believe that people who listen to their soul's yearnings get empowered in their forties to find a new life—not the life they thought they should live, but the life they truly love to live."

Although reinvention isn't uniquely American, we probably have more passion for it than more traditional cultures that flourish in other parts of the world. Call it the pioneer spirit, or say it's in our DNA, as two psychiatry professors have recently claimed. John D. Gartner of Johns Hopkins Medical School and Peter C. Whybrow of UCLA argue that immigrants, who are gutsy enough to change homelands, carry a gene for risk taking. Both have written books examining the dark side of this lively, competitive spirit, but the silver lining is the willingness to make a big, scary change. I believe we're seeing this gene in action with the midlife changes rippling across America.

The Domino Effect

As I talked to more and more people, a few themes kept coming up. A big one was the power of the September 11 experience. Many people mentioned the terrorist attacks as a motivator for making a big change. On September 11, 2001, the entire nation was reminded how fragile our lives are. As we tried to make sense of the tragedy, men and women across America were turning to each other and saying, "If not now, when?"

Another dynamic I hadn't considered when editing reinvention stories for a women's magazine was the impact on a couple when one of them decided to throw away life's old rules and write a new set. Often it sets the spouse on a path toward his or her own reinvention. When Barbara Wild moved to Boston to pursue a graduate degree, it energized her husband, Michael Nelson, to reevaluate and relaunch his career as a photographer. When Kirk Kvetko quit his job to spend four years exploring other areas of his life before returning to work, it inspired his wife, Colleen, to leave her own job at the peak of her career and reexamine what work really means to her.

There was a domino effect in many reinventers' lives. One reinvention would lead to another. Ellen Delathouder got a face-lift, then found a wonderful new boyfriend. When Jon Weisberg moved to a new city in the West, it motivated him to begin a new sideline career as a teacher and a new avocation as an artist.

Sometimes all it takes to break the inertia of an okay-but-not-outstanding existence is one small step. A little change that feels great can lead to others. So I've included suggestions of modest changes: *Fifty Ways to Jumpstart Your Life: Little Reinventions with Big Payoffs.* They're scattered throughout the book to get you thinking about how to make your life more satisfying or more exciting. Maybe adopting a baby or switching careers is too big a step. Executing the right mini change can make you more comfortable with risk taking, it can give you a chance to test-drive a bigger change, or it can be all you need to do, adding just the right seasoning of novelty to your life.

Some of the men and women in this book moved from one satisfying life to another, morphing from one true expression of themselves to another. For others, it was a matter not of changing but of becoming. At the end of class, my yoga instructor says, "May you become the person you always thought you could be." For some of the people in this book, for the first time in their lives, this is happening for them—on the far side of forty. Whether it's discovering a new path, or finally finding the road you should have been on all along, these Life Entrepreneurs know what's important: The quality of our days is measured by the experience we've accumulated, not the stuff we own. Remember the old joke, "He who dies with the most toys wins"? For these Life Entrepreneurs, it couldn't ring more false.

Doing the reporting for this book has been one of the most pleasurable experiences of my work life. All day, every day, I would talk to people who are optimistic and excited about their future. All of them are smart enough to focus on what they're gaining rather than what they're giving up. Every afternoon, I left the little studio where I work with a smile. I hope I've managed to capture their essence so that readers can feel the same inspiration. I hope their stories make you smile, too. And think about your life.

Are You a Life Entrepreneur? If you're making changes, too, I'd love to hear about them, maybe even tell your story in a future book. You can e-mail me about your reinvention at susancrandell.com.

THINKING
ABOUT
TOMORROW

"If there is a path, it is someone else's path and you are not on the adventure."

—Joseph Campbell

CHAPTER 1

Work That Works for You

THE FIRST GENERATION to go to college en masse, we baby boomers had an unprecedented opportunity to choose rewarding work. So it may seem surprising that at midlife so many of us are dumping career number one and moving on to career number two. Of course, some of this migration can be credited to restlessness: Even in a fulfilling profession, twenty years on the job can ignite a craving for something new. But many of the career changers I've spoken with tell me that their first profession simply never thrilled them.

Problem was, back in our twenties when we were starting out, a lot of us just didn't know how to find work that works for us. I'm a prime example. Like many of my college buddies, I drifted into a profession almost at random. I adored college, but was no student. Thrilled to find myself living on my own for the first time, in a dorm filled with smart, funny women, I majored in friendship, with a minor in jug wine. Remember Almaden? I loved the lazy afternoons when half a dozen of us would gather in someone's room and talk for hours. Or the all-nighters we'd pull, not studying but playing hearts. I knew that when college ended, I would go to work, but somehow I never formed anything remotely resembling a plan. I majored in history, for no reason except that there were some terrific professors in the department.

What Should I Do with My Life?

My senior year, the reality hit—*Ohmigod, I need a job, maybe even a career.* My first impulse was a delaying tactic. I applied to law school. This was less about law—I had only the dimmest idea of what an attorney did all day—than about extending the pleasurable lifestyle that was school. I would have made a terrible lawyer. I aced the English portion of the LSATs and failed miserably at reasoning out the sample legal cases the test presented. This fact, along with my middling GPA—let's say I did a lot worse than Bill Clinton, a little better than George Bush—underwhelmed the three law schools to which I'd applied. I can't say I was crushed; in my heart of hearts I knew law school was a holding action, not a life plan.

A job was inevitable. But which job? On what possible basis would I choose? Like the thousands of other liberal arts majors graduating that year, I had no professional training, nothing that would point me in any direction. My roommate's father said the one thing that gave my search a point of view. Robin's dad was one of the most accomplished people I knew, a senior VP at a big textile manufacturing firm in the South. We were having dinner at their country club one evening after graduation while Robin and I were holed up at her family home in North Carolina, postponing the inevitable. The conversation turned to careers, in a desperate attempt by Robin's parents to jump-start our lives. When her father remarked that his job was routine, I was stunned. The daughter of a small-business owner and a schoolteacher, I had always figured that anybody who had an important, high-paying position like his must rush off to work every morning filled with enthusiasm for the fascinating things he would do that day. But he said that one week was largely like another, his work a matter of making the same kinds of decisions over and over again.

Learn to meditate. Science shows that meditation can boost the immune system and even ward off stress-related illnesses such as heart disease, high blood pressure, and depression. You can find a class at a local yoga school, or try the book *Meditation Made Easy* by Lorin Roche, who has been teaching meditation for three decades.

After that conversation, I had one goal: Don't be bored. I'd been told by my professors that I had some talent for writing, and I knew I loved to read. So I set my sights on a job in magazine publishing, figuring it couldn't become repetitive since there'd be a new issue along every month. And that's largely how it turned out. Every time I edited an article, I learned something new. For me, the creative work never stopped being satisfying. Until I was fifty-two, I never considered any job but magazine editor, and I still haven't considered any industry but publishing.

The Career Ice Age: Before Counselors Walked the Earth

I got lucky with my career choice, but it was really a fluke. When we boomers were in college, nobody was giving us much advice. At my college, career counseling was conducted out of a single office in a building I visited exactly once. Many of us just stumbled into the next phase of our lives. After graduation, a lot of my friends moved to Boston—the next best thing to college is a big college town—and got jobs, whatever was available (one of them, who'd scored 740 on the law boards, handed out pirate garb and gorilla masks at a costume store) and would pay the rent. Nobody was giving us Myers-Briggs personality tests that would reveal what kind of job would play to our strengths. There were no life coaches or self-help books to point the way. We just flailed around. The fortunate few happened upon something they were good at and enjoyed.

Whether we loved our job or hated it, time marched on. Our lives got busy and complicated, rich and full. We married, had babies, and the spotlight shined on our families. We were preoccupied with our relationships, or with bringing up our kids. For many of us, work took a backseat; if it wasn't perfect, the dissatisfaction was relegated to background static that we lived with. Then one morning, we'd wake up and think, *Wait a minute, there's got to be more.* The trigger might be a raise or promotion denied, a landmark birthday or the realization that this life isn't eternal, so we'd better optimize our activities while we're here.

Over the years, the size of the shadow work casts across our lives can make a merely humdrum job seem intolerable. Our generation spends more time working than doing just about anything else. Hours at our desks easily eclipse family time, and unless we're champion sleepers, we probably log more hours at the office—and getting there—than we do in bed. Work occupies a majority share of our days, and yet a surprising number of us are not enchanted with our jobs. When we did a survey at *More* magazine, I was stunned to find that nearly three-quarters of the forty- and fiftysomething women in our upscale, educated audience weren't crazy about what they did for a living. These were people with options, people who'd had the benefit of college and even graduate school, along with a fair share of authority and flexibility in their chosen work. I expected them to be thriving. But the majority were just doing it for the dough. A study by a division of Ajilon Professional Staffing, in Saddle Brook, New Jersey, came to a slightly brighter conclusion, finding that 40 percent of the men and women they surveyed loved their jobs—which still leaves the majority less than enamored.

What's going on? Why isn't work working for us? We were the generation with the education, the opportunity. Did we all choose the wrong profession, or are there other issues at play?

Brave New Idea: Work Should Be Fun

It's a relatively recent concept that work should be fulfilling. In centuries past, most children moved into their parents' profession, whether it was farming, blacksmithing, or running the general store. Children born into work that engaged and satisfied them were lucky indeed. The freedom to choose a career is largely a twentieth-century development, and the thought that work should be rewarding, even fun, is still newer. The idea got traction in 1980 with the publication of the book *Work Redesign,* in which authors Richard Hackman and Greg Oldham maintained that to do a job well, people need to find their work meaningful.

Sometimes it isn't the work itself that disappoints, but the working conditions. Maybe that fourteen-year-old boy wasn't wrong when he dreamed of becoming an architect, but three decades later he finds his workday isn't spent solving design problems and sketching soaring skyscrapers, as he'd imagined. No, his commissions more often run to cookie-cutter-design Chinese restaurants in malls, and he puts in many hours dealing with staffing and budget issues, responding to clients' unrealistic expectations, and juggling an overload of work.

In the past two decades, technology has upped the ante on

time pressure, creating what I call instant-itis. Remember the old Federal Express slogan, "When it absolutely, positively has to get there overnight"? These days, that would be the slow-boat service. Now that we have instant modes of communication, everything must be done instantly. Suddenly, even a fax becomes snail service; you've got to e-mail it, and you've got to e-mail it right now.

To compound the stress, there's no downtime anymore. In a world of beepers and BlackBerries, an increasing number of us are on call twenty-four hours a day, seven days a week. Even doctors, the classic example of "on all the time," unplug when a colleague is covering. In a recent poll of New Year's resolutions, several executives mentioned stepping away from their 24/7 addiction to BlackBerries and Treos. Many of us are asking ourselves: When did we sign up to be available to the office all the time? Wasn't that the deal we struck when we decided to become parents? Why is work suddenly oozing into our family time?

As I talked with boomers who've launched their own businesses, I realized that a big motivation to remake their careers was laying claim to their own time. Some found themselves working longer hours than they had in a corporate job, particularly during their fledgling firm's launch. But it was maximum hours with minimum stress because they approached their tasks with a new mind-set: They were in control, and they could decide when to knock off.

The New York Times reported that Americans now work an additional 172 hours a year, on average, than we did the year I graduated from college, 1973. In a survey by the Families and Work Institute, a nonprofit research group based in New York City, 37 percent of boomers said that they are chronically overworked, almost a third more than other age groups. Experts point to the high-level—and high-stress—jobs boomers are more likely to hold, as well as lifestyle issues we uniquely face, including caring for elderly parents and hosting boomerang kids who have moved back home as adults. Toss a Gen-X boss into the mix, and you've got Excedrin headache number 9-2-5—the overwork special.

What happened to those innocent grammar school dreams, when we couldn't wait to be a firefighter or a nurse or an astronaut? How did work turn into an obligation rather than a joy?

Staging a Second Act That Shines

That question has led an unprecedented number of boomers to remake their work life. Some are launching businesses, some are telecommuting to tame the time crunch, others are boldly moving into new industries, still others are downshifting to part time. Traditionally, your forties and fifties are the decades when you've earned the right to coast a bit, to cut back on your work hours, let the younger go-getters carry the bulk of the load. I remember the early days of my career when the more senior you were, the earlier you left the office at the end of the day. But downsizing and increased productivity demands have canceled all that. Now many boomers are working harder at fifty-six than they did at twenty-six.

There's another factor that makes midlife an ideal time to initiate a big change. With more years of saving behind them, boomers have more resources to cushion a risky career move. Furthermore, with a lightening of day-to-day family responsibilities, they have more time to consider a new direction.

> **Volunteer as a firefighter.** Learn a new skill, make new pals,
> help your community. Need I say more?

Ironically, that very same time-served/money-in-the-bank phenomenon can make it harder to summon the courage to reinvent a career. At this stage, with two or three decades invested in a chosen field, there's a lot at stake. When you're young, it's relatively easy to opt for a big switch. In the 1990s, when the dot-com craze was exploding, I lost several talented young editors to Internet jobs. As one of them said to me, "I may be crazy, but how can I not take this chance at twenty-five, when I'm single and have no family responsibilities? I have no one to answer to but me." For her, the risk didn't feel that big; if she needed to make a U-turn back to magazines, there were a lot of jobs at her level. But for someone in a senior position, the kind you work decades to get, it's a much bigger deal to throw it all over in pursuit of a dream.

Nevertheless, more and more boomers are doing just that, seeking work that really speaks to their soul. In talking with people for this book, over and over I heard them say, "I needed to find something that felt right for me, at the deepest level." For some, discovering work that resonates was possible only now: It had taken them forty or fifty years to truly know themselves. They gloried in their strengths, understood their limitations, had logged enough life experiences to know what would be satisfying.

You Can Go Your Own Way

"My boss is an asshole, but I can work with him because I know him so well." That's the self-deprecating joke Portland, Oregon, native Steve Weiner cracks, describing his feelings about becoming his own boss after twenty-two years of corporate life. But he's utterly serious about the satisfaction of being a small-business owner. The freedom and control are intoxicating, he says; he could never, ever go back.

Steve speaks for a big share of our generation. For us, the urge to launch a business and call our own shots is a powerful motivator. An AARP study found that men and women over age fifty make up 25 percent of the total workforce, but a whopping 40 percent of the self-employed. Among the self-employed one out of three took the plunge after turning fifty. It stands to reason that the urge to be our own bosses should sharpen as we mature and grow accustomed to holding the reins, whether it's bringing up children or taking on more authority at a corporate job. We've tested our ability as decision makers. At midlife, we approach a solo venture with a heightened degree of confidence. Most of us have ridden our share of rough road, and our judgment has been honed by our failures as well as our successes.

Some, like me, may be surprised to find themselves thriving as captain of their own ship. I vowed I would never own a small business, having watched my dad run a company that sold travel trailers and camping supplies with reasonable success but no real joy. By his late fifties, he was so burned out, he retired happily to a series of what he called "nothing jobs"—working on the loading dock of a newspaper company or in the parts department of an automobile dealership—relieved to finally shed the stress of running Crandell Sales.

As a child, seeing him struggle with the anxieties and pressure of business ownership, I knew I wasn't cut out to be an entrepreneur. As an adult, I was grateful for the paycheck that arrived every other week, whether business was good or bad, and I appreciated the corporate health plan and the 401(k) with company-matched contributions. If you had asked me when I was in my thirties whether I'd ever work for myself, I would have said "Hell, no." Then at fifty-two, I became the sole proprietor of another Crandell Sales, with just one product to market—me. Two qualities I share with many of my boomer peers made this improbable shift possible: personal growth and a sizable network of contacts. By my early fifties, I had worked at half a dozen magazines and knew lots of editors to whom I could pitch article ideas. By the same token, I was confident that as a freelance writer, I understood what editors want, having sat so long on the other side of the desk assigning articles.

The intersection of those two priceless commodities—contacts and seasoning—can be a boon to midlifers who are launching businesses in the same arena. Becoming a consultant in your industry is a lot easier than making the leap to a completely different line of work. Even if you're entering a new field, your background can be important. Louisiana resident George Oldenburg is one of the Life Entrepreneurs profiled in this chapter. At first blush, his transition from bank executive to zoo owner at forty-five seems about as radical as a career change can get. But George credits his financial background with helping him manage the annual budget for a highly cyclical business, when the lion's share of revenues flow in during just a few high-season months.

So we come at new occupations with special qualities that help us succeed. Often midlife is the first time we have the wherewithal to start a business, whether it's from an inheritance, a severance package, or a plump 401(k) we're willing to bust. Of course, we're gambling with our futures, and the stakes are higher because we can see the potential infirmities of old age ahead. The new-business owners I've talked with don't deny the risks, but they don't dwell on them either. Like Steve Weiner, they're too busy glorying in being the boss.

Calling a Time-Out

Sometimes job burnout hits so hard, there's nothing to do but remove yourself from the workforce for a while. Once regarded as career suicide, this is now an increasingly common strategy for catching your breath. Some people use their time-out to explore a new path, while others rediscover a passion for their job. The lucky ones work for a company like Nike or Intel that offers paid sabbaticals, or a firm such as Procter & Gamble, which grants the time unpaid. According to a 2005 study from the Society for Human Resource Management, 17 percent of all US companies were offering some kind of extended leave.

In her midforties, Mary Lou Quinlan took a five-week sabbatical from her job running one of the top advertising agencies in New York, and ended up leaving her high-powered position to launch her own boutique ad agency, Just Ask a Woman. She wrote about what she called "my walkabout" for us at *More,* published a book on the subject of sabbaticals, *Time Off for Good Behavior,* and appears as a judge on the reality show *American Inventor.* Another article we published, "Leaving at the Top," profiled powerful women who'd become disenchanted enough to quit. Some of them walked away from the workplace, but most simply took some contemplative time to figure out their next career move. Ann Fudge famously left a top post at Kraft Foods, then two years later returned to the fray as CEO of Young & Rubicam Brands.

For one of the couples I interviewed, Kirk and Colleen Kvetko of Naples, Florida, one sabbatical led to another. Kirk was the first to bail out of a job, leaving a twenty-three-year career at FedEx, worn out from being on call 24/7. He wanted to climb a mountain, compete in triathlons, and play lots and lots of golf. It was four years before someone offered him a position enticing enough to draw him back into the workforce. No sooner was he behind a desk again than Colleen called her own time-out, quitting a big-deal bank job to clear her mind and discover a new path. When she started her sabbatical, her husband wrote Colleen a letter telling her to "Smell the roses, listen to the birds, relax and do what you enjoy."

Not everybody can afford a long stretch without pay, and many may find the risk of job hunting without a current job too high a price to pay. But sometimes a valued employee can negotiate some unpaid time away, even at a company without a formal policy. It's worth looking into if you crave a break in the routine but can't afford to jeopardize your job.

The Myth of the Omega Job

When I was in my early forties, I used to talk about the Omega Job. I thought of the working world as an oversize game of musical chairs: When the music stopped, you'd better be sure you had somewhere to sit. As far as I was concerned, the music stopped at fifty. At that point, I needed to be in a position I wouldn't age out of, a job I could keep until I was ready to retire, because by then I'd be too old to find a new one.

When I did turn fifty, I was perched on what seemed like the perfect seat. In a notoriously ageist industry, I had landed at one of the few magazines in America that wasn't youth-obsessed. As the standard-bearer for *More,* I was the perfect age. Unless I screwed up, I could probably keep that job right through my fifties.

When I resigned two years later, I had already begun revising my theory of the Omega Job. The world had changed, and I no longer felt that UNEMPLOYABLE was tattooed across my back. As the leading edge of the boomer generation turned sixty, I could see the rules beginning to bend. Age discrimination hasn't gone away—ask anybody over fifty who's hunted for a new job—but a new way of thinking is starting to emerge. In some industries, we boomers are actually moving into a buyer's market. In 2008, the oldest boomers will be eligible for early Social

Security benefits (that is, if Congress doesn't redo the math and raise the age at which you qualify), and a growing number of companies are worried enough about this potential brain drain that they're offering surprising incentives to attract and keep experienced employees. For example, *Fortune* reports that Charles Stark Draper Laboratory in Cambridge, Massachusetts, is wooing its senior scientists with up to six months a year off, or flexible workdays. And Home Depot touts "snowbird special" jobs, working winters in Florida and summers in Maine.

Home Depot was one of the original thirteen "featured employers" on a growing list AARP has posted on its Web site since February 2005—companies that are friendly to older workers. Others included MetLife, Pitney Bowes, Borders, Principal Financial, and Walgreens. More than seventy-one thousand people checked out the listings in the first month of the program. Increasingly, companies are recognizing that we have job skills and work ethics that can make us the top pick for many positions. We're healthy and able—and unlike our parents, we don't dream of disappearing to an Arizona retirement village.

The New American Success Story: Balancing the Life–Work Equation

When I was forty-six, I interviewed for a job at *Ladies' Home Journal.* Over goat cheese salads at a Manhattan restaurant, I told the editor in chief, Myrna Blyth, that there was one problem with hiring me: I wasn't hungry for her job. If she brought me on staff as her number two, she wouldn't be ensuring an orderly succession. In fact, I told her, I was a born executive editor who thrived on running the staff and putting together a vital, engaging magazine. I had no interest in hammering out budgets, playing politics within the parent company to secure resources for the magazine, working such long hours that my family spent more time with Katie Couric than me, or handling all the other administrative and lobbying functions that take an editor in chief far from the work he or she joined magazine publishing to do. Fair enough, she said, and offered me the job.

Six years later, we'd launched *More,* and now Myrna was retiring. She called me into her office and said, "Congratulations, you're editor in chief." Neither of us mentioned the no-promotion ultimatum I'd delivered so long ago. I knew that if I didn't take the big job, I'd get a new boss, and then I'd be out. The arriving editor in chief would want a handpicked number two to carry out her vision for the magazine. That's the way it works.

Swap iPods. Trade with a friend for a week, and listen to his or her playlist, not yours. Expand your horizons beyond the Beatles and the Stones.

And I can't say I'm sorry I said yes. I had the chance to run a national magazine at a critical stage in its life. It was gratifying to be the chief visionary of a publication that inspired enormous devotion among its readers. But the best thing about nabbing the number one job was that it inspired me to quit. If I'd never been pushed out of the cozy nest as Myrna's second in command into a job about which I had ambivalent feelings, I'd probably still be there. I'd have missed the chance to remake my work life, returning to reporting and writing, which I love, and quitting a punishing commute that I can no longer believe I once made every day.

Over the years, I seldom confided my lack of ambition, even to my friends. My generation of women had fought so hard to be considered for the top positions that not to want one seemed like a character flaw. I thought I was an anomaly, an oddball. Shouldn't I be grateful to be offered the big-cheese job? Once again, I belatedly discovered that my ambivalent feelings re-flected a generational trend among both women and men. A Burson-Marsteller survey reported in *Business Week* in March 2005 found that an increasing number of executives don't want the CEO job—the "thanks but no thanks" crowd grew from 27 percent in 2001 to 60 percent in 2004. Other workplace observers confirm a "the promotion's not worth it" wave. Since the make-your-life-count wake-up call of 9/11, people eager to strike the right work–home balance are willing to sacrifice money and status. They'd rather be the sales associate who doesn't miss any of the kids' soccer games than the office man-ager who can't leave work.

It's Not the Money, Honey

When we're young, salary figures high among our work-world concerns, often trumping our title or even our job description. We need money to launch ourselves in life—to buy a car, pur-chase a house, and pay for a growing family. How much we earn influences how good we feel about ourselves. By midlife, the picture has changed. Money has paled as a motivator among the men and women I interviewed; we no longer define our worth by our tax bracket, and we've had plenty of years of hard labor to prove that an enviable salary won't buy you happiness at work. Not a single person I talked to mentioned financial suc-cess as a reason to remake his or her career. These second choices came from the heart. Job 2.0 had to satisfy at a much deeper level than the number of digits on a W-4. Some people are working longer hours in their reinvented job, but it doesn't matter, because they love their work. Others have finally found the confidence to lay down the terms of their new employment. Some, like Ellen and Michael Albertson, made significant finan-cial sacrifices to bankroll a transition to more rewarding work.

This Boston-based duo quit a lucrative gig writing books and making media appearances together as The Cooking Couple, and are living on Ellen's income as a personal trainer while Michael launches a stand-up comedy career. Every one of the career changers I talked to felt the timing of their sea change was no accident. It wasn't until midlife that they had all the psychological tools and attitude to succeed at the new venture— and the confidence to make a big change. Helen Hand, a psychotherapist who took over as president of the university her brother had founded, told me that when she was younger, "I didn't see myself as a leader."

At midlife, we have context, perspective, and a longer view. When we bump up against an obstacle, we know that there's smoother road ahead—if we take the proper turnoff. And if we make a false step, we're better at not only recognizing the mistake, but also correcting it.

Perhaps the best payoff of all for remaking our work life is the message it sends to our kids. When we refuse to settle for a humdrum job or trade dollars for satisfaction, we're showing the next generation what it means to have fulfilling work. George Oldenburg's son has watched his father put in long hours at the Zoo of Acadiana, coming home at night dirty, exhausted—and happier than he's ever been. One day, his son hopes to run the zoo himself.

The Life Entrepreneurs

Animal Farm

At forty-five, Louisiana native George Oldenburg quit a banking career to buy a small-town zoo.

George's Lesson: Owning a business can mean longer hours than you'd ever imagined working, but suddenly that's more than okay. There's a new calculus when you're doing something you love.

GEORGE OLDENBURG ALWAYS said that the best job he ever had was working at a pet shop while he was in high school. Little did he know that three decades later, his career would come full circle when he purchased a pet shop extraordinaire—a small-town zoo near Lafayette, Louisiana. At forty-five, he became the proud father of Willie the lion, Henrietta the pygmy hippopotamus, and Humphrey the camel, just a few of the star attractions among the more than three hundred animals at the forty-two-acre Zoo of Acadiana.

Today, with three years of zoo ownership behind him, George's voice is still colored with the enthusiasm of a new venture as he describes his plans to develop the thirteen-year-old zoo into a don't-miss for tourists and a gathering place for Louisiana locals.

Nothing in George's life suggested such an unconventional career step. Growing up in Lafayette in a family of five kids, his pets were plentiful but pedestrian: dogs and cats, hamsters and gerbils, a turtle and an aquarium full of fish. After earning a degree in horticulture at the University of Louisiana, he got a job working for the USDA, making loans to farmers. A few years later when he had a chance to move into banking, he grabbed it. "I had just gotten married, and felt it would be a more secure position," George remembers. He was good at the new job and enjoyed the work. His family thrived, and so did his career. He moved up through the ranks, supervising the bank's various branches, overseeing consumer loans and credit card business. It was a full life, including a board presidency at the school his boys attended and rewarding work on a chamber of commerce project to revive downtown Lafayette. But after twenty years, it wasn't enough. "I put a lot of people into business who were very successful and happy," George says. "Whenever I'd make a loan, I'd think, *Boy, it'd be nice to work for myself.*"

When the zoo was put up for sale five years ago, George considered making an offer, but felt that with a young family, the time wasn't right. Two years later, when the opportunity came again, he didn't hesitate. "I called my wife and told her I wanted to buy the zoo." She was enthusiastic, and their three boys—then ten, twelve, and fourteen—were so excited they could hardly keep the secret until the deal had closed. George's parents were a harder sell. "We took my mom and dad out for a dinner of boiled crawfish to make the big announcement," he recalls. "They thought I was insane."

George admits that beyond the rosy glow of the dream lay a few dark doubts. "At the start, I did a lot of worrying about buying a business where your assets can die," he says. "And I had to resign from the bank before I could even make an offer, so there'd be no conflict of interest. It was risky to quit my job, *then* apply for a loan." After thirty days of unemployment, his $1.2 million purchase price was accepted and the bank loan approved. The die was cast; George was a zookeeper.

Since then, he's busier than ever—and happier, too. Working at the zoo is never dull, and George relishes pitching in on almost any job. "I can do electrical work or plumbing, build fences, work with animals, or plan a wedding reception." If a driver calls in sick, he runs the zoo train.

But the best part has been learning about the animals. "I can walk through the zoo now and immediately spot something that's not right." He's equally delighted that the animals recognize him. "If a particular tiger spots me, she'll walk up to the fence and make a chuffing noise."

Doing PR for the zoo, occasionally he's gotten to know the

animals a little too well. "On a local morning show, I was talking away to the host and had no idea that the parrot sitting on my shoulder was eating my microphone. After the segment, the producer said, 'Thanks for coming, and you owe us four hundred dollars.'" On another TV appearance, an eight-foot Burmese python worked its way up into his pants. One day he took an important new acquisition, a baby white tiger, to do a school presentation. "There I was, in front of the class, when Jolie decided to take a bite out of my leg. It hurt bad, but I didn't want to let on in front of the kids."

Cat nips aside, George says he's never been healthier. "Since I bought the zoo, I've lost weight, and I haven't taken a single sick day. My wife says I've had a personality change; I come home a lot dirtier, but a lot happier." It's seeing the big smiles on guests' faces that makes all the hard work worthwhile. One of George's new attendance boosters is a Snore 'n' Roar program that brings scouting groups to the zoo. They take a twilight tour of the exhibits, camp out overnight, and in the morning enjoy a backstage peek at the daily vet clinic and kitchen. One enraptured young boy told George, "This is the best day of my life."

October 3, 2002, was not the best day of George's life. Three years later, he still remembers the dread. "When Hurricane Lili headed our way, I knew it could wipe me out." He and his staff moved animals, boarded up exhibits, and hoped for the best. George even brought home a favorite goat from the petting zoo and some snakes and birds. After the storm, the zoo was littered with broken tree limbs—"It looked horrible," George says—but all the animals were alive. It only took George's team three days to get the place in order and open again, but it took months for people in Lafayette to rebuild their houses. Until then, they weren't even thinking about going to the zoo. "The storm took a big chunk out of our business that year," George says.

Despite this setback, George's new programs have revitalized the zoo, which turned a profit in 2004. He still doesn't draw a salary, preferring to reinvest the money in the property. His family lives on his wife Marleen's earnings as a registered nurse plus income from some rental properties they own. "I couldn't have done this without my banking background," George says. In spring, when attendance peaks, there's a lot of money coming in. "I could go crazy buying animals and building exhibits. But come August when school starts, we're pretty slow, and I have to plan for that."

Running the zoo has become a family affair. "My boys are learning what hard work is," he notes. George's oldest son dreams of taking over the zoo one day. This, of course, delights his dad.

"I could have stayed at the bank another twenty years," George says. "But I'm building just as much equity in the zoo as I'd have in my 401(k)." At times, George brings work home. "We got a six-week-old white tiger last year, and she required bottle-feeding every four hours." For three months, she went home with George every night, and he and Marleen would take turns getting up. "It was a once-in-a-lifetime experience."

When pressed, George admits he's working more than ever before, and seldom takes a vacation day. But it doesn't matter when work feels like fun. "At the bank, I was starting to count the hours; now it's more like a hobby than a job."

His career reinvention had to be a midlife event. "I wouldn't have bought the zoo at thirty-five. My children were small, and I didn't feel that secure in my abilities," he says. "At forty-five, I was looking for a change. My brother-in-law was killed in a plane crash the year before I bought the zoo, and it made me think: *I could die tomorrow and miss out on something I really wanted to do.*" That's all George has time to say; he's off to check on the spider monkeys.

The Pause That Refreshes

At forty-five, Kirk Kvetko jumped ship from a twenty-three-year career at FedEx to climb South America's highest peak. Four years later, he's back at work, and his wife, Colleen, has called her own time-out from a high-flying banking career.

Kirk and Colleen's Lesson: *Saying sayonara to an excellent job can be the smartest career move of all. A sabbatical is a nourishing recess period when you take time to develop a clear picture of what kind of work you want to do.*

AT FIFTY, COLLEEN Kvetko turned her back on a supersuccessful thirty-four-year career (yes, she'd been working in banking since she was sixteen), quit her job, and accepted a retirement package without the slightest intention of retiring. "I'm taking some time to reinvent myself, asking myself these questions: *What skills do I have? Do I want to go back into banking or do I want to put my energy somewhere else?*" she says, clearly enjoying the fact that no holds are barred, the sky's the limit.

Her husband, Kirk, wasn't a bit surprised when Colleen announced her decision one evening when they were taking a walk near their Naples, Florida, home. Five years earlier, he had retired from a two-decade career at FedEx.

So are they spending golden afternoons together, sipping iced tea on their lanai? Not a chance. Kirk is back at work, running operations for a company that sells financial services to seniors. And he says of Colleen, "She's got more hustle. She won't last as long as I did. I give her six months." But neither of them would trade their sabbaticals for anything.

"I have to have passion for what I do," Colleen says. "I hit fifty, and I said to myself, *Let's step back and rethink it.* I'm in that muddy water right now."

Listening to the calm and humor in her voice, it's hard to imagine the tortured six months that preceded her decision. Hers was not an easy job to leave. President of the Fifth Third Bank for thirteen years, she'd been named the fifth most powerful woman in banking by *US Banker* magazine. "My bank agreed to buy another bank last summer, and I knew my role would change," Colleen says. "I promised myself if I didn't love coming to work every day, I was out of there." But following through on that promise was tough. "I'd wake up in the middle of the night. I did more crying in that six months than in our entire twenty-seven years of marriage." She was haunted by the thought of abandoning the two hundred people who worked for her. "I was on the fence: Give up that big salary, that title, that position, the career I had since I was sixteen? Was I letting down all the women in the bank world to whom I was a role model?"

Sign up for a fund-raiser walk. Name a cause, and there's a walk to raise money. The distances are doable even for the workout-challenged. Just Google the cause of your choice.

Those considerations were all too familiar to Kirk. "The day it hit me, I was at a national sales event in Nashville, where I was to give a presentation to thousands of FedEx employees." He had been passed over for a promotion, but, more than that, he was weary from twenty-three years of being on call day and night. "I went up to my room, had a cigar on the balcony, and thought, *I'm not enjoying this. It's time to check out.*" He delegated his presentation to a colleague and caught a flight home. That night he wrote his letter of resignation.

"FedEx is a fabulous company, but twenty-three years there is like forty years somewhere else. I did everything—ran call centers, business service centers, the drop box network. It's a 24/7 business. Many nights I slept in the office," he says. "I wanted to enter triathlons, bike across America, climb a mountain."

During their early years together, Kirk and Colleen had a single financial goal: to get to the point where either one of them could say, "I quit." "When Kirk and I got married," Colleen recalls, "we decided that no matter what, we would live on one paycheck and bank the other." Through those lean years, Colleen moonlighted at a card store at night, and Kirk mowed lawns. Month after month, paycheck by paycheck, their savings mounted. "I drove a Corvair with a rotten floorboard," Kirk recalls. "We bought handyman-special houses and fixed them up. We sold the first one for a sixty-thousand-dollar profit, I'll never forget that."

When Kirk walked away from his job, he didn't have to worry about making ends meet, even if he never worked again. "Money isn't everything," he says, "but it certainly dictates what you can do." Without his job, he wasn't bored for a minute. He threw himself into running the house. "I told Colleen, 'You just work, I'll take care of everything else.' My brother-in-law bought me a shirt that said CABANA BOY." He paid the bills, ironed Colleen's blouses, sent out birthday cards.

Kirk had a few other things on his to-do list, most notably climbing Aconcagua, the highest mountain in South America, with a reputation for brutally changeable weather. "We lost our cook, a very experienced climber in his early twenties, who got hypoxia and literally walked off the mountain," Kirk says. There were nineteen people in the party; only three made it to the 22,841-foot summit. Kirk turned back just twelve hundred feet below, amid seventy-mile-an-hour wind gusts and a snowstorm blowing in. "I could see the flag; that's how close I was. It's a lonely feeling, after all that training, but you have to do the

smart thing." The real victory was the $330,000 the group raised
for two charities.

Last year, when Kirk was offered the job he now holds, he
approached the decision employing a new methodology born
of lessons he'd learned on his sabbatical. "If I went back, I was
going to do it on my terms." He asked to shadow the CEO who
was courting him. For nine weeks he traveled with him, attending meetings and meeting the staff before accepting the job.
"I bought all the air tickets, the hotel rooms; I didn't want any
obligation." Then Kirk put off the start date for two months
while he and Colleen took a Mediterranean cruise and he went
fly fishing in Montana. Back in the office, he now works smart,
not hard. "I have raised productivity way past the goals we set,
but I check out every day by four."

The day Colleen retired, Kirk advised her to reclaim her life.
In her banking days, Colleen was out at business dinners every
night. "The new rule should be, if someone calls and you don't
want to do it, you don't," he says.

"The next six months are going to be one part planning, one
part serendipity," Colleen adds. "I'm very goal-oriented; I like to
feel productive. But that might be adding value to my body, by
working out with a trainer every day." She's also overseeing the
design of a smaller house, so they can simply lock the door and
head off on trips. Over the next few months, Colleen plans a
visit to her family in Ohio and a niece in LA, girlfriend trips to
Yosemite and a South Carolina spa, an Alaska cruise and an
African safari with Kirk.

She hasn't lost any time getting a new career on track; even
before she left the bank, she was studying for a real estate license. "That way, I'll have something to jump into right away if
I start getting bored," she says. "I know the community, the
mortgage market, the legal side." Her friends are horrified, seeing this as a road right back to fourteen-hour workdays. "They

know how I am," she laughs. "But I'm going to try to avoid that this time." She may sell houses, or become a mortgage broker. Or then again, she may not. At this point, she's preparing for everything, committing to nothing. "When the time comes, I'll know what the right thing is.

"I'm a risk taker in pretty much everything I do," she says. "When I'm on the golf course, and I've got a 160-yard second shot over a big lagoon, I'm not going to lay up, I'm going to go for it." She's eager to see how the next chapter of her life turns out. However the plot line proceeds, it will include a very powerful marriage. "I'm so lucky," Colleen says. "We're best friends and we have so much fun together. Twenty-seven years later, I'm still as much in love with Kirk as the day I married him."

Colleen drives an aqua Thunderbird convertible, and she's just changed the license to GO plus her initials, slightly disappointed that her first choice, GO GIRL, was taken. When she was working at the bank, she couldn't put the top down. "I was always driving to an appointment so my hair couldn't be messed up." Now, she reports, the top has not been up since she called time out. At last, Colleen can feel the wind in her hair.

Going Back to College—As President

After her brother was killed, psychotherapist Helen Hand found solace and satisfaction running the university he founded.

Helen's Lesson: *If you're considering a new direction, don't be shy: Think big. Intending to simply jazz up her job, Helen was bowled over by the rewards of making the complete career change that fate presented to her.*

WHEN HELEN HAND got the phone call, she couldn't believe what she was hearing. Her older brother, John, had been murdered the previous night, attacked at random by a young woman wielding a knife. "I was in total disbelief," she says. "It was the most devastating thing that had ever happened to me." It was a particularly horrible blow because Helen had always been close to her only sibling. "He was the big brother, the guy who blazed the trail for me," she remembers. As she mourned his death, she could never have predicted that this tragedy would set her own life on a completely different course.

When they were teens, Helen followed John to Duke University. When they graduated, brother and sister both returned to Denver, Helen to graduate school in psychology, John to seek a profession. John was a searcher, a visionary, Helen says. He got a real estate license, became a leader of an ashram, and worked as a program director for Denver Free University in the 1970s. A decade later, John started his own adult education university. "He was the sort of guy who didn't wait until he had the credentials to do something," Helen says. "He'd cast his line way out there, and then pull himself toward it." Colorado Free University, which he founded in 1987, prospered to become one of the biggest adult education schools in the country, offering four hundred courses to more than twenty-five thousand students.

Meantime Helen won a fellowship to earn her doctorate at the University of Denver. In short order, she married a lawyer, opened a psychotherapy practice, and had the first of their three children. She loved her work, feeling she was made for the role. "Growing up, I was the one in the family who tried to figure everybody else out, the peacemaker who always wanted to understand all points of view." Her client list grew, and she practiced happily for twenty-five years.

Then, in her early fifties, she became restless, yearning for a new challenge. A month before John's death, she attended a Boston conference on running psychotherapy workshops. "I was looking to jazz my job up," she says, "maybe starting a women's institute to run weekend workshops where people could reconnect with parts of themselves they'd lost." While she was retooling her profession, a new career presented itself.

Try a driver education day. Take your car out on a local racetrack and hammer. Check the track's Web sites for opportunities, or the local chapter of your marque's owner's club.

"A month after John died, I was talking to his number two at Colorado Free University, who was struggling to hold everything together," Helen recalls. "She said an extraordinary thing to me: 'Why don't you take John's place and run the school?'" Helen was flabbergasted. "My first reaction was, 'I could no more do that than fly to the moon.'" A couple of weeks later, the business trustee for the school mentioned it again. "That time it clicked," Helen says. "Partly it was a sense that my life was already utterly changed. My brother had been my touchstone, my soul buddy. Now the world was upside down and inside out. It felt like a tsunami taking me somewhere, and that I should go with it." She liked the idea of staying connected to John by continuing his work. Still, it wasn't an easy decision to make. Her brother's salary was much less than Helen made, and she felt a strong sense of responsibility to her long-term patients. Helen and her husband talked it over and agreed that she'd take the job, but instead of closing her practice, she'd cut back her hours to ten a week.

At Colorado Free University, she inherited a shell-shocked staff, still grieving their boss's death. Though people were welcoming, the transition was tough. "I had to run the school my way, not John's," Helen says, "and I met some resistance when I changed people's duties and the structure of the staff." One employee left. To make matters worse, when Helen took the reins in 2004, the school had hit a rough patch. Revenue was dropping 2 percent a year, and the balance sheet hovered at the profit–loss line. "It was really challenging," Helen says. In his will, John had left a broad-strokes mission statement for the school, but as the architect of CFU's future she was largely on her own. "A lot of the time I was flying by the seat of my pants, making it up as I went along." It was scary, but exhilarating, too. "It's been amazing to feel my own creativity popping."

Helen's new role answered her restlessness on many levels. Accustomed to doing things on her own, whether it was billing patients or dealing with their insurance companies, she now found herself a consensus builder. "I went back to my roots as the peacemaker," she says. And she learned how productive collaboration can be. "Whenever I interview a new teacher, I come up with a bunch of ideas for courses."

In her first year at the helm, not all of Helen's initiatives have taken wing, but she's learning whether to revamp or discard the ones that don't fly. It's all part of the challenge, part of the fun. "I've been delighted to find out how much energy I have," Helen says. "I can feel parts of my brain waking up. I'm discovering all kinds of dormant knowledge, things I've picked up through life experience. We all have this stuff stored away, but we don't realize it until we use it. As a psychologist, I know that different parts of ourselves come forward when we interact with different people—our spouses, our co-workers, our friends. When we take on new challenges, a similar thing happens: Different dimensions of ourselves step forward. Feeling a new skill set awakening gave me courage to believe in myself.

"Being fifty-three is a great help," she continues. "I don't think I could have done this in my thirties. Back then, I didn't see myself as a leader." Now, Helen says, she's drawing on her life experiences and coming into her own. "The challenges of a blended family with stepkids from my husband's first marriage prepared me. We had to invent things as we went along." She also credits her psychology practice with providing the knowledge and confidence she needs. "There are moments with clients when you think, *Oh heavens, I don't know how to deal with this.* There's an old joke among psychologists that you'll sit there with a patient saying to yourself, *Boy, you need professional help,* and then you realize you *are* the professional help. Life-and-death issues, suicide risks—the buck stops here."

Helen's family has given her great support. "All my kids adored my brother, and they can see that I'm into the new job." Even the friends who were concerned that she might be doing it for the wrong reasons, out of grief or a misplaced sense of responsibility, have been won over by her excitement. "Most days, I'm having a blast," Helen says. "I hope to be doing this a long, long time."

Giving Up Glamour, Rolling the Dice

Michael and Ellen Albertson found fame and fortune as The Cooking Couple, but they abandoned their lucrative gig to pursue separate dreams. Michael's now doing stand-up comedy; Ellen's a personal trainer.

Michael and Ellen's Lesson: *One of the pieces of wisdom that midlife brings is realizing that being successful isn't the same thing as being happy. A career that sounds perfect on paper may not feel that way. Sometimes you have to gamble on happiness.*

MICHAEL AND ELLEN Albertson had a career many people dream of. Authors of a successful cookbook, they hosted their own syndicated radio show and traveled around the country giving speeches and appearing on TV. It was glamorous, it was exciting, there was plenty of money coming in. Then one day they turned their back on the limousines and the cameras. In the most grown-up decision they'd ever made, they set their lives on a risky new course.

Their story begins, appropriately enough, with a romantic encounter over food. "Michael picked me up in a grocery store," Ellen says, laughing. When they married in 1993, Michael, a former chef, was staging concerts and corporate events for a Boston company, and Ellen worked as a hospital dietitian. One night, Ellen mentioned that she'd like to write a cookbook. She knew nutrition; Michael knew media and marketing. "So we just did it," Michael says. "Remember the old Judy Garland–Mickey Rooney movies—'Hey kids, let's put on a show'? That was us." They came up with a great title—*Food as Foreplay*—and wrote a lighthearted book backed by serious science, celebrating the crossroads of cuisine and romance. They published the book themselves, contracting with a distributor and filling orders from a sea of cartons in the basement of their suburban Boston home. "To our shock, the book was a big success," Michael says. In the first year, *Food as Foreplay* sold a hundred thousand copies, sparking three hundred radio interviews and dozens of TV appearances. Ellen and Michael quit their jobs to launch a joint career, billing themselves as The Cooking Couple. "It wasn't scary at all," Ellen remembers, "because I could feel the universe pulling us in this very exciting direction." They started a Boston radio show, which multiplied among Massachusetts stations, then went national.

When the media blitz struck, Ellen was pregnant with their first child, and her swelling belly became part of the schtick. "See," Michael would say when they appeared on TV. "Food as foreplay: It works." Several major publishers took notice of all the excitement, and the Albertsons signed a six-figure deal for a second book. It would be a crash project to produce the book in time for Valentine's Day 2002. Once again, amid all the hub-bub, Ellen and Michael decided to have a child. After giving birth to their son, Ellen took four days off, then returned to a punishing schedule creating the book. "I was breast-feeding, writing, breast-feeding, writing," she says. "The entire summer was a blur."

If the timing was ideal for *Food as Foreplay,* it couldn't have been worse for *Temptations: Igniting the Pleasure and Power of Aphrodisiacs.* Between spring 2001 when they signed the deal and the following February when *Temptations* was released, al-Qaeda attacked the United States and the stock market bot-tomed out. "It changed the whole mood of the country," Michael says. "People were no longer asking 'What's going to happen to my orgasm?' They were asking 'What's going to hap-pen to my life?'" *Temptations* fell short of sales goals, and the publisher didn't renew their contract.

The Cooking Couple were far from washed up. "Our radio show was going gangbusters in over a hundred markets," Michael says, and they were picking up lucrative product en-dorsements, from companies as diverse as CorningWare, Glen Ellen wines, and Dunkin' Donuts. They'd had overtures from production companies to create a TV series starring The Cook-ing Couple. But signing a deal meant giving up ownership of the trademark. "Ellen was forty, I was older than that, and we're no fools," Michael says. "I always felt the agenda was to make us executive producers and hire some blonde and a hot young stud to go on air."

The golden life was beginning to lose its luster. Ellen and Michael were always on the go, crisscrossing the country to ap-pear at product promotions and wedding shows. The turning point came on the return from a ten-day trip. When Ellen reached down to pick up her baby son, he crawled backward into the nanny's lap. "It was heartbreaking," Ellen says. "I thought, *What are we doing, leaving our kids with strangers, and my son is scared of me?*" Michael adds, "That's when we both knew we had to get off the bicycle we'd been madly pedaling for eight years.

"Would we have quit The Cooking Couple at thirty-two? Absolutely not," he continues. "It takes the experience of another decade to ask yourself whether this is the roller coaster you want to be on. When you're thirty-two, any roller coaster is a good one. But we had become windup toys; everybody wanted The Cooking Couple schtick. We didn't want to be telling people how to gum their aphrodisiacs twenty years from now."

Ellen and Michael shut down the radio show, cut way back on their appearances, and began to envision the next chapter of their lives. "We spent a lot of time visualizing where we wanted to be in five years and then backing up into how we'd get there," Ellen recalls. Michael had always wanted to accomplish two things: write a novel and do stand-up comedy. Ellen didn't want to work as a dietitian anymore. One day she got a postcard in the mail advertising a home-study course to become a personal trainer. "It was just a little three-by-five card, but it changed my life," she says. "I'd always been a jock. I ran competitively in high school, and in college I was a dancer." Ellen got accredited as a trainer, figuring she'd have the extra thunder of advising her clients on nutrition. It proved to be a winning combination, and soon her calendar was filled with appointments. The work is fulfilling. "I'm training a forty-year-old schizophrenic who's lost thirty-five pounds and doesn't suffer from sleep apnea anymore. It's turned his life around."

Her clients appreciate not just the depth of her knowledge but the maturity of her outlook as well. "Baby boomers want someone who's educated and can talk about a variety of subjects—museums, books, raising kids. And they like my philosophy: feeding your body to be healthy, not denying it to lose weight."

A year ago, Ellen added the title of Reiki Master to her credentials. "It's a form of energy healing. When you touch someone, you're a funnel for universal life force energy. It's my spiritual practice; I tune myself up every day with Reiki."

Right now, Ellen's earnings pay the bills, and they live frugally while Michael builds his future. Most mornings, he gets up at 5 AM and heads down to the basement, which is no longer packed with cartons of *Food as Foreplay,* to work on a completely different kind of book. He's writing a romantic spy thriller about a down-and-out rock star who's trying to resurrect his career. *Rock Spy* has been two years in the making. The manuscript will go to his agent in two months. Sure, there are dark days when the work isn't going well. "After I finished the first draft, I bought a book on how to write a best-selling novel. When I realized how many problems my manuscript had, that was a black day. A black week," he says. "Then you realize the only way out of the blues is to set the alarm, make a pot of coffee, go down to the office, and get to work."

When he isn't plotting *Rock Spy*'s future, he's plotting his own. For six months, Michael has been polishing his stand-up routine at Boston comedy clubs, putting together material for larger sets he can take to New York. "So far, the response has been excellent," Michael says. "My angle is 'bad dad' humor. My audience is people like me, boomer dads." The common wisdom may call comedy a young man's game, but Michael sees virtue in his seniority. "The club owners look down on the kids with their baseball caps on backward, doing dick jokes and gay bashing. I'm a professional. I show up on time, make their clubs look good, and attract a better class of customer.

"Why am I trying something only one in a million people succeed at? I don't know. But my new hero is Rodney Dangerfield.

He started doing stand-up at forty-eight, and became one of the biggest stars in comedy," says Michael, who's now forty-seven. "Even as a child, I always believed that whatever I do, I'm going to succeed." Some of his humor draws on his mixed-race heritage. His mother was half black and worked as a book-keeper. His father was Jewish and a union organizer in New York. "The FBI would camp outside our door, and our house was firebombed when I was eight. My father went to work in a bulletproof vest. Maybe I'm so confident because I survived that stuff."

Run for office. Or get appointed. Serving as a member of the local school board in a small town can introduce you to a whole new cast of characters, and could even fuel bigger political ambitions.

It was tough at times, straddling two races, but the sense of humor that would fuel Michael's stand-up career was already serving him well. "My freshman year of high school, the black kids were beating me up. When they walked up, I'd say, 'Why don't I just stuff myself in my locker and save you the trouble.' I'd start to do it and they'd laugh." Within a year, the guys on the football team had become friends and protectors.

These days, neither Ellen nor Michael is afraid to dream big—really big. "My goal is to be one of the best trainers and holistic health counselors in the country, the Jack La Lanne for the new millennium," Ellen says. "I want to write books and have a large enough media presence to reach a lot of people. Michael joked that I should try out for *Survivor,* and I'm going to." Michael's dream for stand-up is eight thousand people at Carnegie Hall, or a slot on Letterman; if *Rock Spy* finds a read-ership, it will become a series, maybe a movie. Meanwhile, Ellen and Michael don't mind living the simple life. "People who aren't satisfied fill their lives with stuff," Ellen says. "Struggling to be happy, they get into this standard of living where they need a bigger house, a second van." Ellen and Michael's idea of a hot date is a home-cooked dinner and a DVD. They're working their schedules so that they don't need a nanny; one of them is always available to take care of the kids, who are now eight and four. They are confident that their financial future will work out, and that if either of them hits it big, the kids will be older and it'll be okay to climb back on the media merry-go-round. As Ellen puts it, "You throw your kids out of the nest, then you jump out yourself."

In the Driver's Seat

Getting downsized at forty-eight after twenty-two years as a TV cameraman turned out to be a lucky break for Steve Weiner. Now he runs a business building Porsche race cars.

Steve's Lesson: *Don't be afraid to launch yourself out of the comfort zone of a salaried job if you dream of running your own show. There is life after corporate America.*

STEVE WEINER HAD worked at the NBC affiliate in Portland, Oregon, for more than two decades, and he loved his job. As a cameraman and sound engineer, he didn't just film traffic accidents and house fires. When a national story broke anywhere in the Northwest or California, he'd cover the action in the station's satellite truck. "The big earthquake in San Francisco—I was there. When the Unabomber was found in Montana—I was there. When the Olympic Torch went around the country, we chased it," he says. "For a guy like me who's really interested in news, it was the catbird seat."

So it came as a shock the day Steve's manager called him in and told him they were reducing staff. Steve, the second most senior person in his department, was out of work. "After twenty two years, I got two weeks' severance," he says. "No parachute whatsoever." It was a body blow to his family's finances. His wife was on disability after a work-related illness, and Steve bartended nights to make ends meet.

There were two obvious directions Steve could take: look for another job in television, or ramp up the sideline business he'd run for twenty years, tuning and repairing race cars. He chose to hedge his bets by pursuing both options, but he was a middle-aged man looking for work in a shrinking job market. "Here I was almost fifty, and TV stations were shedding staff," he says. He sent out forty résumés to TV stations and related businesses. "I spent nine months answering ads, and got one interview." At that point, Steve says, the utter futility of trying to buck age discrimination sank in.

At the same time, Steve was moving ahead full throttle to build his little moonlighting business into a big enough operation to support his wife and him. "I loved working on Porsche race cars and high-performance street cars." Fueling the growth would require a substantial outlay of capital for equipment. Steve needed a partner. Luckily, he already knew the perfect person, a technician at an independent repair shop. "He's an immensely gifted mechanic," Steve says. "He, too, had been talking about wanting to go off on his own. When I got laid off, we both said, 'Let's do it together.'" They found a piece of property, signed a lease, and hired a couple of mechanics. For the kind of operation they planned, they'd have to attract a nationwide clientele of Porsche enthusiasts who would ship their cars to Portland, FedEx the engine or transmission to be overhauled, or order parts. One of the most critical, and most frustrating, early tasks was building a Web site that could form the backbone of the mail-order business. "People of my generation do not grasp computers very easily," Steve jokes. "But I knew if I didn't learn, we were screwed." He taught himself to build pages and put them on the Web.

Rennsport Systems grew slowly at first. "Some weeks, I'd pay the property lease and the employees' salaries, make my house payment, and realize there was nothing left over for groceries," Steve recalls. "I'd be a terrible liar if I said I didn't second-guess myself a few times." Eventually, he realized that nearly everyone who launches a business lives under this pressure, and even experiences moments of panic. "It was three years before the business was solid enough that I didn't worry about paying the bills."

There was no question that Steve was well suited to the work itself. He'd been a car nut since the age of thirteen when one of his older brother's friends turned him on to hot rods. "I helped work on his cars, and by the time I got to high school, I knew a fair amount," he says. His folks took a dim view of grease monkeys, so Steve kept a lid on his activities, renting a garage from an elderly lady in the neighborhood where he stashed his cars and tools. All the money he earned working at a local gas station and bagging at a grocery store was poured into his hot rods. He usually had two tucked away in the secret garage—one he was working on, plus a parts car. "My parents didn't have a clue," he says. "Toward the end of high school, when they finally figured out what I was doing, they weren't happy. When you grow up in a middle-class Jewish household, building race cars is not acceptable."

After high school, Steve started racing sports cars while working at a British car dealer as an apprentice mechanic. "I bought a little Bugeye Austin-Healey Sprite, got my SCCA competition license, and raced it for a year." He sold the Sprite and purchased a '67 Mini Cooper, which he rebuilt for the track and raced until he got called up to Vietnam as an air force pilot. Back home after a year, flying two-seat O-1s on dangerous low-level missions over Laos and Cambodia, he started working on Porsches. He and a buddy went pro, entering Trans-Am races, a series for highly modified pure race-car versions of Mustangs, Camaros, Jaguars, and the like. "Guys like us with minimal experience out there on the track—these days, they'd never let you do it," Steve says. "When I think about it, it's a wonder we survived." The prize money wasn't great, but Steve learned something priceless—that he loved working on Porsches.

While Steve was honing his racing skills, he was also building a career as a sound- and cameraman. After his tour in Vietnam, he landed a job at a Portland radio station. A few years later, when an opportunity came to move to TV, he took it. "It was more money, more glamour, a chance to meet interesting people," he says. At the same time, he was working on cars for a growing number of racer friends.

Today Rennsport Systems is one of the country's most highly regarded builders of extremely powerful modified Porsche 911s. Steve enjoys the role of guru, and is well known among Porsche fans not only for the supercars he builds, but also for the advice he freely gives to enthusiasts. After almost a decade running his own show, Steve says he's unfit to return to corporate life. "Being your own boss, you get an attitude. You don't suffer fools anymore. Now, if I had to work for somebody else, I couldn't keep my mouth shut, which means I'd be back on the street."

Nine years after the fateful day that upended his TV career, Steve says flatly, "Getting fired was the best thing that ever happened to me." It pushed him to make a decision he admits he never would have reached on his own. "You sit in that comfort zone where you get a paycheck, you have health insurance, vacation. Life is good; you don't have to think. But another word for 'comfort zone' is *rut*. I'll gladly trade income for freedom."

There is one downside to owning Rennsport: virtually no time off. "You have to be around to answer the phone, handle your customers' needs, put out fires. I'm like a shark that will drown if it doesn't keep swimming. Going at it six to seven days a week is tough." Steve hasn't taken a vacation since he launched Rennsport, and he fantasizes about spending a few weeks in Europe with his wife. Still, he's content doing what he loves. "It's a lot more fun than the TV business. Corny as it sounds, I'd advise people to follow a passion, whether it's tuning race cars or mixing concrete. If you don't go to work every day with a big smile on your face, it's time to look in the mirror and ask yourself, *What does really melt my butter?*"

CHAPTER 2

Health Makeovers

WHEN I WAS in junior high, everybody knew right where to find me at any school sporting event: on the bench. In seventh and eighth grade, I went out for every team that had uniforms and a ball. Field hockey, basketball, baseball, tennis—you name it, I was there. I so wanted to be an athlete and sew one of those big blue-and-gold letters onto a jacket. There was just one problem: I'm a klutz. Pass the ball to me, and I'll fumble it. Count on me to block a goal and you might as well just post the new score on the board.

By high school, I'd given up on team sports. Turning in my jerseys with regret, I joined the yearbook staff and faced up to the fact that when it came to athletics, I didn't have the right stuff.

Fast-forward four decades, and now, in my midfifties, I am proud to call myself a jock. No, I have not achieved some miraculous late-blooming athletic finesse. I would still be the last pick for any team sport you could name. What I have belatedly discovered are my true athletic assets: What I lack in co-ordination, I make up for in stamina and strength. So if I choose an activity wisely, I can not only participate but occasionally excel. Over the past ten years, I've met a lot of other late-to-the-party athletes out on my bike routes and in the weight room of my gym. Some, like me, needed to figure out what sports they could effectively play, while others just needed to be given the chance.

An Accidental Athlete

The late-dawning realization that I'm not a total loser at sports began in a most unlikely way. I was thirty years old and had just returned to work after two years at home raising my daughter, Brook. Now my husband was going to be the on-duty parent while I resumed commuting to New York City. The only problem was, I wasn't holding up my end. I was so exhausted, I was ready to collapse. When I lay down with Brook to read a story at bedtime, I was asleep by page three.

Steve sent me to the doctor with this message: "I like my wife. I want her back." My internist gave me the most valuable piece of medical advice I've ever received. "I'm not surprised you're run down," he told me. "You have a two-year-old child who's still getting you up at night, a stressful job, and a hellish commute. Why don't you start a workout routine? That should jump-start your energy."

The following day, a buddy and I joined a gym two blocks from our office. The Jane Fonda–style exercise classes had us collapsing in laughter at the back of the room as we missed the beat, lifted the wrong leg, shuffled when we should have stepped. Carol let her membership run out, but for some reason I stuck with it. Against all logic, I kept going, and eventually I was able to follow the routines with precision, if not grace. My body got stronger, and I began to notice actual muscles in my arms.

Then, when I was in my late thirties, my husband bought me a used mountain bike that an editor friend had tested for a magazine. Steve and I explored the quiet country roads near our home and signed on for cycling trips in rural Vermont and California's wine country. Too dumb to realize we had the wrong bikes for road riding, we did a century ride—a hundred miles through Westchester County's bucolic back roads—on heavy, slow mountain bikes in ninety-six-degree heat. Steve came to his senses immediately. It was the last century he ever rode.

> **Start a book club.** Invite your most adventuresome friends to join, then read books about risk takers. That way the book club can moonlight as a support group for Life Entrepreneurs.

But I loved the Zen of slipping silently through pastoral landscapes, the miracle of my legs propelling me to distances I'd never imagined I could go. The year I turned forty, to prove to myself I wasn't over the hill, I rode a double-metric—two hundred kilometers or 124 miles, plus 7 bonus miles to correct a wrong turn I made. Fifteen years later, I still complete at least one hundred-mile ride every year.

During my forties, I discovered another great lifestyle sport when I began hiking with a friend every weekend in the forest preserve behind our house. A longtime backpacker who'd camped under the stars in the Rockies, Chris taught me to follow trail blazes and the value of wearing the right hiking shoes. We still do four or five miles together twice a week, escorting her water-loving golden retriever from lake to lake.

At fifty, I reentered the world of competitive sports, but this time with lowered expectations. Running *More*, I was engaged in a love–hate relationship with my job. My friend Sarah was having her own struggles with a top editor's job at another magazine. Friday lunch together was sacrosanct. We had a standing therapy appointment—with each other. No matter how hectic work got, at high noon on Friday we'd head to a nearby gym for a squash game and a sauna. Neither of us ever developed racquet skills worth boasting about, but we loved to work up a sweat and considered the day a success if we each got off a few good shots. We cared so little about who won that we seldom could remember the score. After an hour on the court, we baked in the sauna, working out our minds as we soothed our muscles. We vented about issues at work, coached each other through the tricky patches—ultimately convincing ourselves to reinvent our lives. Sarah acted first, quitting her job two months after 9/11 and moving her two kids to a small town in Maine, where she's found a much happier life freelance writing. She was a Life Entrepreneur role model for me.

Since I've been working at home, I now spend a borderline-obsessive amount of time at the gym every day—an hour in the weight room, another hour on the cardio equipment. People actually admire the definition in my legs. This continues to astonish me. I attribute it to finally figuring out what I'm good at: I'm a perfect candidate for simple sports like biking and hiking and weight lifting, where you can substitute dedication and strength for agility and finesse.

I tell this story because it's so typical of my generation, in which a lot of athletes have bloomed late. Too old for legislated equal treatment on the athletic field under Title IX, many boomer women discovered the pleasure of sports far into life. For men who weren't born athletes, success at sports was just as elusive. On fiercely competitive teams, they were out of the running. Now they're right beside me in the weight room, grunting the big barbells into the air, or kayaking, or engaging in any number of "lifestyle sports." For some, like Jim Koeppel, discovering physical activity has become much more than a rewarding way to pass leisure hours. He had suffered debilitating bouts of back pain for almost thirty years. But since he began practicing Pilates at forty, his back has been healthy and strong. Now he's carrying the torch, teaching Pilates to others.

Form Versus Function:
Knowing What Truly Counts

They don't call boomers the Peter Pan generation for nothing. In many ways, we refuse to acknowledge that we've aged. When I asked the people I interviewed how old they felt, quite a few of them mentioned a number in the twenties. In the focus groups we did at *More,* and in all the surveys I've read interviewing both men and women, boomers say they feel at least five, often ten years younger than their age. In fact, the joke about these surveys is that typically, when asked to specify the age when "old" begins, boomers offer a number a few years past their life expectancy. *Young at heart* is a cliché that rings true for us. I know I feel that way. Occasionally I catch a glimpse of my reflection in a store window and I don't even recognize myself. Who is that woman staring back at me, with the crow's-feet and softening jawline? That's not how I see myself at all. My mind's eye automatically subtracts a decade of wrinkles. Remember Jack Benny's joke about remaining an eternal thirty-nine? We're living it.

I find that this illusion is neatly fostered by never really looking at yourself, an unconscious shift that several of my friends confirm. When I floss my teeth or brush my hair these days, I'm not really registering what the mirror tells me. Keeping track of reading glasses may be a pain, but isn't it convenient that our near vision starts to give out around the same time gravity has its way with our faces? Maybe it's a sign that we're not supposed to worry about it all that much.

My standard line about biking is, "I may not look as good in Lycra anymore, but I can still go the distance." I can't say I wouldn't happily reclaim the flat belly of my thirties, but if I have to make a choice, function trumps form any day. I'd rather be able to do the ride than to look hot in the outfit, and I'm grateful that I haven't aged out of any of the sports I truly care about.

Recently, I was debating whether to buy a pricey new bike, wondering aloud how many years I'd be able to ride it. "Mom! Get a grip. You sound like some oldster constantly fretting about impending death," my daughter said. "Buy the bike. Trust me, it'll get plenty of use." She's right. It's all too easy to short-change ourselves in this way. We don't have a lot of role models for late-in-life athleticism; it's our generation that's going to prove just how far we can go. So we have to hang tough. I'm dealing with a bout of heel pain right now. I cheer myself up by remembering that Banana George Blair didn't start barefoot water skiing until he was forty-six—and at ninety, he's still going strong. Jack La Lanne, who launched his first TV exercise show the year I was born, is still giving motivational speeches.

I'm feeling bullish about the decades of fitness yet to come, for me and for my generational peers. And if I ever get terminally discouraged about the lines on my face, there is no shortage of professionals who can help.

Mirror, Mirror: Can I Turn Back the Clock?

Medical advances and the prospect of marketing to the biggest, richest generation in American history have granted boomers an unprecedented opportunity to "keep our looks," as my great-aunt Helen used to say. A generation ago, a face-lift was a face-lift—take it or leave it. It was a rare treat, affordable for only the affluent. Today there's a whole menu of products and procedures to choose from—laser resurfacing to exorcise wrinkles, Botox to relax them, all kinds of injectables to plump them up. You can even have Gore-Tex installed in your face.

It's no surprise that women are flocking to these procedures, but so are the guys. According to the American Society of Plastic Surgeons, cosmetic surgery procedures for men in the United States have skyrocketed from a mere 47,000 in 1994 to nearly 1.2 million in 2004. In the same ten-year period, women's surgeries have grown from 345,000 to 1.7 million. Add in another 7.4 million minimally invasive procedures (resurfacing, injectables)—eight billion dollars' worth a year—and you can see just how far the urge to look younger is reaching across our generation. Between 2004 and 2005, the total number of procedures jumped 11 percent, to 10.2 million.

People can get a little crazy with this stuff. I recently read an article about hymen-reconstruction surgery, and two of the women who had the procedure are old enough to know better. A forty-year-old had the five-thousand-dollar procedure as "the ultimate gift" to her husband. A fifty-one-year-old went one step farther, adding vaginal tightening, to "add sparkle" to her marriage.

Still, as the procedures multiply, our attitudes change. "How do you like my eye lift?" a friend recently asked me. Unimaginable a generation ago, it's a comment more and more of us are hearing from our colleagues and friends. At *More,* one of our contributing editors, former NBC News reporter Connie Collins, came in for an idea meeting a mere week after her face-lift. She wrote an unflinching report of her recovery for us and also taped a mini documentary for the Discovery Health Channel. A beautiful woman whose face was etched with lines from youthful smoking and sun damage, Connie looked amazing after the lift. It was great girlish fun to ooh and ahh, sharing the experience with her. Call it the new female bonding. We're excited about the opportunities to look as good as we feel, and it's wonderful to share the joy.

Men aren't as forthcoming yet, but they're on their way. In an article we did about men's face-lifts in 2004, about half of the guys we interviewed were willing to go on the record and give their name, including a New Jersey construction worker who'd had liposuction. "If somebody wants to say something, I'll smack the crap out of them," he told us.

To Cut or Not to Cut?

So far, I'm sticking with what nature gave me. I haven't tried Botox or contemplated a face-lift. I don't even use anti-aging cosmetics. My morning and night routine is still Cetaphil with a Neutrogena chaser. When people ask me whether I've had any cosmetic procedures (when I was editor of *More,* the question was fair game and many reporters did), I laugh and say, "With so many people having face-lifts these days, somebody's got to volunteer for the control group." I'm saying no right now, but I'll never say never.

I might well have been driven to the surgeon's office had I continued to work in New York. As more and more people opt for anti-aging procedures, the norm is changing. What fifty looks like these days among professional circles in big cities isn't a naturally aging face. It's tauter, smoother, surgically enhanced. So many women have opted for anti-aging procedures that those of us who've forgone such treatments are beginning to look out of step—prematurely old. Meantime, before-and-after TV shows such as *Extreme Makeover* are demystifying and popularizing plastic surgery. Cosmetic dentistry has so taken the country by storm that the media story on tooth whitening has shifted from "Should you?" to "How often is too often?"

Book an Earthwatch trip. The leading volunteer vacation agency, this nonprofit deploys do-gooders trips worldwide—excavating at the Olduvai Gorge, monitoring turtle populations in the Great Barrier Reef, or assessing the impact of climate change on Portuguese seabirds. Choose from 130 trips in forty-seven countries (www.earthwatch.org).

While it's been great fun to share the excitement of friends who've loved their new looks, I do worry that our culture is getting plastic-surgery-crazed. Years ago, some urban, upscale parents would give their daughter a nose job as a sweet-sixteen gift. I always wondered about the message this sent; now kids are turning the tables, buying plastic surgery for their moms, like the fifteen-thousand-dollar face- and eyelid lift one daughter gave her fifty-four-year-old mother recently. A New York City facial surgeon sent a press release listing "gifts of beauty" that included a hundred-thousand-dollar makeover. Are we really so far gone that we need a six-figure operation to be happy again? As treatments proliferate, are we raising the bar on what it takes to look good?

These are tough questions that our generation, with its unprecedented access to surgical enhancements, is going to have to sort out. By talking about her visual reinvention for this book, Ellen Delathouder has contributed to the dialogue. She has complicated feelings about the procedures she chose, and wanted to go on record about both the pluses and the minuses. When the bandages came off from her face-lift at fifty-eight, she wasn't thrilled with what she saw—it just didn't look like her face. Being a woman of action, she went back to the surgeon and had some adjustments made until she had a look that she liked.

Color Me Sassy: The Hair Dye Effect

I may still be a holdout on the plastic surgery front, but I'm forever wedded to another anti-aging cosmetic: hair dye. Other than a telltale whisper of gray at the roots, I haven't seen the actual color of my hair in six years—and I hope never to again. The effect of having shiny auburn locks—dusted with blond if I'm in the mood—is powerful. It makes me feel vibrant and young. Almost every woman I know also dyes her hair, as do a few of the men.

I don't think anybody's stopped to consider the enormity of the hair color effect. For many boomers, it transforms how we feel about ourselves at midlife. The impact of a youthful mane is so potent that—from a distance, and from the back—I was once mistaken for one of my daughter's college friends.

All of these look-better options, from henna rinses to forehead lifts, affect far more than our mood. If we see ourselves as vital, attractive people, we act that way. Enriching our looks can enrich our attitude and then our lives, in a delightful domino effect. We just have to figure out where to draw the line between having fun with our looks and desperately clinging to a youthfulness we cannot rightly claim. Easy stuff, huh?

A Generation of Gym Rats

Let's move from the outside to the inside—from beauty to vitality. By the time we're in our forties, most of us have had some kind of health wake-up call—a friend or sibling who's been treated for cancer, the death of a parent. That first hint of our own mortality can send us to the drugstore for a regimen of anti-aging vitamins and supplements, or lead us to revamp our diet and start an exercise program.

Looking down the line of treadmills at my gym, I'm not

surprised to learn that the average age of a health club member is forty-one. According to research by the International Health, Racquet & Sportsclub Association, membership among thirty-five- through fifty-four-year-olds grew 79 percent between 1993 and 2004; for men and women fifty-five and over, the increase was a whopping 467 percent. No wonder there's not an idle cardio machine in sight.

We've long known that regular exercise can help control chronic health conditions like diabetes and heart disease. In 2005, a Swedish study revealed that regular exercise can help ward off dementia and Alzheimer's disease. Those who had exercised at least twice a week during middle age had half the risk of developing dementia and a 60 percent lower incidence of Alzheimer's. Other research has shown exercise to be a potent weapon against depression.

Weighty Matters: Is Ten Pounds a Decade Inevitable?

Which raises the question: If we're spending so much time at the gym, why aren't we svelte? According to Centers for Disease Control and Prevention statistics, American men and women are an inch taller than the 1960 norm. We also weigh more—a lot more. Men ages forty through sixty are carrying an additional twenty-seven pounds, and women in that age group weigh twenty-four pounds more than our parents did at our age. A long-term study, published in *The Annals of Internal Medicine,* that followed four thousand people for three decades came to the depressing conclusion that eventually nine out of ten men and seven out of ten women will become overweight. Even those who've maintained a healthy weight into middle age remain at risk.

For women, hormonal changes at midlife can make it harder

than ever to lose unwanted weight. Some studies say that the decrease in estrogen makes it easier for us to put on pounds—*ten a decade* is a depressing shorthand we're all familiar with. And as we get rounder, Hollywood stars get skinnier and skinnier, making us feel even worse.

At *More,* I got a front-row seat on a landmark event in the struggles against unrealistic body images. We were about to shoot Jamie Lee Curtis for our September 2002 cover when she phoned us (for a celebrity to place her own calls is almost unheard of, but as you'll see, Jamie is one of a kind) and said she had an idea for our photo shoot. She was doing the *More* cover to promote *I'm Gonna Like Me,* her new children's book on self-esteem. "If I'm going to talk the talk, I should walk the walk," she said.

At forty-three, Jamie no longer had the body that had emblemized "perfect" in the movie of the same title. In her own words, "I don't have great thighs. I have very big breasts and a soft, fatty little tummy." It was time, she told us, to peel away the myth of the perfect Jamie; she wanted women across America, who measured themselves against Hollywood celebrities, to realize how much artifice goes into the look. She wanted them to know that she had gained weight but she felt great, better than ever in fact. She ate well, exercised, and this is what her body looked like at forty-three.

Jamie proposed that we photograph her in her skivvies, without makeup or special lighting. A second, conventional celebrity photograph would be taken, too—after three hours of ministration by a crew of thirteen, including hair and makeup pros, lighting experts, and a manicurist. We agreed immediately, knowing that this brave act mirrored the mission of the magazine—to reflect the celebratory spirit of women at midlife—and that the unretouched photo of Jamie would get big play in the press. I remember telling the magazine's PR director, "Prepare yourself. This is going to be big."

We had no idea how big. The day the issue went on sale, Jamie and I appeared on *Today*. After that, the phone never stopped ringing. *Dateline* came to the office and filmed, Jamie did every talk show on TV, and there was a whirlwind of coverage in magazines, newspapers, and TV shows worldwide. When the dust settled, more than nine hundred million people had heard about the story.

Hundreds of e-mails and letters streamed into my office from readers who were electrified by the coverage. They all said two things: "Jamie Lee is my hero," and "Ohmigod, she looks like me." The director of an eating disorders treatment center wrote to say she was incorporating Jamie's story in her program, and the aunt of an anorexic teen said Jamie's brave act had made a big impression on her niece. We even had letters from men, applauding both Jamie's message and her new, softer curves.

Ironically, the "real Jamie" photo shoot led to a reversal of the life reinvention the Hollywood star had announced in *More*. In the interview, she told us she was leaving filmmaking to concentrate on her best-selling series of children's books, citing a lack of compelling roles for women her age. Then as a result of the article and the firestorm of publicity it ignited, she got a film offer she couldn't refuse: playing Lindsay Lohan's mom in a remake of *Freaky Friday*. It was a great role that played to her comedic talent—and won her a Golden Globe nod. Since then, she's continued to act when the role is right, and is still writing excellent children's books, too.

Jamie's message—that healthy habits are important, and that the number, whether it's on the scale or inside the waistband of your pants, is not—has been underscored by recent research that suggests being a bit overweight is not a bad thing. In fact, people who exceeded the target body mass index range by a little had a lower risk of death than either extremely fat or extremely thin people did. This is heartening news for those of us constantly fighting to lose ten or fifteen pounds. Then just as we're relaxing in the knowledge that they truly are vanity pounds, along comes another study finding greater longevity for skinny couch potatoes than people who are pudgy and in shape. It's always something!

While scientists sort out the true health implications of extra weight, some overweight boomers are discovering that midlife can be the time to take charge. There's a powerful reason why boomers are finally shedding excess weight they've carried since childhood or childbearing: They're moving into the decades when it can make the difference between an active life and a premature surrender to chronic disease. As I write this, the current poster boy for weight loss success is the governor of Arkansas, Mike Huckabee, who lost more than a hundred pounds and then ran a marathon. He's now a spokesperson for the American Heart Association. Donna Wade, who shared her story for this book, is another example of someone who fought being overweight since her teens, finally finding the motivation and inspiration to lose ninety pounds after forty. As the pounds dropped away and she felt better about herself, she discovered a latent athletic ability. Today she's an active triathlete who's training for an Ironman competition. As she sets higher and higher goals for herself, it motivates her to stay with the meal plan that's kept her at a healthy weight. At five foot two and 140 pounds, she admits that she's not Hollywood sleek. But that's fine with Donna. She's content with her weight because it represents a healthy number. Function, not form!

Welcome to the Lifestyle Pharmacy

Cosmetic surgeons aren't the only health professionals courting the vast boomer market. Drug companies have seen the potential of selling a whole new category of pharmaceuticals designed not to stave off death but to improve our lifestyle. First there was Rogaine, promising to restore a youthful head of hair; then, in the late 1990s, Viagra burst onto the scene, quickly becoming one of the best-selling drugs in America. Both of these treatments, aimed at men, have spawned companion pharmaceuticals for women, to improve thickness of their hair and the reliability of their sexual response. Now there's a drug in development to lower our weight "set point," making it easier to lose pounds, and another that may trick our stomachs into feeling full. One industry consultant, AdvanceTech Monitor, puts the lifestyle pharmaceutical business at a whopping twenty-three billion dollars a year.

What this means for boomers is that we have more and more power to affect our looks, and will have to decide what price beauty, what price youth—or at least, the appearance of youth—we are willing to pay.

Fighting Disease on a Bigger Stage

Despite our best efforts to stay healthy, midlife is when a lot of diseases strike—from breast cancer, which is the number one killer of women in this age group, to heart disease, the number one killer overall. For many boomers, the first stirrings of a serious health problem become a call to arms to reinvent their health—eating healthier foods, exercising regularly. But many are taking action on a far broader scale. They're mobilizing to become part of the team for the cure. Boomer women have led the charge to fund-raise for breast cancer research, providing a template for fighting many other diseases. Now if you Google "breast cancer fundraising events," you'll get more than two million hits. No slow learners among the men: A decade ago, prostate cancer was the disease that dared not speak its name; today there are more than 140,000 events—walks, races, dinners, tennis and golf matches—to bankroll a cure.

When the disease that strikes is a chronic condition with daily visual manifestations, like multiple sclerosis or Parkinson's, it presents a special array of worries and concerns. *How long will I be healthy? What effects will the symptoms I'm experiencing have on my life? Will I be able to continue doing my job? How will my loved ones react? If I'm single, will anyone date me?* Some boomers who are wrestling with these difficult issues are not getting bogged down in their personal response to the disease; they're pledging to become part of the solution. Marlene Kahan, who was diagnosed with Parkinson's at age fifty, was shocked and horrified. She resolved to become as smart as her doctors about her disease. Hitting the Web, she discovered a fund-raiser walk in her city that would take place in two months. In that short time, working her personal and professional connections, she was able to mobilize a team of forty friends and colleagues who walked with her and solicited nearly sixty-thousand dollars in donations, becoming the number one fund-raiser for the event.

Attend a religious service. If you're a lapsed church-, temple-, or mosquegoer, or a nonbeliever who simply wants to see how the other half lives, it can be a meaningful experience. Even if you're a regular attendee, visiting another denomination can give you new perspective on your own beliefs. If it doesn't deepen your faith, it will at least broaden your knowledge.

It's a long and victorious journey from the 1970s, when NBC correspondent Betty Rollins couldn't find a publisher for her landmark book about surviving breast cancer, *First You Cry*. Today, as boomers age into prime years for the early warnings of heart disease—high cholesterol, high blood pressure—we're seeing a similar metamorphosis in the publicity campaign. A decade ago, celebrity spokespeople were loath to appear under the "heart disease banner," but today big-name stars like Toni Braxton, Bill Cosby, Melanie Griffith, and Antonio Banderas are participating in the American Heart Association's fund-raising programs.

Whether it's taking responsibility for our own health, or pledging to help others through awareness and fund-raising, the boomer generation is ensuring a healthier midlife for themselves and a healthier game plan for generations to come.

The Life Entrepreneurs

The Biggest Loser

Donna Wade shed ninety pounds, discovered the gym—and became a triathlete.

Donna's Lesson: *It took turning forty to achieve a mature perspective on her weight. Her insight: You have to stop thinking about losing weight as a diet. It's not a temporary solution, it's a new life plan.*

DONNA WADE WAS a chubby teenager, and for most of her adult life she hovered between 180 and 200 pounds. "I'm only five foot two, so that was a lot of weight," she says. Donna, who is single, grew up in Ohio and now lives in Greer, South Carolina. Like so many Americans who are overweight, she tried every diet that came along. Ironically, all that dieting kept her fat. "When a weight loss plan failed—and they all did—it was easy for me to say that I just can't lose weight."

When Donna turned forty, she finally found the courage and inspiration to turn her life around, dropping ninety pounds and transforming herself into a competitive athlete. A trip to New Orleans to celebrate the big birthday brought her to the decision point. A year earlier, Donna had had a hysterectomy, and recuperating from surgery pushed her weight to a lifetime high of 230. When she went shopping for clothes for the trip, sticker shock struck. "I'd worn size 1X for a long time," Donna recalls. "But now I had to buy 2X clothes. That was a major wake-up call." When she developed the photographs from the trip, Donna was stunned to see how heavy she looked. "When you're really overweight, you know it, but somehow you don't think you look like that. It was a real 'Ohmigod!' moment."

Donna told herself it was now or never. "I knew it would only get harder to lose weight as I aged," she says. She made two basic changes in the way she ate: switching to fresh, healthy foods, and cutting portion size. Within three months, she had lost thirty pounds.

Now Donna was feeling better about herself, but she needed a new motivator to recharge her weight loss plan. As a nurse practitioner, she knew that the flip side of the weight loss coin featured a barbell: "I realized I had to exercise." Around this time, a reunion with a friend from grade school underlined the importance of keeping her new life plan on track. "My friend had come through a mastectomy and a bone marrow transplant with flying colors," Donna says. "But within two years, she discovered she had MS. Now she's spending an increasing amount of time in a wheelchair." Donna had always taken her own good health for granted. She redoubled her efforts to achieve a healthy weight by joining a gym.

At the fitness center, Donna had that typical new-member fish-out-of-water feel, facing a bewildering array of gleaming metal machines. "I couldn't even figure out how to turn the elliptical machine on," she recalls. Donna persevered, and the elliptical trainer ended up becoming her favorite. The other key to success was starting small. "This is where a lot of people set themselves up to fail," she says. "When you're at square one, you don't have the stamina to stay on the machine for forty-five minutes. If you try to, you're too discouraged to come back. I began doing twenty minutes, and increased my time by just five minutes each week." At first, the weight room seemed too intimidating—"I thought only muscle heads used free weights"—but after a few training sessions, she learned to like it.

Adding gym visits four days a week to her healthy eating plan did the trick. Over the next six months, Donna lost another forty-five pounds and figured out the principle that has allowed her to maintain a healthy weight for three years. "I couldn't think of it as something temporary I was doing to get my weight down," she says. "I wasn't dieting, I was changing my life."

Even so, as the pounds continued to peel off, Donna was losing something else—her motivation to go to the gym. "I knew I was fitter, but I needed something more to inspire me." A friend suggested that she train for a marathon. "It seemed ridiculous," Donna says. "I couldn't run one mile, so how could I run twenty-six?" Still, she was intrigued enough to go online and check it out. She began reading about triathlons, which sounded like fun. "I hadn't swum or biked much since I was a kid, but the idea of having three sports to work on really excited me." She started training on her own, reading books and following the guidelines. "When I discovered how much I liked it, I hired a coach," she says. At forty-three, in her first season, she competed in ten races. "No Ironmans," she hastens to add.

"They were all shorter distances—maybe a half-mile swim, a fifteen-mile bike ride, and a three-mile run. I loved it."

Through her triathlon training, Donna lost another 15 pounds, dropping to her current weight of 140. "I suppose in a perfect world, I'd like to lose another ten," she says, "but I have a lot of muscle mass. I'm not skinny, but it's a healthy weight for me." Shopping for clothes has become fun. "At the weight I was, you don't buy what you like, you buy what fits." Now a size 10, Donna has the run of the store. Because her medical test numbers were healthy to begin with, she hasn't seen the dramatic change some other weight losers do. But she's proud of her resting heart rate of fifty, a true athlete's number.

"I'm never going to win a triathlon, but I've taken a first and two thirds in my age group," Donna says. This has spurred her to accomplish the once impossible dream: a marathon. "The training was brutal, and when race day came, I was afraid. I didn't know if I could do it. When I crossed the finish line, I started to cry. I was just so thrilled to be standing there."

True to form, no sooner had she completed the Kiawah Island Marathon than she was plotting her next conquest: a half Ironman—a 1.2-mile swim, 61-mile bike ride, and 13-mile run. Four weeks before the race, Donna experienced her first major setback. She had to withdraw when she suffered pain in her left hip. "It's disappointing, but it wasn't worth the risk that overtraining could make the bursitis chronic." She remembers seeing an eighty-year-old woman compete. "When she completed the race, everybody applauded, and I thought, *I want to be doing this when I'm eighty.*" These days, instead of running, Donna's taking her two dogs, a golden retriever and a black Lab mix, on long walks. Chances are, she won't be sidelined for long. She's already targeted a half Ironman race for the coming spring.

In setting out to change her weight, Donna achieved a much bigger goal: transforming her life. These days, a lot of her socializing revolves around fitness—meeting people for a bike ride or running with a friend once a week. "It's much more significant to me than going out to dinner," she says. But she's careful to keep in touch with her old buddies, too. "It's easy for someone like me who's seen such incredible benefits to go overboard and reach the point of obsession. I have to step back sometimes and realize I haven't seen my nonfitness friends for a while. It's a balancing act."

After several years at her target weight, eating right is something Donna must be mindful of every day. "Even now, if I'm stressed, I'll think I'm hungry," she says. "I have to tell myself, *No, you're not. You just want to eat.*" After a race, she'll treat herself to an order of french fries or a gooey dessert, but then it's right back on the wagon. Working out helps keep her food choices in line. "If you're logging the training time, you want to put food into your body that will help you meet your goals." Donna eats small meals five times a day, so "I never get to that place where I'm starving and will eat anything I can get my hands on as soon as I walk through the door.

"I'm a happier person these days, easier to be around," Donna, who's now forty-four, continues. She thrives on the compliments her new appearance invites. Her whole life, people have commented on Donna's hearty laugh, which bubbles up repeatedly during our conversation. But she wasn't always as happy as she seemed. "When you keep trying to do something and fail over and over again, there's an emptiness," she says. Now there's a real depth to her laugh. Donna is happy inside and out. After the half Ironman next spring, she's planning to go for the whole enchilada next year—a full Ironman. "I think to myself, *How can I run a marathon after swimming 2.4 miles and biking 112?* But my experience has taught me that you can train to do it. Cause and effect. It's all about setting and reaching goals."

Putting Parkinson's in Its Place

When Marlene Kahan was diagnosed with Parkinson's, she transformed discouraging medical news into the inspiration to help find a cure.

Marlene's Lesson: *Middle age is when many chronic diseases strike. Getting beyond your own situation—say, fundraising for research—can help you thrive despite having a condition that will never go away.*

AFTER MARLENE KAHAN turned fifty, she began noticing a few anomalies. Some days, she felt a tightness in her legs, or a tremor. Other times, there was no way she could position her body to be comfortable. Since the symptoms seemed to pop up at the same time in her hormonal cycle each month, she figured perimenopause was the cause. "It was enough to get my attention, but not enough to make me worry," she says. Her work as the executive director of the American Society of Magazine Editors kept her too busy to dwell on these odd symptoms.

Then one October afternoon two years ago, she was giving a speech at a national conference when her head started wobbling. "It was so weird," Marlene recalls. "I felt like a bobblehead doll." Nobody seemed to notice, and Marlene chalked it up to stage fright. Still, this upsetting new development was enough to send her to the doctor. Her internist referred her to a neurologist. "He diagnosed my condition as 'essential tremors,' prescribed beta-blockers, and told me to live with it." As the shaking got worse, Marlene toughed it out. Finally, eight months later, she consulted another neurologist, the top man at a New York City hospital, who took her complaints seriously.

He asked her to fill out a detailed questionnaire and followed up with a two-hour physical exam. At the end, he said bluntly: "You've got Parkinson's." Marlene was stunned. "I went to the appointment alone because I never expected to hear something like that. Every sad scenario you could think of ran through my head—a wheelchair, not being able to do anything for myself." Somehow she found her way back to work, went to her office, and shut the door. "I just sobbed," she says. "I felt that my life was over."

Trace your ancestors' travels. National Geographic has partnered with IBM on a research project to trace human migration paths across the world. For $99.99, they'll send you a DNA kit: You swab your cheek, and they identify what migration path your ancient ancestors pursued out of Africa (www.nationalgeographic.com/genographic).

The diagnosis carried such a feeling of finality, Marlene could never have imagined that six months later, this dreaded disease would thrust her life into an exciting new phase, inspiring her to take steps to preserve her health and to find great satisfaction working for a cure.

But first, she had to come to terms with the fact that she had a chronic disease that would affect the rest of her life. She trolled the Internet learning about Parkinson's. She knew the disease was in its early stages, and her manifestations suggested that it would not progress quickly.

That weekend, she and her boyfriend, Ken, drove to his cabin upstate, hoping to escape the city and the bad news. "I tried so hard to accept the diagnosis, but I just couldn't." For the first time in her life, she felt hopeless and depressed. A psychiatrist she consulted didn't help. "She was very cold, wanted to do the take-me-back-to-birth routine," Marlene says. "What I needed were the tools to handle this illness." In the end, Marlene found them on her own, by reading about Parkinson's and talking to her friends. "When I started telling people, their love and caring was my medicine. With each person I told, I felt better," she says. At her organization's national convention the following year, she decided to go public. "When people asked, 'How are you?' I'd say, 'I'm pretty good but I was diagnosed with Parkinson's this year.' There'd be a wide-eyed look, I'd get a hug, and we'd go on from there."

It wasn't long before Marlene's natural resilience kicked in. "I'm stubborn and independent," she says. "As a kid, I never had a lot of cheerleading or much support. Everything I've accomplished I've done on my own. I determined that I would take this on, too."

Cruising Parkinson's Web sites, she learned about an upcoming fund-raising walk in Central Park. She signed on, giving herself a thousand-dollar goal. "I e-mailed everybody in the universe, and the first day I had two thousand dollars in pledges." She kept raising the bar, clearing it, and raising it again. "It got to be fun. Everybody was so generous," she says. As the networking circles rippled outward, she met more and more people who'd been touched by the disease. She was buoyed by the positive stories people told her—like an uncle with Parkinson's who at eighty was still playing tennis. And she was grateful when she could help a fellow patient. "I met a woman who'd been fired after she told her boss she had Parkinson's," Marlene recalls. "When I told her I was out in public, doing the walk, she was inspired to tell her new boss, who was fine about it."

As Marlene told friends and colleagues about the fund-raiser, she was pulling in more and more donations. On a sunny April day, forty people walked with her, all wearing MAG QUEEN team hats. Afterward, Marlene threw a party at her apartment.

"It was a gorgeous day. I was so happy to see people come out on my behalf." When the donations were tallied up, Marlene was the number one fund-raiser, pulling in close to sixty thousand dollars. It was a real turning point for dealing with the disease. "I couldn't believe I had come out of nowhere and taken over this walk," she says. The warmth and support of colleagues and friends were healing her depression; now feeling the power she had to fight this disease by raising research funds showed her the way to turn misfortune into opportunity.

Meantime her symptoms had progressed. "There's a stiffness, and the tremors are more consistent than I'd like," she notes. "Sometimes my legs are going a million miles a second, like I'm running a marathon sitting in my desk chair." When she notices a change, she calls the doctor, who adjusts her medication. It's a delicate balance, because some of the drugs have unwelcome side effects, including nausea and jerky movements.

Even when there's bad news, Marlene can handle it because she's taking control. She hired a personal trainer, who works with her twice a week. "I used to be very bad about the gym, but now I exercise religiously." She's popping vitamins and using acupuncture to ease symptoms, with her doctor's endorsement. "I probably should talk to a nutritionist, too, but one thing at a time," she says. "It's only been a year."

Parkinson's has put a strain on Marlene's love life. "I had just started going out with Ken when I was diagnosed. Horrible timing," she says. "We met on Match.com and really clicked." A year into the relationship, he broke it off. "I couldn't blame him for pulling away. He had been supportive, taken care of me when I was diagnosed, but it just got to be too much." Five weeks later, they met for drinks, talked things through, and got back together. Now they keep communication channels wide open. "We're playing it by ear, seeing where the relationship goes."

The most difficult thing is knowing this disease will never go away. "It's very hard to think that I'm going to spend every day for the rest of my life being uncomfortable and wondering about the progression. I try to keep all that far back in my mind." Instead she focuses on the fact that stem cell research may brighten her future. "I'm hoping that in ten years there will be major changes in treatment, even a cure." And she credits her maturity for leveling out her moods. "If this had happened when I was younger, it would have been more difficult," Marlene says. "I'm smarter now, and I have better resources to handle it." In many ways, she can't believe she's in her fifties. "I feel like a kid most of the time, and when people tell me I look radiant, healthy, and young, I tell myself at least the outside is holding up."

At the deepest level, Marlene knows she's tough. "My father was a prisoner at Auschwitz, and if he could survive that, I can survive this. But I wish he were still around to talk to me about it," she says. Marlene keeps an aphorism a friend gave her from Indian mystic Shantideva: "If you can do something about it, why waste time getting upset? If you can't do anything about it, why bother getting upset on top of it?"

"I can't say I'm more spiritual, but I have a new understanding of the importance of living in the now. I'd always dwelled on the past or worried about the future. Now I know we have nothing greater than this particular moment." She's finding positive solutions to the problems that Parkinson's presents: "I'm getting my hair straightened tomorrow by that five-hour Japanese technique, a big move," she reports. "I don't like the frizzies all the time, and it's too hard to handle a blow dryer."

Marlene's fund-raising work has given her an uplifting focus for her life. "Since the Parkinson's walk, I've had calls from the Michael J. Fox Foundation, and I may do some work with them.

I want to organize fund-raisers on my own." She's brainstorming even as she talks: "Maybe I could get my magazine editor friends to publish articles during Parkinson's Awareness Month, the way they do for breast cancer in October." Nine months before the next Central Park walk, Marlene has already registered her team with the goal of topping the sixty thousand dollars she raised her first time around. "Sure, there are days when I'm miserable, but the do-good factor helps," Marlene concludes. "I have this disease for a reason: I'm meant to help others. That's what gives me the strength to stay positive."

Banishing Back Pain

At forty, Jim Koeppel launched a new career that cured his chronic back problem.

Jim's Lesson: *Making over your health can ignite a bigger life change. Taking Pilates classes to feel better led to a new profession as an instructor.*

"I'VE BEEN CHANGING my mind about what I want to do with my life since I was sixteen," Jim Koeppel says. When he was a boy, he wanted to be a pilot, so he started taking flying lessons at fifteen. On the verge of making his first solo flight, he got beaten up outside his Queens, New York, high school. The attack left him with a fractured skull and double vision—dashing his dreams of a career in aviation.

When Jim went to college, he was so ambivalent about his future, he never declared a major. He dropped out for a semester to start a punk rock band and transferred to the University of Colorado for a semester before earning his BA. "My degree was from the Gallatin University Without Walls at New York University. I called it the institute for the terminally undecided," he says. Over the years, Jim worked as a truck driver, an oyster shucker, a guitarist, a substitute teacher, sales and marketing director for a software company, a freelance writer, and a bartender. Some jobs he hated, others he enjoyed, but nothing really stuck.

Then, at forty, Jim found himself. He discovered a discipline that has offered him good health, newfound strength in body and mind, and what looks to be a lifelong career. Here's how it happened.

At the time of this breakthrough, Jim was in the throes of a way-too-busy life. A doting at-home dad to two-year-old daughter Naomi, Jim would rush off to a gig when his wife got home from work. He'd been playing music since the age of twelve, when his parents gave him a guitar to ward off boredom while a broken leg mended. Now he played in three bands—rock, jazz, and blues—taught guitar at a music store on Sundays, and was finishing up a master's degree in music. "I got up with Naomi one morning at four and thought, *I can't do this anymore.*" Beyond a basic lack of sleep, carrying amps back and forth from basement to car was taking a toll on his body, exacerbating a back problem he'd had all his life. One night during a performance, his back just gave out. "We were in the middle of a song when I fell to the floor," Jim says. "I couldn't stand, so I finished the song on my knees. My bass player had to pick me up and walk me to my car."

Jim knew he had to take action. "Ever since I was a teenager, my back had gone out three or four times a year, putting me in bed for days." His brother had also suffered from chronic back pain and was on the verge of scheduling an operation when his surgeon suggested that he try Pilates, a system of exercise and physical manipulation designed to increase core strength and improve posture and alignment. Pilates worked so well in alleviating his brother's back pain that Jim decided to give it a try. After three one-on-one sessions at a spa in Irvington, New York, where he lives, Jim's back felt great. As long as he practiced Pilates for an hour three times a week, it stayed great.

"I've been doing Pilates for two years now, and my back has not gone out once. That's a miracle." Jim started doing research on Joseph Pilates, a boxer and acrobat who developed the techniques to treat fellow prisoners at an internment camp in England during World War I. "He was really the first physical therapist." Intrigued by the changes that practicing Pilates had wrought on his body, he wanted to learn more. "They started calling me Mr. Pilates at the spa, because I was the only guy," he says. "The owner told me, 'If you get certified, you've got a job here.'" A number of factors convinced him to take the plunge: "The private sessions were expensive, but if I didn't do it, I didn't feel good." Naomi was about to enroll in preschool, so his time would be freed up to do the necessary course work. "Basically, I studied Pilates so I could improve my self-practice."

Enroll at a university you couldn't get into at eighteen. Top schools, including Harvard, run continuing education programs that employ their regular faculty and curriculum. Check the Web site of the best college near you.

He signed up for a three-day anatomy workshop run by the Kane School of Core Integration in New York City. He dug into studying, realizing he had some catching up to do. "A lot of the people in the class were personal trainers, dancers, massage therapists, or chiropractors—they'd already studied anatomy." But Jim persevered. Two more weekend workshops taught him to train clients on mats. After ten hours of supervised teaching, twenty hours of self-practice, and a written exam ("which I failed the first time"), Jim was certified as a Pilates instructor; he could teach classes or offer personal training sessions. The next level of certification, for working with clients on Pilates machines, involves hundreds of hours of supervised teaching and self-practice.

Two years after that first weekend workshop, Jim expects to attain his Pilates machine certification in about six months. Meantime, he's bought the equipment and set it up in a Brooklyn studio, which he also rents out to other instructors. He is finding that leading Pilates classes is the most challenging, most rewarding work of his life. "I taught at SUNY Purchase as part of my master's program and I have no problem getting in front of people," he says. "But private Pilates sessions can be really draining. You're one-on-one, it's intimate, people start telling you their problems. You have to touch them to perform a manual release on a tight muscle or tendon."

Touching didn't come easily to Jim, but he was a natural at reading the body's anatomy. "I was really uncomfortable in my first mat workshop, the only guy among twenty-six women in leotards." Once he overcame his timidity, assessments were easy to do. "In one workshop, we'd put our hands over someone else's and try to intuit their emotions. I got it right every time," he says. "It sounds flaky, but the instructor said I had a really powerful connection."

The work is gratifying when he can help someone the way Pilates helped him. "One client told me that after two weeks of sessions, she didn't feel the sciatica in her leg that had been plaguing her for years," he says. "I see a conductor regularly. When he first came in, his head was tilted to the right from the asymmetric posture of holding a baton. Now his neck is straight and aligned."

Jim's long-term plan, once Naomi is in school all day, is to earn his living teaching Pilates, perhaps opening his own studio, while reserving some energy to play music again. For now he's basking in the benefits Pilates has brought. "I'm a maniac. I practice seven to ten hours a week. I also do Gyrotonic exercises, a sister discipline in which the motion is more fluid and circular, and I take trapeze lessons every other week." Jim feels stronger and healthier than he did as a teenager. "People constantly tell me how different I look," he says. After a month of Pilates, Jim's pants were too big. When he saw his father after four months, "My dad said, 'I think I'm shrinking.'" Jim told him, "'No, you're not. I'm growing. By standing straighter, I'm an inch taller than I used to be.' Pilates has totally transformed my life."

A New Face on the Future

Ellen Delathouder had second thoughts about her face-lift, but ultimately the operation was a success. It gave her a new look and a new outlook on life.

Ellen's Lesson: *Even with the wisdom of fifty-plus years, it's easy not to anticipate that the change wrought by cosmetic surgery is much more than skin-deep. Be smart enough to know that when things get tough, regrets are useless; you have to move ahead.*

"I ALWAYS REMEMBER what Gloria Steinem said: When women start telling their stories, they begin owning those stories and their lives," Ellen Delathouder says. And that is precisely why she talks with rare honesty about the face-lift she had at fifty-eight. "It's the last bastion where women don't share. After I had the surgery, several people I know really well confessed that they'd had face-lifts, too. Because they'd never told anyone, they missed out on the support of other women." Ellen's face-lift was not the Cinderella tale that reality TV makeover shows would lead you to assume is the norm. It was a long, tough road to "happily ever after."

Like so many women of her generation, in her thirties Ellen used to say, "A face-lift? Never." In her forties, "never" became "probably not." By the time she got to "Well, maybe," she was making appointments with doctors in Des Moines, Iowa, where she is a VP of marketing at a media company. She knew all the reasons to say no. "It's a battle against aging you're not going to win," she says. "I've seen some bad jobs, and I went through that *I can't have a face-lift because I'm a feminist* thing."

Ellen's a complicated woman—a self-described Mother Earth type who's a Unitarian ("and you know we're all old hippies") with friends who are professors and intellectuals. But she has always worn makeup everywhere, kept her lustrous blond hair in a stylish cut, chosen chic and unusual clothes that complement her lithe, five-foot-eleven frame. "Growing up, I was the pretty one," she says. "My brothers and sisters were brilliant, valedictorians, PhDs. Everybody always said to me, 'Oh, you'll be a model.'" For a long time, Ellen thought that looking good would make people like her, and she didn't have the confidence to flex her considerable intelligence until she found a mentor who saw Ellen's potential and encouraged her career.

Oddly enough, it was her first mentor who also got Ellen thinking about plastic surgery. "Back when I was in my midforties, she asked me if I would ever have a face-lift," Ellen recalls. "Shocked, I blurted, 'Do you think I need one?'" Yes, her mentor told her, if she wanted to stay in business, but not yet. Ellen's mentor, who was in her sixties, had already had two.

Ellen didn't seriously consider a face-lift until another decade had passed. She knew she didn't need one to keep her job. When she'd tried to leave in her midfifties, the CEO had invited her to write her own job description. Over the years, Ellen had simply gotten fed up with what gravity was doing to her face. "I didn't want to look younger," she says. "I just wanted my skin to stop sagging." Like many other women, she went to the doctor asking about an eye lift, then found herself trading up. The first time she met with the surgeon she ultimately chose, he suggested a whole palette of procedures—eye, brow, and face-lifts, and puffing up her lips with belly fat. She left his office vowing never to return. But after seeing two other physicians, she found herself back in his office. "At first, it sounded overwhelming. But I'm a creative person who sees the entire composition. I know that sometimes when you fix one thing, you break everything else." Getting the works was beginning to sound good. "And I had the money," she notes. "Would I have borrowed to do it? Probably not. But I had put my three kids through college, and they're all independent now. It wouldn't put my retirement in jeopardy." She'd been divorced for twelve years, and it was her money to spend.

Still, she wavered. When the doctor gave her a tentative date for the procedure, she said she'd have to get back to him. A few weeks later, she discovered a colleague had had a face-lift by the same doctor. "She was beautiful, and I would never have dreamed anybody had touched her face." As soon as she left the meeting, Ellen confirmed the date.

"Once I made the commitment, I told myself, *No matter what happens, you can't turn back.*" She feared disfiguration, anesthesia, that she wouldn't like the results, that other people wouldn't like her new look. The only thing she didn't fear was the recovery. "I wasn't listening when the doctor told me it would be a two-year healing process. I was so naive. I figured, *Two weeks, I'll be back to normal,*" she says. "I didn't know how bad the worst would be. It was a *long* journey of healing."

Ellen had never had major surgery. "When I woke up I was so thirsty and I couldn't breathe. These are normal reactions to anesthesia, but I thought I was dying." Before she could regain her equilibrium, she was out the door; she had opted to spend the first night at home with two attendants, a friend who stayed overnight and her thirty-four-year-old son, Yancy, who lived next door. "I had tubes, I was in pain, I was out of it, I was scared. It would have been so easy to wish I'd never had it done, but I just wouldn't let myself go there." Yancy never let on how shaken he was to see his mother this way. He lay down next to her and held her hand. For the next week, her friends gave her foot rubs, delivered meals, and offered encouragement. When Ellen saw herself in a mirror a few days after the operation, she felt so sick she didn't even care how red and swollen her face was. And she felt guilty that she'd brought this all on herself. Denying her feelings, she threw herself back into work, conducting meetings by phone, and even having her staff over to her house.

Look up an old friend or flame. We all have mysteries in our background—those once rich relationships that broke up in a flash of temper, or just whispered away. Find them on Google or Classmates.com, and rekindle romance, reconnoiter your past.

Two weeks after the surgery, she was back at the office, still not happy with her new look. "I felt like I had somebody else's face. I'd look in the mirror and my eyes would try to adjust the image back to the old me." She couldn't feel the top of her head or the sides of her face. She got through the days by reminding herself that she had to look forward because there was no going back.

While Ellen was facing down her own doubts, she wasn't getting rave reviews from all quarters. Most of her friends were supportive, but she still recalls one comment that stung. "A supposed buddy told me she was going to get an eye lift, but that she certainly wouldn't use my doctor." And she still regrets not telling her twenty-two-year-old daughter, Ann Marie, who drove down from Minneapolis for a visit five weeks after surgery. "When she walked in the door, I was acting like nothing had happened. I was naive enough to think she might not notice," Ellen said. Ann Marie told her mother that she resented being out of the loop and that she liked the way she'd looked before. "She went off like a rocket," Ellen says, "behaved exactly the way I didn't want to deal with." Ellen was calm but firm. "You're you and I'm me. At my age, you may make a different decision. In fact, I hope you do," Ellen told her daughter. "I wasn't promoting face-lifts at that time."

But the months went by, her skin relaxed, the swelling went down, little creases returned here and there. Gradually, Ellen grew accustomed to her new face. Two years later, she loves it. Her doctor has fine-tuned her lips to a contour she's comfortable with, and she's learning to accent her plush new mouth with bolder shades of lipstick. "He was great to work with," Ellen says. "He always spent time with me, made sure that ultimately I got the result I wanted."

The face-lift has helped Ellen feel beautiful again, but in a much different way. "Now it's a bonus, not something I need to feel okay about myself. It's given me a new spirit of girly fun." Her newfound confidence delivered another bonanza: Playing to this spirit of adventure, she's found a new man, and he's inspired her to take up biking and skiing. "I met him a year and a half after the surgery, when I was feeling pretty and flirtatious. Jim is three years younger, the kindest, sweetest, most compassionate man." The face-lift has led to another surprising change: Ellen is no longer fashion-model thin—and she's as thrilled with her voluptuous new shape as with her updated face. "I've got twenty more pounds. Some of it's biking muscle," she's quick to add. "And I feel more sensual. It's all part of the new way I see myself, especially since I began a relationship with this wonderful guy."

Will she go back into the OR for a refresher someday? "Nope," Ellen says flatly. "I invested in it, I got my money's worth. I'm done."

Becoming a Woman

At fifty, Dana Beyer finally found the courage to have surgery she'd dreamed of since she was a teen—to change her gender.

Dana's Lesson: *You have to listen to your heart and respect your own needs, instead of worrying about what other people will think.*

IT'S HARD TO imagine a more extreme health makeover than the one Dana Beyer embarked upon at midlife. For as long as she can remember, Dana felt she was a female with a male's body. "The psychiatric diagnosis, gender identity disorder, is a complete misnomer. I've never had any doubt about my gender identity," she says. "But growing up, my friends made fun of me whenever I would show anything outside our code of masculinity. I was taunted, pushed around, shamed in the boys' locker room—but I didn't feel like I belonged there, so there was a sense of bringing it on myself, too." It wasn't until she was on the verge of fifty that she summoned the courage to act on her conviction and have the sex reassignment surgery that transformed her life.

In an outer borough of New York during the 1950s and '60s, she squashed down her feelings about her sexuality and grew up as a boy. It was just too lonely, too hard, to do anything else. "In those years, when people thought of cross-dressers or any kind of transgressive sexuality, Norman Bates in *Psycho* was the image in their minds," she recalls. It wasn't until an eighth-grade trip to Washington, DC, that Dana learned she—in those days, he—was not alone. "On the bus with my quote-unquote girl-friend, I picked up *True Confessions,* and there was an article ti-tled 'Sixteen, and I Had to Change My Sex.' I thought, *Ohmigod, that's me.* Then I spent the next thirty years running away from it because it was just too scary."

Dana went to medical school and became an opthalmolo-gist like transsexual pioneer Renee Richards. Continuing to live as a man, she married her junior high school sweetheart, the girl on the bus, who knew about Dana's gender crisis. "She prom-ised she would never tell anyone, and to her credit, for almost thirty years she never did." They traveled the world together and had two sons. But all the while, Dana says, living in the wrong body just got harder and harder. Jennifer, née James, Boylan, who wrote a book about transitioning at midlife, *She's Not There,* describes it in a way that rings true for Dana. "Jenny called it an erosion of her old self, the one she projected into the world. The sand keeps crumbling until one day, the beach is gone. This is common for women like me who've delayed their transition." Before Dana reached her own tipping point, she divorced and married again, and conducted a successful eye surgery practice in Mississippi. "I spent all those years hoping I was just a cross-dresser, that I could manage with that, and ig-nore who I was."

As with many of the life changers I talked with, September 11 forced her decision. It was at the Manhattan wedding of a childhood friend, in sight of the smoldering ruins of the World Trade Center, that Dana, who had already begun taking estro-gen, decided to go for the transgender surgery. "I'm sitting at the reception thinking, *What are these people, whom I've known for forty years, going to think when they find out?* That's what had been stopping me all along. I was afraid of losing everybody." This was not an unrealistic fear. Dana had read medical literature about people who had transitioned and emerged from the operation friendless and alone. The wedding was only nine days after the terrorist attacks, and Dana could see the pall of smoke hanging over the rubble. Looking out the window at that ominous gray cloud and reflecting on the fragility of human life, she realized she needed to act.

Dana's wife helped her break the news to her parents. "My mother said she wished that I would wait to transition until they were dead." After Dana had her first surgery, to feminize her face, she went to visit them. "The man who rarely held me even as a child greeted me with a big hug," she recalls. "My mother couldn't get over my constant smile. She said, 'I can't remember you ever smiling,' and I told her, 'Yes, that is the point.'" Since then, Dana's parents have offered to help others in the same circumstances.

> **Don't eat after dinner.** TV's prime time is peak hours for refrigerator raiding. Breaking one big bad food rule can be the tipping point to a new lifelong eating plan. Don't revamp your diet all at once; just make one commitment and stick to it. A month later, you'll be ready for another change.

Then Dana sent out two hundred e-mails and letters explaining why she was transitioning. "I told my rabbi, not knowing whether I'd ever be welcome in the synagogue again."

Dana was stunned and delighted by the way her friends rallied around her. "I have a hard time thinking of anybody who didn't," she says. "One woman who runs a local restaurant and is Eastern Orthodox told me, 'This is difficult, you're going to have to give me some time.' But even she came around."

There's another reason Dana waited so long to transition:

Worried about the effect on her kids, she didn't want to make the change until they were out of high school. In the end, her two boys were fine with dad-turned-mom, Dana thinks, because they'd been expecting it all along. "I told my kids when they were six and three that 'Your dad's different, he likes doing girl stuff, too.' When I had electrolysis and shaved my mustache, they asked why, and I said, 'I'm more comfortable this way.' As the years went by, I'd drop hints here or there." When they heard their dad would be undergoing genital reconstructive surgery, both boys were supportive. "The younger one did have to put up with some taunting at school. But once he said, 'If you don't stop, I'll belt you,' that was the end of it." Dana's older son wrote his college essay about his father's transition; he's now a sophomore at an Ivy League school. "They'd probably rather have their father," Dana says, "but they accept things and like me better in many ways, since I'm much happier."

Changing gender was a two-year process, starting with hormone treatment; Dana's first operation was a relatively new specialty, facial feminization surgery. "Some people had posted before-and-after photos on the Web. I looked at them and said, *Wow. I could look the way I've always wanted to, like my sister.*" It was a ten-hour, thirty-thousand-dollar procedure in which the forehead is recontoured, the chin and jawline reshaped. The results were so convincing that "Once I took the bandages off, there was no going back," she says. "I put on a skirt and makeup, and that was it." Dana recalls feeling a tremendous rush of liberation, and relief that she was finally herself. She grew her hair into a strawberry-blond bob. Six months later, the genital surgery was almost an anticlimax.

Dana was a DES baby, and her research into the effects of this drug, given to five million pregnant women in the United States between 1948 and 1971 to prevent miscarriage, has convinced her that it's the culprit in her gender woes. "You got DES once you knew you were pregnant, around eight weeks. The testes develop in week seven, but brain sexuality doesn't occur until the beginning of the second trimester." Giving a potent hormone such as DES in between—effectively bathing the fetus in estrogen—Dana believes, produces fetuses with male genitals, female brain chemistry.

When she was twelve, Dana began bleeding from the penis. Terrifying, to be sure, but in a strange way also encouraging to the boy who felt he was a girl. "It was awful, painful, a terrible experience. But I figured I should be menstruating. I was hoping my breasts would grow and that everyone would finally recognize that I was a girl." Now Dana knows that the bleeding came from uterine remnants in her body. At the time, the only solution the doctor could offer was five months of excruciatingly painful cauterization of the urethra. Dana recalls, "I'd come out of the treatments crying, and my father would say, 'Be a man.'" At one point, she developed septic shock and nearly died. "When I was recovering from surgery, I remember telling my mother I was going to become a doctor so this would never happen to anybody again."

No longer practicing medicine, Dana now devotes her time to activism. While the effects of DES on daughters are well known (infertility and pregnancy complications, vaginal and cervical cancer, structural anomalies of the reproductive tract), the effects on sons are far less documented. "My friend Scott Kerlin, who has a social sciences PhD, started DES Sons International Network six years ago to get the word out. A year later, I joined the group as medical consultant." This is not an issue that will recede as the years go by. For one thing, DES reaches down through the generations to affect DES grandchildren, too, and it's similar in chemical action to a number of pesticides, including DDT. Dana gives talks and grants media interviews. "People say I'm effective because I'm not angry anymore," she says.

She may not be angry, but other people are. While our culture is getting more comfortable with homosexuality—consider the proliferation of same-sex spousal rights laws, and the popularity of network sitcoms such as *Will & Grace*—transgender isn't even knocking at the door of mass-culture acceptability yet. Gay cowboy movie *Brokeback Mountain* became a surprise success in early 2006, while *Transamerica,* which profiles a man on the brink of transitioning, achieved critical acclaim but found no footing at the box office. For transsexuals, this can be frightening as well as sad. Hate crimes are a constant worry. "My older son keeps telling me that I should upgrade my alarm system now that I'm out publicly and speaking," Dana says. "There are a lot of crazy people, but I don't worry about it. I know that even if something were to happen, I did the right thing."

Dana's second wife supported her through the transition, but moved out after the final surgery. "It was very difficult for her," Dana says. "I think Jessica Lange used the metaphor in the movie *Normal* that you watch your husband die." Since then, Dana has dated, which brings up a host of issues—basically, what do you tell him, and when? "I have a third-date rule," she says. "If things are working well, and we've got a connection, I tell the guy. Generally, he says, 'That's fascinating,' and then he's history." Right now Dana is living with another transwoman, whom she met in Hollywood while performing in the first all-transgender cast of *The Vagina Monologues.* Ever candid, Dana says, "I like sex with men better, but I'd prefer to live with a woman."

For Dana, transitioning isn't so much a reinvention at midlife as a "becoming"—finally expressing the person she has been inside all along. "I know people who transitioned in their twenties. I respect them greatly and wonder where their courage came from. Their response to me is, We don't know where you got the courage to keep playing the game, being responsible to the people you were responsible to—your spouse, your parents, your children, your profession—for all those years." In fact, Dana says, she'd been living her life for other people, not for herself. It took the wisdom and maturity of midlife—as well as a wake-up call from the September 11 terrorist attacks—to make the change.

CHAPTER 3

Redefining Family

RECENTLY, I HAD a front-row seat at an event that high-lighted one of the many ways boomers are reinventing family life. On a rainy Saturday afternoon, I joined a circle of graying women in a suburban living room, most of us parents of kids in their teens and twenties. If you had to guess what we were up to, a Botox party would be the logical choice. But we were defying age in a completely different way—with a baby shower for our fifty-one-year-old friend Claire Gruppo. As we oohed and ahhed over tiny powder-blue sweaters and marveled at a newfangled baby gadget, the Diaper Genie, our hostess passed out flutes of champagne. Even Claire could drink be-cause she was having her baby not only at an unusual age, but in an unusual way: A surrogate was pregnant with donor sperm. In four days, Claire would fly down to Florida for the birth.

Her son Connor is now a chubby six-month-old with a goofy smile and a crafty gleam of mischief in his eyes, and Claire's life has been overturned in a most delightful way. As the hard-driving president of an investment banking firm, she used to be on the road half the time, on call 24/7. Since becoming a mom, she's knocking off work early to hurry home and play with her son and plotting to throttle back to a four-day week. *Quality time* is no longer defined as the hour she sits in a conference room hammering out a multimillion-dollar deal; it's the hour she spends cross-legged on her living room floor in a sea of brightly colored Fisher-Price toys.

> **Become a tourist in your town.** I've lived near New York City for thirty years and I've never been to Ellis Island. Correct one of your own lapses with a day trip to a local site and experience your community in a new way.

She's not alone. With a leg up from medical science, we baby boomers are launching our own midlife baby boom. The birthrate for women forty-five and over more than doubled between 1990 and 2002, according to a Centers for Disease Control and Prevention report. Adoption at midlife is on the rise, too. China, which allows single parents up to age fifty to adopt, as well as couples up to age sixty-five, has seen the rate increase 39 percent in just two years, from 2002 to 2004.

Having babies at an age when previous generations became grandparents is yet another manifestation of the boomer credo that rules are for somebody else. Women who dedicated themselves to their careers until they were well into their forties are refusing to say, "It's too late for me." So are couples who married late in life and want to share their love with a baby. Some high-profile parents may have gotten the ball rolling. Diane Keaton adopted her two children as a single mom in her fifties. Joan Lunden had two sets of twins by surrogate, the first pair born when she was fifty-two, the second two years later. Vice presidential candidate John Edwards and his wife, Elizabeth's, youngest children, Emma Claire and Jack, were born when Elizabeth was in her fifties.

Better Late than Never:
The Boomers' Baby Boom

When Connor was born last spring, I had just begun reporting a story about families having children at midlife. As I called new parents and adoption attorneys around the country, I expected to discover a tribe of trophy babies, the ultimate arm candy of the Peter Pan generation who put off growing up so long that they arrived at parenthood desperately late. I envisioned legions of nannies and baby nurses insulating the new moms and dads from the exhausting realities of parenthood—multiple middle-of-the-night feedings, piles of smelly diapers. I figured these miracle babies would be the spawn of wealthy couples who had thrown money at the project, producing offspring courtesy of Star Wars fertility techniques.

Boy, was I wrong. I interviewed more than a dozen new mothers and dads in their forties and fifties, and every last one of them was hopelessly in love with their late-bloomer babies, delighted to devote their so-called retirement years to changing diapers and carpooling to soccer games. Several of the fathers were planning early retirement so that they could be the on-duty parent while their wives returned to work after maternity leave.

What I hadn't taken into account in formulating my initial rather cynical view was the tremendous effort required to create a child at this age. No woman tosses her diaphragm away at fifty and delivers a baby nine months later the way many of us could at twenty-five. These children are hard won through costly, time-consuming medical and/or adoption procedures.

When Claire, who underwent years of fertility treatments and adoption efforts before deciding on surrogacy, calls Connor her million-dollar baby, she's joking, but not entirely.

This is not a trend for the fainthearted; late-bloomer parents must face down a vocal cadre of critics who accuse them of putting their own happiness and fulfillment ahead of their child's. The parents themselves admit that some issues loom larger for them. Will they be around to see their sons and daughters finish college and marry? Will they get to meet their grandchildren? The parents I talked to had committed to staying healthy—Claire had a complete medical exam before embarking on the surrogate project—and were optimistic about their prospects of staying the course for a good long while. Most had consulted actuarial charts and could quote you both the statistical norm and the names of their longest-lived uncles and aunts.

Often later-in-life parents are finally realizing a long-held dream, and they dive into parenthood with more gusto than their decades-younger peers. At *More,* one of our contributing editors wrote an essay on a social phenomenon born of the midlife baby boom. She had noticed a new breed of mom whose kids were entering school in the affluent New York City suburb where she lived. She called them Suburban Supermoms. These women had worked tirelessly for decades, fighting gender stereotypes to climb the corporate ladder. Now senior executives at the nation's biggest companies, they had given up the power and the glory to stay home with their kids. In their late forties and early fifties, these moms entered full-time motherhood with an aggressiveness that matched their former business style—dispatching faxes of the week's carpooling schedule, coordinating volunteers for a bake sale on their BlackBerries. In short, they were running the PTA like a Fortune 500 company—and often running afoul of the traditional at-home moms who'd been handling the job quite nicely before the American business superheroes parachuted in. It made for some interesting social clashes in the bedroom communities of major cities across the United States, and pointed to the ardor with which these better-late-than-never babies were being greeted.

My daughter was born when I was twenty-seven, and I believed that having her early in life kept me young. Indeed she has, egging me on in a variety of healthful activities like hiking and biking, as well as a few death-defying ones, such as skydiving and mountain climbing. But I notice a glow of youthfulness among the midlife parents of toddlers, too. Tina Georgeou, a friend who gave birth at fifty-one, told me that when her daughter Lauren was born, the child in herself was reborn.

That's Grandma in the Mini Skirt

While a small cadre of boomers is widening the window on parenthood, another group, who had their kids when they were in their teens and twenties, is remaking the roles of Grandma and Granddad. When I was a kid, grandmothers had short gray hair frozen into a corona of permanent-wave frizz. They stayed home, cooking and cleaning in an extremely unflattering article of clothing we actually called a housedress. Grandfathers went to work and spent weekends slouched in front of the ball game on TV; grandchildren were beloved but seldom played with. Grampa patted you on the head when you visited and, if you were lucky, slipped a crisp dollar bill into your pocket.

Boomer grandparents are a whole new breed. Twenty-first-century grandmas wear sleek dresses and jeans, and they fit grooming appointments—manicures, hair color treatments, even Botox injections—between business meetings. Boomer granddads are as likely to play a pickup game of basketball as a round of golf. Furthermore, this generation's men are hands-on grandparents, competing with their wives for babysitting assignments. A small but growing number of grandparents are playing a leading role in their grandchildren's lives right from the start—in the delivery room when their grandbabies are born. My brother-in-law and sister-in-law were the first to tell me about this miraculous experience, witnessing the birth of their first grandchild. A few months later, when a friend was invited to attend her grandchild's birth, I knew something was going on. A writer at *More* found enough other cases to do a trend story for us, which we titled "Grandmas in the Delivery Room." From my experience, the granddads have a little catching up to do—my brother-in-law is still the only guy I know who's had the experience.

It's an intimate beginning to a close relationship. When I was growing up, the grandparents of a few lucky friends took them on a celebratory trip to Europe after they graduated from high school or college. Now a vital and vibrant generation of grandparents is whisking their grandchildren off on trips from an early age. It's spawned an industry of travel companies eager to court their business. There's even a word for it—*grandtravel*. Google "grandparent grandchild vacations" and you'll get tens of thousands of hits, from traditional choices like Disney World to horseback riding and windsurfing. A friend of mine is eagerly counting the years until her six-year-old grandson is old enough to go on safari with her.

Ours is the most affluent generation in history, and those who've made out well in the world are underwriting more and more of their grandkids' lives. They're paying for private school tuition, summer camp, tutoring. They're also giving their kids the down payment for a place to live. It's all part of a new cross-generational relationship.

The Buddy System: Parenting the Boomer Way

One reason we're being invited into the birthing room to participate in one of the most intimate moments of our children's lives is because we've retooled our relationship with them. We often get a bad rap for being pals to our kids instead of take-charge parents. A generation reluctant to accept our own adulthood, we were sometimes more eager to win our children's approval than their cooperation. Maybe it's not all that surprising that we shied away from the "authority figure" role, defined by a term we applied with a sneer of derision back in the 1960s. Some of us weren't the finest disciplinarians during the turbulent teen years when our kids were experimenting with liquor and sex. As our generation's kids entered junior high school, parenting magazines had a new issue to grapple with: what to say when your teen asked you if you'd ever smoked a joint. But a laissez-faire approach can begin to pay dividends when our children reach their twenties and morph into peers. We have an easier time loosening the reins and allowing them to be adults, since we never had such a firm grip anyway.

I remember popping a beer with my freshman college roommate to toast our newfound freedom as we watched the taillights of my mother's Country Squire fade away. Independence was intoxicating, and we were going to misbehave as soon and as often as we could. I had terrific parents, a no-complaints childhood, and still, doing the opposite of whatever they advised was standard operating procedure for me. If I'd listened, I would never have married husband number one (and if he'd paid attention to his folks, he would have run from me as fast as he could). When I moved into my first apartment, I packed the car and drove there by myself. My parents never even saw the place. For me, it was a declaration of independence, and if they mourned a missed opportunity, they never let on.

> **Raise a service dog.** It's a bona fide act of good works, and a neat way to test-drive adding a pet to your life. Guidedogs.com gives a good explanation of what's required, and ability.org/Guide_Dogs.html has a contact list of organizations to connect with nationwide. You can even raise a future bomb sniffer.

Fast-forward a generation, and you'd find Steve and me making our daughter's move into her first apartment a festive family weekend. We helped her pack and paint. When she and I made an emergency run to Bed Bath & Beyond, she actually asked which shower curtain I liked, and I was invited to share the first night in her new place. Where I was so uncertain about my independence that I had to flaunt it at every opportunity, Brook is confident enough to seek her parents' counsel—and then disregard it if she so chooses.

This new model for parent–child relationships—call it the buddy system—has spawned some interesting demographic trends, among them summer camps for parents and kids. When I was growing up, camp was a place parents sent their children, to expose them to new sports and crafts and some fresh country air—and to buy themselves some quiet couple time free of sibling squabbles and childhood demands. Now parents are enrolling in camp with their kids. With so many two-career families, mothers and fathers may yearn for romantic time together, but many are even hungrier for time with their children. Twenty-three percent of the accredited summer camps in the United States offer programs to bring Mom and Dad along, from the US Space & Rocket Center in Huntsville, Alabama, where campers fly a jet fighter simulator, to the Bar 717 Ranch near

Hayfork, California, which offers a classic camp blend of swimming, horseback riding, pottery, and wood-shop classes. It's easy to see why we parents are on board for this—days spent together in the wilds of Montana learning to ride are true quality time with our offspring. A week free of beepers, cell phones, and life's other interrupters—both theirs and ours—are a siren call to many parents. Apparently, our kids like us well enough to allow us along on their summer vacations.

An even more surprising trend is the increasing number of boomers who are sending their teens off to prep school—and following them there. At Choate Rosemary Hall, thirty families have moved to the Wallingford, Connecticut, area so their kids can benefit from a first-rate boarding school education while still living at home. A dozen families have relocated to Andover, Massachusetts, while their children attend Phillips Academy. The parents cite the closeness they feel with their kids; they could never send them off to dorm life at thirteen. Far from being embarrassed to be living with Mom and Dad, these kids are not only content, they're enthusiastic, citing a lower-stress environment, not to mention the home-cooked meals.

Hi, Mom, I'm Home! Our Boomerang Kids

Those trends may surprise you, but I'm sure you're acquainted with boomerang kids—you may even have one inhabiting the back bedroom right now. "Hi, Mom, I'm home," is a call being heard from Sarasota to San Francisco as a surprising number of twenty- and even thirtysomethings move back to the family manse. The number of boomerang kids has doubled over the past fifty years. Now one in ten kids over the age of twenty-five live with their parents, according to the National Survey of Families and Households. This figure is likely to keep growing, according to a survey of college students by MonsterTRAK, an online job service, which found that 60 percent of respondents planned to live with their parents after graduation.

The reasons for coming home are many. It may be a simple matter of economics: By living free, or paying a modest rent, the kids can save money or pay down college loans. For some boomerangers, their childhood home is a familiar refuge from the storms of life: losing a job or a failed marriage. But it's the new buddy-system relationship that makes it appealing for a child to repopulate the empty nest.

Still, living with a fully independent adult child can require a new set of guidelines, even for laissez-faire boomer parents. Everything from who does the laundry to whose TV shows we watch can become a field of battle. I've talked to many boomer parents who, like me, were able to sleep just fine while their kids were away at college, going who knows where and coming home who knows how late. But once they move back home, we lie awake watching the numbers on the digital clock change until we finally hear the crunch of gravel in the driveway. Despite such stressors, every parent I've talked to has savored those bonus years with a child.

Steve and I were boomerang parents for a while. Brook spent the year after graduation traveling around the world, then lived at home until she found a job and an apartment in New York. At twenty-three, she was more experienced and street-smart than Steve and I, having lived for a year out of a backpack and by her wits. On September 11, 2001, she landed in Beijing, traveling alone, not knowing a soul. Saddened by the tragedy, she remained calm and resourceful, connecting with a friend of a friend. Meanwhile, Steve and I were scrambling trying to figure out how to airlift her out of there while no planes were flying. Fortunately, she never realized how unhinged we were until months later, when she finally arrived home.

When Brook moved back into her old bedroom, like

boomerang families everywhere, we had to write a new script for ourselves, one that acknowledged her savvy and smarts, while allowing her the privacy and independence of a card-carrying adult. The spirit was willing, but the flesh was weak. Steve and I were too full of opinions for her own good, suffering from an overwhelming desire to micromanage her life. Should she postpone a job search to complete a book manuscript she'd been working on about her travels? Or should she start scouting for a position right away? Steve championed the job hunt, I was boosting the book, and poor Brook just sat there at the dinner table watching the two of us argue about her life. Ultimately, she did what she wanted, which was the most sensible course—continuing to work on her manuscript while she sent out résumés.

A funny subset are the boomerang kids living with their parents in retirement communities. Aimed squarely at the boomer market, "younger" communities for active adults are multiplying fast, from just 204 nationwide in 1995 to 1,274 in 2004. One developer in New Jersey estimates that 5 percent of the residents have grown children in the household. The kids may suffer the kind of razzing Cameron Diaz's character endured in the movie *In Her Shoes* for living in her grandmother's retirement village. But they're laughing all the way to the bank, paying off college loans while taking advantage of recreational facilities—tennis courts, golf courses, and pools—they could never afford were they living on their own.

At Last, True Love

We may have established a new standard for parent–child intimacy, but we have not set the best record in affairs of the heart. The most divorced generation in history, boomers more than doubled the marriage-breakup rate of our parents' generation, along the way launching a new mega-trend: Singletons are now the most common type of household in America. We may have invented living together back in the 1960s, but apparently a goodly group of us never moved on to tying the knot. A record-setting number of boomers—12.9 percent—have never been married, versus only 3.9 percent of Americans over sixty-five.

Divorce is the classic fallout of a midlife crisis. Sometimes it's as simple as this: Your life doesn't measure up, so you start looking around for somebody to blame. Or maybe the road to splitsville is signposted REINVENTION: You're changing, trying new things, and your partner just isn't along for the ride. Couples who have stayed together for the kids reward themselves with freedom once the last one packs for college. There are so many reasons for love to falter at midlife. We did some research on marriage trends at *More* and found a spike in divorces, which led to a story we called "The 17-Year Itch."

In researching this book, I've seen divorce acting as both cause and effect: Sometimes ending a marriage kick-starts a life reinvention; other times, divorce occurs as a side effect of a big life change. And in some cases, it's a classic egg–chicken controversy: You simply can't tell which came first—the reinvention or the divorce. When you shed your spouse, it forces you to take a new look at your life. Some friendships don't survive the split; with others, it deepens the relationship. You move to a new neighborhood, you begin going out by yourself. Naturally, sometimes without any special intent, you begin to reexamine other choices you've made.

Divorce is never easy, always sad, and often disillusioning. Nevertheless, many of us remain romantics, searching for the perfect partner in life. The whole concept of a love match is relatively new, a product of the Enlightenment in the 1700s, as Stephanie Coontz, author of *Marriage, a History: From Obedience to Intimacy or How Love Conquered Marriage,* points out.

Before that, marriages were economic constructs, arranged for the fiscal betterment of the sponsoring families. It was all about alliances and inheritances. Coontz, who has contributed to a boomer romance trend herself by marrying her college sweetheart when she was in her forties, maintains that marriage has changed more in the past thirty years than in the previous three thousand. These days, it's a partnership where the couple, no longer shackled by society's gender expectations, are free to create their own roles within the relationship.

Reuniting with an old love is an increasingly popular manifestation of the love-at-midlife phenomenon. Donna Hanover, who married her college boyfriend after divorcing New York City mayor Rudy Giuliani, wrote a whole book of encore love stories with the delicious title *My Boyfriend's Back.* Psychologist Nancy Kalish, who also wrote a book on the subject, *Lost and Found Lovers: Facts and Fantasies of Rekindled Romances,* turned up more than a thousand reunited couples. There's something comforting about loving somebody who knew you back when. Bonus points: It short-circuits those awkward getting-to-know-you first dates. You share memories and friends; your families know each other. And of course, there once was that spark. One woman who fell in love with a high school buddy in her forties told me, "We're joined at the hip in every way. We talk about everything. Having that shared history makes everything so easy."

Nostalgic sites like Classmates.com and Reunion.com have helped former lovers reconnect, and e-mail offers an unscary way to get a conversation going. Other boomers are using technology to look forward, not back, hitting the Web in record numbers to seek a partner in romance and life. Membership in online dating leader Match.com tripled between 2000 and 2005 among men and women over fifty. The AARP magazine's column "Modern Love" is written by a man who teaches seminars on online dating. A former co-worker of mine resigned her job and moved cross-country at forty to live with a man she met on JDate.com, a Web site that helps Jewish singles find each other. Another friend in her forties fell in love with a younger man she met on Match.com; after two years of dating, they've just gotten married. In fact, most of the midlife love stories I've heard recently involve a modem and a mouse.

Create an adventure fund. Earmark an annual amount of money that won't break the bank, and devote it to having a new experience—from taking a drawing class to exploring Bhutan.

What's different about marrying at midlife? An AARP survey of one thousand recently divorced men and women between forty and sixty-nine found that, most of all, they were looking for a partner who shared their values. A psychoanalyst who married in her fifties told me that at midlife, "You're driven by common goals, looking for companionship rather than a relationship that pivots on hormones." Other newlyweds talked about finding someone they'd be happy to grow old with. When we were twenty-four, "until death us do part" echoed through multiple decades into an unforeseeable future. When you're fifty-four, it's a phrase that really gets your attention—in ten years we could find ourselves taking care of an incapacitated spouse. This sobers us, but doesn't seem to put us off.

Romantic love is as powerful a force as ever, with several couples confiding that their sex life at middle age is the best it's ever been. In our generation's checkered history of love, pharmaceuticals have been there just in time. The free love movement was launched after the first birth control pill was approved in May 1960; now our sex lives reap the benefits of Viagra and other sexual function drugs.

dren, a lot of them yearned to know what had happened to that baby they gave up. No matter how fulfilling the rest of their lives had been, there was a hole at the center of their hearts. A record number of women have addressed that longing and completed their families at midlfe by tracking down the baby they gave away. Sperm donors, too, have gone to the trouble to find the children they sired anonymously so long ago. For the lucky ones like Marie, a wonderful relationship has followed. Tens of thousands of birth parents have been reunited with their sons and daughters, enough to have sparked an industry of helpers—private investigators, support groups, even reunion Web sites. Adoption.com, a nonprofit site, offers a reunion registration service where birth parents and kids can reconnect.

Whether it's having a baby or finding one you reluctantly gave up decades ago, falling in love or forging a new-style relationship with your grown-up kids and grandkids, a growing number of boomers are redefining family in a rewarding way at midlife.

The Life Entrepreneurs

After Fifty, a Baby

Marrying in their forties, Steve and Tina Georgeou were late to the altar, but they still wanted to have a child. Tina gave birth when she was fifty-one.

Tina and Steve's Lesson: *Never, ever say that little life-limiting phrase,* It's too late. *Having a baby at midlife is an excellent way to ensure that you'll be exhausted—and feel younger and happier than you have in years.*

TINA AND STEVE Georgeou thought about having a baby for years, but when they finally decided to quit considering and start conceiving, it might have been too late had they been members of any generation before the boomers. But with modern medical techniques pushing the envelope on aging, the number of late-in-life moms is rising. In 2003, 323 women over fifty in the United States had babies. Tina was one of them.

Steve and Tina are extremely independent people who spent their early adulthood building their careers, so they got a late start on marriage itself. "When we married, he was forty-eight, and I was forty-three," Tina says. It was the first marriage for both of them, and after a long-distance courtship during which Tina was working in Montreal and Steve in New York, they wanted to take time to enjoy each other before starting a family. As Tina's career in advertising and marketing soared, having a baby kept getting postponed. Finally, in her late forties, Tina knew it was now or never. "Steve's my best friend, and we do everything together, but there was still something missing," she says. "I wondered, *What are we working so hard for? What are we building here?*"

"Tina was the one who pushed for this," Steve confirms. "I imagined I'd have children, but it never felt pressing." Tina serves on the board of trustees for Save the Children, but the Georgeous never considered adopting. "I guess I was stubborn," Tina says. "I really wanted the thrill of being pregnant." Their doctors told the Georgeous that conceiving at Tina's age was a long shot. "They make the odds seem infinitesimally small. But we were very lucky," says Tina. "What's even more amazing is that even this late in life, my body did exactly what it was programmed to do." She gained just nineteen pounds in a pregnancy so smooth, swollen ankles were her worst complaint.

Despite being a statistical anomaly as an over-fifty expectant mom, Tina never felt out of step. "Nobody in the OB office gave me that *What's she doing here?* look," she recalls, adding, "There's something about starting a new life that transcends age barriers. People just said, 'Wow. A miracle child is on the way.'" Steve, too, noted an awed reaction among their friends. "One remarked to me, 'I can't even run a mile and Tina is having a baby.' There's a superwoman aspect to it." Tina placed the call to her mother to announce her pregnancy with a touch of trep- idation. "I thought she might say, *Are you sure this is right for you at this age?*" Tina recalls. "But she was thrilled. She told me, 'This is the one thing you needed to do.'"

They elected to forgo amniocentesis or other tests to screen for birth defects. "There is no way we were going to abort this baby, so there was no point in having the test," Tina says. Their daughter Lauren was born a healthy, vibrant seven pounds, six ounces, when Tina was fifty-one and Steve was fifty-seven. Two years later, Steve, who comes from a big, close Greek family, is still amazed by the experience. "I feel I'm still becoming a fa- ther. I continue to be surprised by the sheer joy of having a child."

Tina, who held a senior marketing position at a major pub- lishing company when she was pregnant, had every intention of returning to work. But after being home with Lauren, her job seemed less and less compelling. "One day, toward the end of my maternity leave, my assistant called and told me she'd booked the corporate jet for an upcoming meeting at our com- pany headquarters in Des Moines. And that's when I said, 'I'm not going to do it.'" She knew Lauren would be her only baby. "It was an experience to revel in, not to share with distractions."

Steve and Tina happily revamped their lives to put their baby girl front and center, in a way younger couples don't al- ways have the freedom or inclination to do. Steve used to keep late hours at the marketing consulting company he owns, but now he makes a point of getting home early enough to spend time with Lauren before bed. Tina has an office at Steve's company where she does project work for publishing companies and ad agencies, on a relaxed schedule that gives her plenty of time with her daughter.

Lauren has transformed their social life, too; these days, they'd rather stay in and play with her than go out on the town. "We used to be restaurant fanatics, eating out at all the new, hot places here in New York, but now we entertain at home," Steve says. "The pleasure is vicarious—we read the reviews."

Walk ten thousand steps a day. That's the number doctors recommend for optimum health. Pick up a pedometer and do ten thousand paces every day for a month, then consider yourself launched on a healthier life. To check out the calorie burn of other daily activities, go to caloriescount.org.

Most of their friends were enthusiastic about the big change in the Georgeous' lives, and for the few who weren't, Steve has a theory: "People who'd had good experiences with their own children were overjoyed for us; the people who warned us we didn't know what we were in for—diapers to change, up all night—hadn't had a great time raising their kids."

Becoming parents has heightened the Georgeous' awareness of their mortality, but they remain optimistic about the future. They have named a guardian and set up a college fund for Lauren. "When you write your will, the lawyer puts the actuarial tables right in your face. We're looking at years of income generation to provide for her when we'd normally be considering retirement," Tina says, admitting, "The fact that you might not be there when she's twenty or when she's thirty-five does hang over your head." Steve says he's now more consciencious about his health. "I lead a pretty clean life. I go to the gym, and am good about medical care. I have an uncle who's ninety-six and still in good shape. I could live well into my eighties." He hasn't gotten the classic "Is that your grandchild?" comment, but he expects it and is ready. "I'll say, 'No, I'm her grandfather's son,' and let them figure it out," he says, laughing.

One downside of parenthood they share with mothers and fathers of all ages is the intrusion of a demanding little creature into their life as a couple. "Tina and I don't have as much time for each other," Steve notes. "But we expected that."

"It's opened my eyes to the tiny things that make you happy, and made me realize that I'd lost touch with the child in me," Tina says. "Getting down on the floor with her triggers memories of my childhood—the imagination and creativity of talking to the vacuum cleaner." When Lauren was a baby, Tina would fall into bed exhausted at the end of the day. "Looking after a small child is so intense. In a meeting, you can sit back and gather energy. As a parent, all your feelers have to be out. It's intense and draining, but being older has made me wiser about conserving my energy."

"Our job is to raise Lauren as an independent person, so she can choose what to do with her life," Steve says. "It definitely helps to be seasoned and self-confident ourselves. People who have kids when they're too young don't have the time to develop as a couple first. They get stressed out, and all that anxiety is transferred to the children. When you're older, you know what's important. We can transmit a certain calmness to Lauren." Tina adds, "I hope we'll show her more attention and love than we would have back when we were worried about climbing the corporate ladder. All I can say is, it was the right time for me.

"If I hadn't done this, I'd still have the very good life I had before," she concludes. "But it's so much fuller and bigger now, with so much to look forward to. Will Lauren learn to play the piano? Will she be a dancer? We can't wait to find out."

Third Time's the Charm

Susan Kushnick and Bruce Page had both been married twice before. Like many couples in their fifties, they met on the Internet. Now they're starting a new life together.

Susan and Bruce's Lesson: *Merging seasoned, complicated lives can be more difficult than growing up together in a young marriage. At midlife, you need to ask smarter questions about a partner—is this the person I want to grow old with, possibly take care of?*

"I'M CRAZY ABOUT this guy." As Susan Kushnick Page tells me this, there's a sense of wonder in her voice. Eight months after her third wedding, at fifty-four, she's still a little startled that her life has turned out so wonderfully well.

Six years ago, it didn't seem possible that she'd ever be truly happy again. Her second husband and the father of their two children, then nine and fifteen, was diagnosed with pancreatic cancer. He was dead in six weeks. "That was a horrible time," she remembers. "I was trying to keep my head above water." Flooded with grief, she struggled to make ends meet. "I had a great job at Yahoo!, but it was all-consuming, and I couldn't afford to leave it." Since Susan worked long hours and traveled, she couldn't be with her children as much as she wanted to be. "Basically, they brought themselves up," she says sadly. Then, when the dot-com mania collapsed, she lost her job. "I was a single parent with growing bills." Determined to turn yet another setback into an advantage, Susan decided to quit commuting two hours a day to New York City and look for work closer to her home in Chappaqua, New York. Not only does she love the job she landed as an administrator for women's apparel maker Eileen Fisher, but it proved to be a turning point in her life. Just a few months later, she met Bruce.

At the time Susan was recovering from the tragedy of her husband's death, Bruce Page seemed just as unlikely to fall in love. After his second marriage ended in divorce and his first wife sued for custody of their two children, he'd pretty much given up on romance. When he won the custody case, he opted to focus his energies on his kids and his work as a Presbyterian minister. "I decided I simply was not interested in relationships until my children were older." he says. "Then one day, I realized they were grown and I *still* wasn't doing anything about it."

Susan and Bruce both did what people at midlife who are serious about finding a partner do—they headed for love's fast lane, the Internet, signing up on Match.com. Their generation is the fastest-growing audience on the site, and, according to a spokeswoman, "They're the least likely to believe that their lives are controlled by destiny." No, Bruce and Susan weren't going to wait for kismet; in their fifties already, they were determined to jump-start the process. "People don't fix you up on dates all that much," Susan says, "and I had reached a point where I didn't want to be alone anymore." For a while, nobody clicked with her, but, she says, "I just kept plugging away." Bruce found several "wonderful women" online, but none of the relationships stuck—one time, geography got in the way; with another woman, he wasn't ready to commit; a third shied away from a deeper relationship. Then he met Susan. They went to a movie, after which they sat and talked for two hours. Sparks flew, and the relationship moved quickly. "By the end of the summer, he had practically moved in with me," Susan says. "Yes, it was head-over-heels like teenage love," Bruce recalls, "but it was more complicated, too. We were each dealing with the lives we had built separately, while we were trying to build something together."

Both were looking for different qualities in a mate at midlife than they had earlier on. "The first time, I just plunged into marriage," Bruce says. "We felt we could make anything work. The second time, I was truly looking for a tender caregiver because I was petrified that I couldn't raise my children alone. With Susan, I really was seeking sanity." He pauses and laughs. "I wanted someone who was independent, who had her own track record in life." That old chestnut—similar interests—was the last thing on Susan's mind. "People always talk about finding someone with the same interests; to me, that's not what you should be looking for. What about the kind of person he is?" she says. "I want someone I can grow old with, somebody I can look at and say, *If his body is broken, if his mind is broken, I could still live with him, I could still love him.*"

Send a long, chatty e-mail to a friend. Friendships wither under technology's onslaught, as we wander around plugged into our personal entertainment systems. Make technology work for you by writing a letter-length e-mail once a week, and really keep in touch with your friends.

These days, she's a better catch herself. "I was much more difficult to live with when I was younger. If I thought something was important, I wouldn't budge," she recalls. "Now I can let things go." Susan and Bruce married on a beautiful fall afternoon, outdoors under a chuppah, or ceremonial canopy, on a property overlooking the Hudson River. A friend of Bruce's from seminary married them, and they incorporated some elements of a Jewish ceremony. "It was the most beautiful wedding ever," Susan says. "Everybody pitched in and brought food because we didn't have a lot of money." People came from all five congregations Bruce had served in the New York area. "We were floating on all that love and happiness," says Bruce.

When people meet Susan and Bruce, they assume the biggest obstacle to a silky-smooth marriage is religion: Bruce is a Presbyterian from Charlotte, North Carolina, with the soft turnings of a Southern accent; Susan is a Jew from New York City, a straight talker with a sharp sense of humor. "I was so nervous the first time I went to his church," she says. "I'd maybe been to a Christian wedding once before. I had to sit by myself, I didn't know anybody, I was terrified." But the congregation welcomed her, and Bruce is so comfortable with their different spiritual paths that he jokes about the time she told him that she wasn't going to convert, to which he replied: "Who asked you!" "Honestly," he says, "it was more perplexing to Susan to consider what it means to be a person of faith leading a community as I do, than for me to confront her not being so sure about this whole God thing."

The number one challenge has been something anyone with children would face: blending the family. Bruce's kids are already living independently or away at college, as is Susan's daughter, but her teenage son lives with them. "Before Bruce, my kids had me exclusively," Susan says. "Everyone knows a fifteen-year-old boy is not an easy human being to deal with." She and Bruce don't always agree about child rearing, whether it's making sure homework is done or setting a curfew. Bruce, who holds a degree in counseling, says he has to be careful not to try to manage the situation like a professional. "We've been seeing a family therapist, which has been helpful." In the end, Susan says, "We're a family. Sometimes families get ugly. You grit your teeth, take a deep breath, and try to fix as much as you can, but realize that some stuff you just have to ride out."

And then there is The Fight. "It's huge," Susan says. For the past eight years, Bruce's life has been directed toward moving back south; he went to graduate school to earn the credentials that would allow him to practice therapy in South Carolina, where it would be cheaper to live and he'd be closer to his family. Charleston is his goal, and he actually broke up with that first Internet girlfriend when he sensed she'd never move there. "It's his dream," Susan acknowledges. "The first date we had, we talked about it." But she worries about finding a job. "I'll be fifty-seven if we move when my son graduates high school." There's a deeper concern, too. "I'm a New York Jew, I don't know that I'm going to be very comfortable down there. We fight about it maybe once a month." Before they got married, they spent a vacation in Bruce's brother's condominium on the ocean. "I thought once she saw Charleston, we would be there sooner or later," he admits. "Now I'm not so sure." But it's not a deal breaker; Bruce knows he's found the woman he wants to spend the rest of his life with, wherever they may end up.

"Susan says if we'd met twenty years ago, we wouldn't have given each other a second look. I do believe that people can meet as teenagers and be soul mates their whole lives, but there's real promise to people who've lurched around life and are finally getting clear about who they are and who they want to be with, at midlife. I hope to keep walking a path with this wonderful woman, wherever it will take us."

Two Dads for Hannah and Rebecca

Mark Frey and Doug Vogel adopted two baby girls, reinventing their family at midlife in a way they could not have imagined a decade before.

Mark and Doug's Lesson: *You can research a decision like this endlessly, attending support groups, babysitting off-*

*spring of friends and family. Ultimately, though, it's a gut
decision: Just screw up your courage and take the plunge.*

DOUG VOGEL AND Mark Frey didn't imagine that anyone
would ever call them "Daddy." "Because I'm gay, when I was
in my thirties and forties, I thought the likelihood of having a
child was remote," says Mark, who's now fifty-two. "It just
wasn't feasible then." Doug, who's forty-four, thought about
having kids when he was very young. "I was the eldest and felt
I had to pass on the family name. But once I came to terms with
my sexuality, I figured it wasn't going to happen for me."

How wrong they were, and how happy and rewarding their
lives turned out to be when they became parents at midlife.

Doug and Mark met on an AIDS fund-raiser bike ride in California in 1999 and fell in love. Doug was riding to honor his
brother, who died of AIDS in 1991; Mark had been doing AIDS
rides for almost a decade. Doug lived in West Hollywood, working as an actor and supporting himself by waiting tables in Los
Angeles. Mark lived in the suburbs and was a sales manager for
an insurance company. The relationship deepened quickly, but
their lives were so different that it took a while for them to decide to live together. "After 9/11, I thought, *What the heck am I
doing?*" Doug says. *"I live in a car with my bags, and I go from
one place to another."* He rented out his condo and moved in
with Mark.

They had already been talking about having a family, a discussion that was kicked off by another AIDS fund-raiser ride,
this time from Fairbanks to Anchorage. "It was horrific," Doug
says. It rained every day, and snowed so hard on Denali Pass
that fifteen hundred riders had to be rescued and bused into
camp. When they finally rode into Anchorage, a group of children were cheering at the finish. "One of them asked me, 'Are
you a superhero?'" Mark remembers, and something clicked. "I

turned to Doug and said, 'We've just conquered the hardest thing. Why limit ourselves in terms of what we can and cannot do?'" Mark knew he wanted to adopt a child.

Doug was a harder sell. "I wasn't opposed, but I was hesitant," he says. "We had two dogs and two horses, and I knew this wasn't like getting another animal. This was life altering." Since Mark had a conventional job with benefits, Doug would be the one at home with a baby. He needed to be sure it was the right step for him. They began talking to gay couples with children and attending meetings of the Pop Luck Club, a group of three hundred same-sex families in West Hollywood. "My hesitancy was that the decision was so huge," Doug says, "but then a friend pointed out, 'All you have to do is agree to the first thing—meet the lawyer. Then you can decide whether to take the next step.'"

On the first anniversary of the September 11 attacks, Mark and Doug walked into the office of an attorney in LA who is a leader in same-sex adoption. Mark and Doug decided that if they had a baby, they would name the child for a friend who'd died in the terrorist attacks. Doug liked the lawyer right away. "He was very high-powered, but down-to-earth, easygoing."

Doug was starting to feel good—very good—about a baby. But adopting was easier said than done. The first birth mother they contacted picked them from four families, but it became obvious that her main objective was to get someone to fund her relocation to LA. The second birth mother also picked them, but had second thoughts about placing her baby with a same-sex couple. Mark and Doug were becoming disheartened by the time they finally got the call. A young woman in Nevada who already had two children was pregnant. Her family finances were stretched to the breaking point, and she could not afford another child. She would give the baby to Doug and Mark.

"There's a saying that you don't find the baby, the baby finds you," Mark says. "We knew this child was meant to be ours."

They flew the birth mother to California, and were in the delivery room for their daughter Hannah Ross's birth. Mark cut the umbilical cord. "She popped out perfect, healthy and beautiful," Doug says. They invited Angela to give the baby her first feeding, and they've sent her photographs and letters regularly ever since.

Both men were head-over-heels for this gorgeous blue-eyed baby girl. Mark took three months of family leave—"the best twelve weeks of my life"—so that he and Doug could bring Hannah to the East Coast for a monthlong visit with Mark's family. "Hannah was baptized by our family priest, who had baptized me," Mark says.

When they got back to LA, Doug became the at-home dad. "It was a huge adjustment," he remembers. "I had never not worked. Suddenly, my day was filled with bottles and diapers." Although he adored the baby, he was struck with a bad case of cabin fever. "When Hannah was six months old, I told Mark I was going crazy. I never talked to adults anymore." They decided to hire a babysitter two afternoons a week. Meantime Doug began taking Hannah to acting auditions from time to time, with one very surprising result.

Doug was trying out for the role of a father in an energy bar commercial when his two-year-old daughter caught the casting director's eye. "Truth be told, I think I got the job because I'm Hannah's father." Hannah took direction like a pro and now has a Screen Actors Guild card.

It wasn't long after Hannah's first birthday that Mark got that look in his eye again. He started talking about a sibling for Hannah. This time, the path to a bigger family was smooth and clear. As luck would have it, Hannah's birth mother became pregnant, and they were able to adopt Hannah's biological sister.

"Our lawyer called me on my fifty-first birthday with the news," Mark recalls. "I knew I'd be seventy when this baby finished high school, and I had visions of people saying, 'Grandpa came to graduation, isn't that nice.' I'm healthy, I work out, and take care of myself. I won't be my parents' seventy. This is the secret to a youthful growing old." In April 2005, they welcomed Rebecca into their family.

Change your name. A friend of mine recently altered the spelling of her first name and added a new middle one, at age fifty-four. Now she's got the name she always wanted. Whether you'd like to restore an ancestral name that was "Americanized" at Ellis Island or simply transfer to a moniker that fits you, it can lead to a new way of looking at yourself. Soyouwanna.com has a good how-to section on legally changing your name.

"Becoming a parent is the best thing that's ever happened to me," Doug says. "It's the hardest thing I've done, hands down. I have now apologized to my parents for every bad thing I did as a kid." "We're different parents because we're older," Mark adds. "We sit and talk to Hannah, explain why we're giving her a time-out. At twenty-five, our parents didn't have the time and energy to do that." Doug maintains that he wouldn't have been a good parent in his twenties or thirties. "I placed far too much importance on whether people liked me, rather than focusing on my goals," he says. "Now I have a better understanding of the world. I wouldn't want to be young again unless I could have that wisdom."

Like parents of all ages, Mark and Doug have made sacrifices to bring these children into their lives. They sold one of their horses after Hannah was born because there was little time to ride. Doug went back to waiting tables on weekends to help pay for Rebecca's adoption. "On a bad day, we'll complain about the sad state of our bank account," he says. "But it's a miracle to have this experience."

Far from fracturing relationships, having these children at midlife has forged a deepening bond with many of the couple's friends. "It's strengthened ties with friends who have kids, are thinking about it, and even people who don't have children but support our decision," Mark says. And it's given them a new appreciation of their own parents. "After Hannah was born, I talked to my mother and father every day," Mark says. "In the summer, when we go back home to visit, my nieces' and nephews' kids play with our girls." Doug adds, "Watching my parents finally become grandparents for the first time is such a joy." Clearly, there's plenty of love to go around. "The first smile, the first hug, the first time Hannah said, 'I love you, Poppa.' How in the world did I get here?" Doug says. "I am so grateful."

Mother-and-Child Reunion

When she was barely out of her teens, Marie Hubschman gave up a child for adoption. Twenty-eight years later, she tracked him down, and made a joyful addition to her family.

Marie's Lesson: *If there's a mystery at the center of your life, don't be afraid to take charge and solve it. It may be reconnecting with an old flame to finally understand what went wrong, or looking up an old friend who dumped you. Even if you don't revive the relationship, there's satisfaction in figuring out a piece of your past.*

ON A BALMY FLORIDA evening in early June, when she was forty-eight years old, Marie Hubschman dialed the phone and changed her life. The number was one she had been wishing to know for twenty-eight years, ever since she gave up her baby boy for adoption. Now she was finally going to call his house and hear his voice. "I was shaking, hyperventilating, my heart was beating so fast," Marie remembers. "I kept thinking, *What if he hangs up or says, 'Never call me again'?*"

Marie's story began on another sunny summer day, at a farm stand on Long Island, New York. "From the time I was fourteen, I'd help out selling fruits and vegetables from my family's farm," she says. One day, a handsome young man cruised in on his Honda and asked if she'd like to take a motorcycle ride. "I was sixteen, and Jim was twenty-seven. My parents weren't too keen on it, but he won them over," she says. Marie and Jim began to date, often taking day trips upstate. "He and his buddies would pick me up at six in the morning, we'd spend the day watching Jim race, then go out for a bite to eat," she says. "I was a young-ster and it was very exciting."

Marie graduated from high school and got a job as a long-distance operator. A year and a half later, she discovered she was pregnant. "I was tired, and then I got very nauseous." When she became so sick she couldn't get out of bed, the fam-ily doctor admitted her to the hospital for tests. "One morning, my mother came into my hospital room saying, 'Why didn't you tell me?' 'Tell you what?' I asked. 'That you're pregnant.'" Marie was dumbfounded; they'd only had unprotected sex once. As-suming that she and Jim would get married, she called him after she was released from the hospital. "I still remember sitting in his car outside my parents' house crying. Jim asked me how I knew it was his child, and when I mentioned getting married, he said, 'No way.'

"It was a disgrace," she continues. "My parents said no one must ever know." She resigned from her job and hid away in the house, disguising her swelling belly under oversize sweat-shirts. Even her younger brothers didn't guess her secret.

As Marie's due date neared, a social worker set up a plan for her to move to a facility for unwed mothers in New York City. "I begged my parents to let me stay with them," she says, "but they told me they couldn't take the chance of somebody seeing me." At the unwed mothers' home, the girls were told not to reveal their last names or to discuss their lives. While they waited out their pregnancies, they did housekeeping chores, read, crocheted, or watched TV. "I remember walking in Central Park every day with one girl. We talked about keeping our babies, told each other that somehow we'd make it work," Marie says. "The nuns said adoption was the best thing for the baby, and that we should go on with our lives, forgetting about this." Marie observed the girls who'd return to the home to collect their belongings after giving birth. "They looked lost, empty, horrible." Marie had never been away from home before. She felt totally alone, lying in bed at night crying.

One day, while she was washing her hair over the sink, her water broke. The next evening, after a short labor, her son was born. Marie told the nurses she wanted to feed him. "I made a big stink until they brought him," she says. All five days she spent in the hospital, Marie insisted on seeing her son. While pregnant, she hadn't found the courage to be assertive; now, with her son's welfare at stake, for the first time in her life she stood up to authority. She refused to sign relinquishment papers. Her son, whom she named Robert, was put in foster care, and she returned home to Long Island. As often as she could, she would take the train into New York to play with her baby, maybe bring him a new outfit.

At the same time, she revived her relationship with Jim. "I was in a dream world, still trying to convince him to marry me," she says. "I'd show him photographs of the baby and remark on how much he resembled Jim." She also fantasized about taking Robert and moving out west. She could say her husband had died. But with no money, no car, no support, she couldn't make it happen. By the time Robert was six months old, Marie realized the happy family of her imagination was never going to form. "I knew my son needed a mother and father to love and care for him. I didn't want him to stay in foster care, so the day after Thanksgiving, I went into New York and signed the papers." A month later, she got a call that Robert had been placed with a family. "I was so hurt, so sad," she says, though she knew she'd done the best she could for her son. She broke off the relationship with Jim. For the next four years, her life was just working at the telephone company and living with her parents.

Trade in your SUV for a convertible. My husband bought me a snappy little gray roadster the year I turned fifty-two. I call it my mood booster. Drop the top, and stress disappears into the slipstream. There's a reason that this is a midlife cliché—it works! Be smarter than I was— go ahead and buy it for yourself.

Then, when she was twenty-four, a friend who was relocating to Florida invited her to come along. Hoping that it would be the fresh start she needed, Marie moved into an apartment outside Miami with her friend and his mother. "The move pulled me out of my shell," she says. She quickly made a group of friends who'd spend weekends at the beach and take cruise vacations together. She wasn't yet ready for romance. "It was quite a few years before I started dating," she says, "and whenever I saw somebody seriously, I told him about my son, that I hoped he would find me someday."

When Marie met her future husband, at the age of thirty-eight, she still thought of Robert every day and pined for more children, but another baby was not in the cards. Her husband had had a vasectomy that couldn't be reversed, and when he broached the subject of adoption, Marie declined. Having given up a child, she didn't feel she had the right to adopt another one. Her life went on, but with a great sorrow at its heart.

That all began to change one night when she watched a TV movie called *The Other Mother.* The story of a woman sent to a home for unwed mothers who reluctantly surrendered her baby for adoption and later reunited with him struck Marie to her core. "It was just like my life," she recalls. Among the credits were contact numbers of support groups for mothers searching for their children. Marie had never realized she could take action, not just wait for Robert to look for her. At a support meeting in Palm Beach, a woman who had started a business helping other birth mothers locate their children told Marie that she could find Robert. "I couldn't believe it," Marie says. "Two weeks later, she gave me Robert's new name, where he worked, his home address and telephone number, everything. I was on cloud nine." On the treadmill after work that evening, though, her elation turned to fear. "This was my only shot. If he rejected me, that's the end of the line." On Monday night, she finally dialed the phone. "I didn't know how to start the conversation, but a woman in the group had given me good advice: *Say 'I gave birth to a baby boy on May 18, 1968.'* That way, you're not even telling him he's adopted, in case he doesn't know." Robert answered the phone, and Marie recited her sentence, in a quavering voice filled with terror and hope. "There was silence for ten seconds, then I heard him say, 'Ohmigod, it's my mother.'" They spent three and a half hours on the phone. "For the first time in my life, I was at peace. I knew we would have a relationship forever." Robert had always wondered about his birth mother. "I know he was curious about me," Marie says. "When the time was right, he would have tried to find me." But Marie got there first.

She flew north to meet Robert six weeks later, and after an emotional, gratifying reunion, he joined his birth mom for a tour of her Long Island hometown, and also met her parents and brothers. "My mother now shakes her head, thinking of what we gave up," Marie says. "When I came out of the closet, no one criticized me. And Robert's parents were wonderful to me. They showed albums of Robert growing up, and let me make copies of the photographs." Nowadays Robert and his family come to Marie's for New Year's dinner, and he invited her to the hospital when his daughter was born. "I'm careful," Marie says. "He has parents who raised him and love him. I don't want to come between them."

Marie believes the growing self-assurance she felt in her forties allowed her to search for her son. "I was a shy little girl afraid to hurt anyone's feelings. I didn't speak up for myself. By the time I had the opportunity to find my son, I was strong enough to do whatever it took." She made a lot of changes in her life when she turned fifty. She and her husband moved back to Long Island, and she now works in Manhattan. "It's heady stuff for a farmer's daughter," she says. A smoker for thirty-five years, she quit on the eve of her fiftieth birthday—because her son asked her to.

The hole in her life at last is gone—and Marie filled it herself. She treasures the inscription on the Mother's Day card Robert gave her the first year after their reunion—THANK YOU FOR FINDING ME. ·

CHAPTER 4

Travel: Springboard for Change

O N   A   CHILLY October night, I slipped out of my tent and
stood under a sky full of Southern Hemisphere stars.
Above me, the glaciers that crown Kilimanjaro glowed under
the full moon, which cast a silvery light across our little en-
campment. I was alone in the chiaroscuro light, sixteen thousand feet above sea level, amazed to find myself three-quarters
of the way up Africa's highest mountain. In two days, I hoped
to stand on the summit. I was a world away from my life and
work in New York. As I marveled that I had made it even this
far, I didn't know that this trip would reinvent me, that experiencing this barren, rock-strewn expanse would throw my life
into relief, forcing me to take a fresh look at the choices I'd
made. Somewhere deep inside, I was incubating a much bigger
challenge than ascending this peak.

Launch Pad to a Happier Life

Climbing Kilimanjaro was the toughest thing I'd ever done—until I quit my job. In both instances, I was journeying far outside my comfort zone. On the Kili ascent, I battled physical demons—headachy bouts of altitude sickness that made me regret I'd ever signed on for the trip. Four months later when I resigned, my demons were mental—whispering that if I gave up my position, I'd never have a job this good again. The fact that I'd faced down the fears and anxiety and discomfort on Africa's tallest mountain gave me the confidence to take on another kind of risk. After the climb, I had a new mantra, which I'd mumble to myself whenever life threw me a wobbly pass—*If I could climb Kili, I can do this.*

To me, that's the magic of travel—stepping so completely out of your day-to-day routine that it gives you a new perspective. You see your life anew. We think of vacations as stress reducers, escapes from the traumas and tensions of everyday life. And they are. But the right trip can offer so much more: a clean slate on which to write new rules for your life, and an uncluttered brain with which to formulate them.

Looking back, I can see signs on Kili that it was time to leave my job. The trip to Tanzania was the longest vacation I had ever taken—three weeks—yet I wasn't the slightest bit interested in what was going on back in New York. On evenings when I'd hear one of my fellow climbers in another tent, chattering on her satellite phone to Florida, it never crossed my mind to borrow it so I could see how the next issue of *More* was shaping up.

I couldn't have cared less. I was grateful to be away, focused totally on a single objective—to get to the top of the mountain. Even after I'd stood proudly arm-in-arm with my twenty-four-year-old daughter grinning at a camera by the

SUMMIT sign, I still couldn't summon up any interest in my work. Sitting by the pool at the pretty coffee plantation resort where we spent a day unwinding after the climb—including the best shower I've ever had—I received a fax. As soon as I saw it was from the office, my stomach began to clench. What manner of bad tidings might this be? Had a big photo shoot fallen through? Did a counted-on story fail to materialize? Had a valued staffer decamped to another job?

"Great news," the fax from my second in command said. "*More* was just named one of the 10 hottest new magazines of the year." I knew I should be thrilled; this was an accolade we'd worked hard to earn. But here in Africa, it seemed like a big "So what?" I didn't feel a wave of homesickness for my job, or even a jolt of enthusiasm for getting back in command. I was much more interested in the week of game viewing in the Ngorongoro Crater that lay ahead. In fact, I was a little annoyed to be interrupted in my three-week campaign to totally ignore work.

Embracing Travel—Or Escaping Life?

A better student of her own mind and emotions would have noticed that all my immediate associations with the office were negative. The first thing I thought of was some calamity I'd have to fix. An entire winter would go by before I finally figured this out. When my vacation was over, I simply reported back to my job.

Four months later, my yearnings and dissatisfactions gelled into a plan, and when I resigned, several prescient people asked me if I'd made the decision on Kilimanjaro. I always said no. It wasn't until after I'd left and really examined my choice that I realized the groundwork for quitting had been laid in Africa. Now I tell people: If you're frantic for a vacation because you need to escape your life, be more thoughtful about it than I was. Ask yourself, *What about my life am I so eager to flee? How can I fix my life rather than escape it?* Then take that time away with a free-and-clear mind so you can revel in the vacation, not cower behind it.

Dye your hair. Here's the theory: Look different, feel different. Whether it's covering gray, adding highlights, or shifting the color you've been wearing for a while, it can recharge your batteries. This goes for you, too, guys.

Some people are smarter than I was about the reinvention potential of travel. One of my friends swears by long car trips for making big life decisions. She and her boyfriend decided to get married en route from Boston to Florida. The birth of each of their three children was kicked off with a *should we–shouldn't we* marathon of car talk. "It's ideal," she says. "You're a captive audience for the duration of the trip, so neither of you can avoid the issues."

It's no coincidence that sabbaticals are often staged in another part of the world. Getting that new angle on life, and having to be resourceful to make your way day-to-day in a country where you don't know the customs and don't speak the language, can give you insight into what's truly important. The first emotion may be frustration, but as you explore a new land, it shades over into enlightenment and finally empowerment.

The Go-Go Generation

We boomers are traveling fools, the first generation to embrace air travel en masse. Laker Airways, which brought the world cheap transatlantic fares in the early 1970s, and People Express, with its no-frills bargain-basement flights a decade later, may have been failed business experiments, but they offered an unprecedented opportunity for boomers to become world travelers, putting us in the air in record numbers. So did student standby half-price fares. When US airlines were deregulated in 1978, the ensuing fare wars opened up air travel to more and more Americans. And we haven't stopped: Baby boomers took 269 million trips in 2003, more than any other demographic group, according to the Travel Industry Association of America.

Suddenly, the world was our playground. The more adventurous among us strapped on backpacks after college, bought a Eurrail pass, and set off across France and Italy and Spain, which were actually cheap for Americans to visit back then. International travel, which our kids regard as a right (more than half of the students at my college now spend their junior year abroad), we prize as an extraordinary privilege.

As the years went by, and we'd seen more and more places, the world shrank. In the search for new horizons, our travel tastes became more adventurous, more exotic. We'd already been to Belgium, so how about Borneo? Instead of returning to France's wine country, why not sample the Merlot they make in Australia's Hunter Valley? When we were kids, the occasional National Geographic special whetted our appetite to see a remote region of the world; now there's an entire cable channel celebrating wild and far-flung places. Round-the-world plane tickets, once the darling of backpackers, have found a new popularity among baby boomers. From 2003 to 2004, United, a big player, saw its revenues from these mega-tickets jump 33 percent.

There's no question that the tragedy of September 11 put a crimp in our globe-trotting plans. After the waves of funerals and memorials, most people didn't feel much like vacationing, and many were afraid to fly. I was in Prague a few weeks after the attacks, and there was nary an American in sight. In Vienna, I passed by a candelit streetside shrine to the Americans who'd perished in Washington, Pennsylvania, and New York. Austrians were leaving messages of sympathy, but Steve and I were the only Americans to read them. Gradually, though, Americans became world travelers again. By 2005, air travel had picked up to pre–September 11 levels.

A Late-Blooming Globe-Trotter

As with athletics, I was a latecomer to travel. I took my first airline trip at sixteen; at the time, it was a very big deal. I flew with my parents to visit family friends who had moved to Arizona. Getting on an airliner back in the days when flight attendants were chosen for their looks and wore two-inch heels was an event worthy of your Sunday clothes. We got all dressed up, did our hair and makeup carefully. The experience was special because it was so rare. Now I fly somewhere once a month, and when I get on the plane I'm wearing the publicly acceptable outfit that most closely approximates pajamas. In an era of shrinking seats, growing lines, disappearing meal service, and bankrupting carriers, the transportation may have lost its cachet, but the trips themselves are getting more and more exciting.

Ten years later, at twenty-seven, I saw Europe for the first time. It was a work/pleasure trip, a delayed honeymoon for Steve and me three months after we married. He was writing an article about BMW, so we flew to Germany and then drove through Austria and Switzerland. I was bowled over by everything we saw. In our Munich hotel, I sank into the first featherbed I had ever slept in; I spent hours in the Englischer Garten, sipping an oversize stein of beer and watching people strolling with their babies or walking their dogs. I wondered at how daily life in another land could feel both so familiar and so strange. Visiting the Nazi prison camp at Dachau gave me a brutal, visceral understanding of the tragedy of the Holocaust. Thirty years later, the memory of prisoners' names carved into the crude wooden bunks still brings tears to my eyes. Salzburg was pretty and magical; the Alps, extraordinary. I knew I'd be back as soon as possible.

Over the years, I traveled whenever I could. If I had a choice between buying a new sofa and a weekend in San Francisco, I'd be on the plane in an instant. (This, by the way, is the final reason I will probably never have plastic surgery: I'd always rather spend the money on a trip.) A lot of my friends are doing the same. Each trip feels like a mini reinvention, even when it doesn't result in an identifiable life change. You see new things, you broaden your perspective.

Adventure, Ho!

More than twenty thousand travelers attempt a Kilimanjaro climb every year, and it's just one manifestation of a new breed of adventure vacation that has boomers taking the world by storm. We have the money, we have the time, and we know we won't be able to take these physically demanding vacations forever. So we're booking them now. The average age of our fifteen climbers on Kili was forty-five, bearing out an industry stat that the average adventure traveler is forty-eight years old. A friend of mine hired a personal trainer to get in shape for a demanding kayaking trip to the South Pacific island republic of Palau.

A whole genre of travel companies has sprung up and thrived serving our wanderlust. Well-known outfitters such as Abercrombie & Kent, Mountain Travel/Sobek, and Wilderness Travel have made their fortunes offering soft adventure—

demanding by day, pampering by night. Hiking the Inca Trail, white-water rafting in Costa Rica, horse-packing Morocco's Atlas Mountains, trekking in Nepal: Boomers are doing all this and more. Our determination to have challenging, exciting vacations has led to double-digit growth among top outdoor outfitters, and the Internet makes it easy to preview and book a trip. Now boomers are pioneering in custom wilderness travel that designs trips to the travelers' specifications—say, combining kayaking and yoga, or a rock-climbing tutorial on an off-the-beaten-path route in the Tetons.

Other trips challenge us culturally. Pushing deep into the forgotten civilizations of Irian Jaya, or to remote villages on the Masai Mara in East Africa, can show us communities so different that they shed light on the way we live our own lives. Even a trip to as familiar a land as England can expose us to new ways of thinking.

The Rise of Feel-Good Vacations

Boomers are leading another big travel trend: spa vacations. After an enormous growth spurt in the past decade, spas in the United States number more than twelve thousand, according to the International Spa Association, and boomers, including a growing number of men, have played a starring role in their emergence as a popular way to vacation. This industry's growth reflects an attitudinal change among the members of our generation. Years ago, spas were either boot camps for weight loss or pampering places for the filthy rich. But with medical research showing the life-enhancing value of a healthy diet and exercise program, spas have shaken off their aura of guilty pleasure and been transformed from indefensible treat to laudable vacation. Indeed, these are worthy getaways, custom-designed to be restorative, and we have come to regard them as a just reward for the hard work we do.

I remember my first trip to a spa, when I was in my early forties. It was a discouraging moment in my professional life. Recently jettisoned from a magazine where the entire senior staff had been fired, I was job hunting and writing from home, where I was way too near the refrigerator. Carrying an unwanted ten pounds, I matched the classic profile of a spa wannabe in need of both physical and spiritual uplifting when I lucked into an assignment to write about Rancho La Puerta, a clutch of villas brightly decorated with Mexican folk art on a gorgeous flower-flooded spread in Baja California. I spent seven blissed-out days there, hiking in the mountains, experimenting with fitness classes from water aerobics to FitBALL, making my first tentative attempts at yoga, and eating a delicious low-cal diet. I returned home lighter in every way, determined to repeat the experience.

Mentor a teen. Put your experience to work helping a boy or girl through that other turbulent time of life (neuroscientists have found similarities in brain activity at adolescence and middle age). The National Mentoring Partnership (mentoring.org) is a clearinghouse for good programs nationwide.

Since I began freelance writing, I've spent a fair amount of time at spas, having the good fortune to be a frequent contributor to *Luxury SpaFinder* magazine. I've done sun salutations on a Mexican beach at Amansala's Bikini Boot Camp, and on the dock at The Island Experience, a Brazilian adventure spa. At The Raj, in Fairfield, Iowa, I've experienced *panchakarma,* an ancient Indian purification technique involving very little food, lots of massages with herbalized oil, and—yikes—enemas. An expert "nose" custom-blended an aromatherapy perfume to complete my spectrum of scents at Green Valley Spa in St. George, Utah. I've taken squash and kayak lessons at Canyon Ranch in Lenox, Massachusetts, and had my hormone levels assessed in the medical center at Canyon Ranch's other home in Tucson, Arizona. I've attended a weekend course in Thai massage techniques at the Miami Mandarin Oriental hotel's award-winning spa. Just that assortment of experiences makes it clear that there's a spa for every fitness level, every taste. Some spas dip into the spiritual and the occult, with energy healing sessions and tarot card readings. Adventure spas emphasize the *yahoo!* factor with rock climbing, zip-line rides, and other high-adrenaline activities. A spa week can be a time for busy boomers to reconnect with loved ones; there are couples weekends and mother–daughter weeks (Brook and I have just booked our third getaway at Rancho La Puerta). It's a chance to experiment, trying healthful new pursuits from Pilates to African dance, without embarrassing yourself in front of your friends at home. More and more spas are playing to the mind–body connection by adding medical programs that emphasize wellness and offer everything from cholesterol testing to apnea clinics. Harvard-educated alternative medicine guru Andrew Weil runs a wellness center at the Miraval spa in Tucson.

We're not yet as enlightened as some European countries, where government-sponsored health plans pay for spa services such as massages. But we recognize the value of eating well and exercising; a week at a spa can get you on the right track. I once read that the average cruise vacationer returns home seven pounds heavier. Most spa-goers emerge from their vacation glowing with vitality.

Big Birthdays Take Flight

As America's first globe-trotter generation, we've raised the ante on the classic new-decade birthday party. Our parents celebrated their fortieth, fiftieth, or sixtieth in their living room or at a local restaurant. For big-thinking boomers, a single day's festivities often just aren't enough. Increasingly, we're marking our entrance into a new decade of life with an entire vacation. When I was in Uganda recently on a gorilla-tracking trip (some days I have the best job in the world), I met a woman who was celebrating her sixtieth birthday with a five-week safari. It was a no-holds-barred, top-flight Abercrombie & Kent itinerary to Tanzania, Kenya, South Africa, and Uganda. She had lost thirty-five pounds to get in shape to track the big apes. What better expression could there be of the concept: "I ain't old and I'm showing it."

My fellow safari-goer is emblematic of a generation of travelers who feel that a milestone birthday needs more than a big party at home. It needs the trip of a lifetime. Often the celebrant wants to mark the day by accomplishing a significant feat. For Mary, it was seeing gorillas in their native habitat among the lush volcanic mountains of southern Uganda. My friend Liz Bredeson also celebrated in Africa, by climbing Kilimanjaro with her twenty-year-old daughter. "Reaching the age of fifty didn't seem like a big achievement, but getting to the top of the mountain did," she says. To mark his fiftieth, another friend feted a small group of buddies at a castle in Scotland. Malachy gave the affair a historical twist, appearing at the big birthday dinner decked out in his clan-plaid regalia of kilt and glengarry cap.

Far-flung weddings are on the rise among baby boomers, too. For many who are marrying in their forties and fifties, it's not the first time. They've already done the traditional deal—big reception, big white dress. And they don't have the same obligation to keep Uncle Bob and Aunt Betsy happy by having an in-town affair. Now they want to do something different, something that expresses their personalities and their passions. Enter the destination wedding. I almost got to attend one in Fiji; two scuba instructors from Tahiti had journeyed over to the sister island group to dive the reefs and have a traditional Fijian wedding. All the other guests at the Cousteau Resort were invited to attend, but my flight left just a few hours too soon. This couple were celebrating their new life by launching it with a memorable shared trip. I met a woman at Canyon Ranch who'd put on a wedding we'd all like to attend. She and her husband-to-be paid all the expenses for a group of fifty friends to fly to a resort in Sedona, Arizona, for a lavish wedding weekend.

Recognizing the power of boomer travel dollars, Abercrombie & Kent has issued its first catalog of celebratory trips—from renting a villa in Tuscany or the English countryside where family and friends can gather to striking out on a rafting trip in the foothills of the Himalayas.

Reinventing the Family Trip

The classic family vacation is the stuff of slapstick—parents and kids forced to coexist 24/7, the plaintive backseat whine, "Are we there yet?" *National Lampoon's Vacation,* which capitalized on the broken dream of a cross-country car trip with the kids, mined a universal enough theme to spawn three sequels and remain in regular rotation on cable channels two decades later. We all know the drill: Adults in the front seat, kids in the back, and nobody is having fun.

Fast-forward to the kind of trips boomers are taking with their families at midlife. We have reinvented the family vacation to suit the new, closer relationship we have with our kids. Those who've had babies late in life are loath to leave their wandering days behind. They're scooping up the diapers and the car seat and packing them onto a plane. Club Med used to be the sole refuge of vacationing families with small children. Now adventuresome parents are taking their kids to foreign cities and to chic hotels, which are rushing to set up on-site programs for kids. Hardworking parents are even inviting the kids on business trips. The publisher of *More,* who was on the road at least a week every month, brought her toddlers along whenever she could. Austin-Lehman Adventures of Billings, Montana, has planned a multigenerational biking and hiking trip in the Canadian Rockies for a family of twenty, ranging in age from five to seventy.

Organize a Scrabble tournament. Ask each person you invite to invite one other friend. That way, you can multitask while you play—warding off dementia *and* making new friends.

My daughter Brook is twenty-six as I write this, and we're experiencing an interesting role reversal: Now she's taking Steve and me on her business trips. Last year, she had an assignment to write about India for the travel magazine where she works. Steve and I were delighted to enjoy a much plusher trip than we would have been able to afford had we been paying the entire tab. As we toured Rajasthan, our guide was baffled. Every time a decision was needed—what time to leave, where to have lunch—he'd turn expectantly to Steve and me, and we would defer to Brook. I could see him thinking, *Strange ways these Americans have, letting the child make all the decisions.* I can't say the trip lacked stressful moments, but what I remember best is the pride I felt that my daughter was so competently handling her reporter's duties, and an appreciation that she was willing to share this time with us (of course, we did bring the one magic parental welcome device: the American Express card).

I guess we checked out okay, because six months later she invited us along again, this time on a trip to Fiji. Steve opted to stay home—way too far to go for a beach vacation, he told us—but I was on Travelocity in a flash buying a ticket. The resort where we stayed had won her magazine's ecotourism award, and at the end of the trip Brook, who'd been traveling incognito, revealed why she was there, and congratulated the owner. Suddenly, I became invisible as all his attention turned to Brook, the most important person in the room. After years when she had gamely come to speeches I'd made, corporate events I'd hosted, it was turnabout time: She was the star of the day. Being rendered invisible has never been so much fun.

The Endless Vacation: Living Overseas

Whenever I go to a foreign country, I like to play the expat game—imagining I live there and trying the destination on for size. Even an idyllic landscape like the Tuscan countryside, to which a friend of mine decamped in his forties and where he is now thriving, seems utterly foreign to me. However much I love it there, I know it could never become my home. American from stem to stern, I am fascinated by people like Frances Mayes, author of *Under the Tuscan Sun*, or Peter Mayle, who's written a series of books about living in Provence, who can sink so thoroughly and happily into a new land.

The closest I've come is New Zealand. Steve and I have been there twice, and we both loved the dramatic scenery, the lively, commonsense people. Our original retirement plan had us spending three or four months there during our winter—their summer. If I'd worked another decade under the corporate yoke, we could have afforded it. But my feet got itchy too soon, so we never got to test out just how homey New Zealand could feel.

It is the ultimate kind of travel—calling a new place home, and making home the place that you go back to visit from time to time. Yet there are more than four million Americans living abroad. That's as many as the entire population of Kentucky. Enough Americans are moving abroad at midlife that *AARP* magazine recently did a feature story on the best places to live worldwide. Patrice Wynne, whose migration to Mexico is chronicled in this chapter, moved to one of the destinations AARP recommends. She's eloquent about the complexities and joys of reinventing your life on foreign soil.

That's one remedy for the only downside of an amazing vacation, the postpartum blues, a syndrome globe-trotting boomers are beginning to complain about. Now that their vacations are so luscious, it's painful to see them end. The other solution is to plan the next one before you get home.

The Life Entrepreneurs

The French Connection

Doug and Barbara Babkirk parlayed their love of France into a small business, running women's retreats in a picturesque corner of the French Alps.

Barbara and Doug's Lesson: *Getting away from the familiar references of home can encourage creative thinking, giving a fresh perspective on life.*

BARBARA AND DOUG Babkirk were having dinner one night six years ago at their Tudor-style house tucked into the woods in Cumberland, Maine. They were both forty-eight, and Kate, their only child and the linchpin of their lives, had just left for college in Connecticut. She was thriving, but their lives were sputtering. "We were sitting at the table, both feeling a little weepy," Doug remembers. "I said, 'Okay, Barbara, we need to get a grip.'"

Barbara knew he was right. "It was very sad when Katie left. My work as a career counselor is very satisfying, and Doug loves his job as an associate dean at U. Maine, but you spend so much energy anticipating a child's needs, and when you don't have to do that on a daily basis, it creates a very big hole in your life." They both realized they needed a new project to energize them.

"You speak French; we both love France and wish we could spend more time there. Why don't you do a women's retreat in Provence?" Doug said. Once he'd voiced the idea, Barbara knew it was a natural. "Doug's mother's family is French, and I grew up in a Franco-American household, majored in French at college." But the touchstone was a trip to France they'd made in 1976, when Doug was in grad school. "I'll never forget getting off the plane," he says. "We both started crying, there was such a sense of coming home." Eleven years later, when Kate was seven, Doug took a sabbatical and the family returned to France. "We ended up in Biot, a little village in the south," Barbara says. "We became fast friends with the owners of the house we rented, and Biot became in our hearts our second home." The rose-colored villa their friends owned near this twelfth-century village on the Côte d'Azur would be perfect for the retreat.

Suddenly, their life was upsizing, not downsizing, as they spread notebooks and brochures across the dining room table. Excitement rose as they brainstormed together, and the idea turned into reality with amazing ease. "We had a ball," Doug says. "Both of us love to create things." Barbara would lead the

Living Together, Twenty-First-Century-Style

When we were in our twenties, living together meant shacking up—the dream was to enjoy all the romance and none of the bonds of marriage. At midlife, living together has taken on another meaning for many of us—a solution to the loneliness that old age can impose. My friends and I joke about forming the Home for Decrepit Editors and Writers. Our vision is to live together in an apartment house just big enough to offer units to each of us, plus a caregiver should one of us start to fail. We can shuffle down the hall on our walkers to visit each other, or rock together on a terrace reminiscing about the old days when people read magazines and books by actually turning the pages. When we talk about the Home, we're only half kidding. We may not enact our plan, but we're dead serious about figuring out an appealing living situation before old age kicks in and removes our choices. We want to be surrounded by friends, in a place that reminds us more of a college dorm than death's waiting room.

There are already murmurs of this. A couple of months ago, I read a newspaper story about a mini trend of midlife friends who are moving in together, with the pledge to take care of each other as needed. So far, it's a stronger urge among women than men (which makes sense, since we do live longer). The article profiled women in their fifties who'd chosen to live together to help each other through future illnesses.

Reunited and It Feels So Good

When we were teens, getting pregnant was a shameful secret, and many girls who found themselves in this predicament— such as Marie Hubschman, whose story is told in this chapter— were sent away to give birth in a home for unwed mothers. Even as they went on with their lives, marrying and raising chil-

weeklong workshop, helping women determine new directions for their lives, and Doug, who loved to cook, would prepare the meals. The planning went smoothly for these college sweet-hearts, who sound like twins when they talk about the retreat, echoing not just ideas but the very phrases they use. "We've always served as each other's mentor/teacher/guide/partner," Doug says. "Probably why we've been together over thirty years."

Take a personal growth day. Skip work on a Friday and do whatever you'd do if you didn't have a job. Take a hike, go to the movies, repaint the porch—whatever moves you. Then find a way to include the activity in your regular life.

They printed up a brochure, Barbara sent it to a couple of colleagues, and—riding the wave of American interest in all things Provençal—nine women signed on for the first retreat in 1998. One woman was about to leave her job, another had divorced and was moving cross-country, a third just needed quiet time to listen to herself. In the mornings, Barbara led workshops on making life changes. "We discussed fears and stereotypes, developed intentions for the week." In the afternoons, Barbara took the women on sightseeing tours to the local markets, artisan villages, and Mediterranean seacoast towns. Meanwhile, Doug was visiting the market, buying fresh meats and produce for dinner that day. "He'd never cooked for nine people before, and the villa didn't have enough dinnerware for this crowd. "I felt like Lucille Ball in the chocolate factory episode, trying to keep everything going, washing plates between courses." At the end of the week, they were exhausted, but they'd learned two important things: The program was a winner, but nine's too many.

They could have found a cozy B&B in Maine to host the

retreat, with a lot less wear and tear. But Barbara and Doug both feel the French connection works not just for them, but for their clients as well. "The Mediterranean culture has a deliberateness that encourages being in the moment," Barbara says, "and the sensual beauty of the environment elicits an openness that moves the women to insights and ideas." "The women are totally out of context here—new language, new environment, new people," Doug adds. "Instead of closing and withdrawing, they open up."

The Babkirks have conducted retreats annually since 1998, limiting the participants to four or five. Barbara runs the show, an arrangement that is more than fine with her husband: "I'm pretty comfortable with my feminine side. And when I serve the meals, I love to see the reaction of women who aren't used to being nurtured by a man." Since that first, oversubscribed session, things have gotten easier.

At the moment, Doug and Barbara are content to continue working at their day jobs. But they anticipate another season of change when Doug becomes eligible for retirement in four years. "We've talked about living in France for the spring and fall," he says. "We'd sell our house of twenty-three years, find something much simpler, like a condo." Barbara would do two retreats a year, and offer individual sabbaticals, too.

Doug is part of a circle of men who have gotten together twice a month for eighteen years to talk about their experiences. "There were originally nine of us, but as some couples have divorced and others have moved away, we're now down to four. We talk about job loss, relationships, our kids leaving home, always looking under the story for the spiritual and emotional level." Given the power of that experience, he's considered doing a retreat for men. "Men are good at connecting around an activity," he says, so he's outlined a program in Provence where they'd swap expertise. "For example, one member of my men's group is a potter; he could teach in the area where the impressionists hung out. Another is a lawyer; he could talk about dealing with conflict in creative ways." One thing's sure: If the men's workshop does come to fruition, running it won't be a simple role swap. "Barbara has made it clear she doesn't want to cook."

In an organic and almost painless way, this empty-nest remedy has blossomed into a plan for the coming decades of their lives. Barbara says she never suffered reinvention angst. "Once we figured out how we'd pull this off, it felt so right. In fact, the biggest lesson for me every year is to surrender to the moment. I think, *I've got everything planned so well,* and then it doesn't happen as planned. You have to roll with it."

Many businesses are launched by dreams of wealth, but there's no pot of gold at the end of the rainbow in Provence, and that's just fine with the Babkirks. "The first year, I made a decent amount of money, with nine women," Barbara says. "Earlier in life earning money was a high priority, but the retreat has come at a time in my life when it's fine if I don't make a lot."

Barbara originally billed the retreat for women at midlife, and most of the participants are in their forties and fifties. "There seems to be a stirring in the second half of life," she says. "You may not have the whole picture in your mind, but you have a sense that there's something out there." Self-examination can be hard sledding, as you come to grips with dreams that aren't to be. "Maybe you're not going to be a ballerina, or have the children you thought you'd have. There's grieving, but there can be reimagining, too." The women on the retreats are willing to dig in and explore the tough stuff; they've taken the first step by signing up. "I often hear women say, 'Jobs have always fallen into my lap. Now they aren't anymore.' They need to figure out a new way of doing their life." One woman developed a retirement time line and plan; another committed to taking time for herself while caring for ill parents; a third decided to launch a new career. "It's not looking outside yourself and asking, *Where can I fit?*; It's looking inside and determining who you are."

Which is exactly how the Provence retreats came about.

Leader of the Pack

Rob Geyer-Sylvia always loved to travel, but life kept getting in the way—until he found a new job at fifty-one, as tour manager.

Rob's Lesson: *The confidence and seasoning of midlife can serve you well, particularly when you're shepherding an unruly group in a place you've never been.*

ONE OF ROB Geyer-Sylvia's best memories of childhood is road trips exploring the cities within range of his Connecticut hometown. "Back in the 1960s, flying was for upper-crust folks, and we were a working-class family," he says. "But that didn't stop us. We'd get in the old Hudson and hit the road."

Ironically, it was the Coast Guard that put Rob into the air for the first time, transporting him to a base in Puerto Rico. "I loved it," he says. "I still think flying is magical." Stationed in San Juan for a year and a half, he rented an apartment in the old city, developing a taste for living in a different place. He married in his midtwenties and had two daughters. Like his parents, Rob and Zelda took the girls on trips whenever they could. When Ruth and Marta were four and two, the family spent three weeks in England, Rob's first trip outside North America. They rented a cottage in Cornwall, drove over to Wales, traveled through the Cotswolds, and soaked up London's pleasures.

Eight years later, they rented a house in Tuscany with two other couples for an idyllic week touring the Italian countryside.

Rob worked as a social worker and then a teacher, and Zelda's career as a health industry executive took them from Vermont to upstate New York, and finally to Ann Arbor, Michigan. Life was busy, and, with saving for college a priority, their next chance to go overseas didn't come until both girls were in high school: Zelda, who runs the University of Michigan's HMO, was invited to host a South American trip for alumni. She agreed, with one condition: that her husband go, too. As it turned out, paying Rob's way was a wise investment; the tour company recruited an able new employee. One of the firm's owners happened to be along, and she and Rob hit it off. At the end of the trip, she asked him if he'd consider hosting other tours. The answer was immediate: "Absolutely."

His first destination was China. As tour manager, Rob would be the majordomo, making sure that the local service providers were doing their jobs—that guides would be there to greet the group, that local transportation arrived on time. He flew to Beijing with a company owner, who returned to the States after five days. "I had no idea I would be on my own," Rob says. "I guess she knew I could do the job. I counted bodies, smoothed a few things over, did a lot of schmoozing. It's patience and common sense. When someone fell at the Great Wall, I got her to the hospital." Rob loved the work, and his job performance earned him an encore invitation.

He was delighted to find himself on the way to Chile and Argentina. "I jumped at this trip," Rob says. "I've got a little Iberian blood, and I was dying to see Patagonia." It was a magical trip, including a lake crossing in Argentina memorialized in Che Guevara's *Motorcycle Diaries*.

Next up was a six-week stint overseeing back-to-back seven-day barge cruises between Amsterdam and Budapest.

Rob had been able to dovetail the other trips with his teaching schedule. But this time he'd miss the start of classes in September. Suddenly, the employment disadvantage of being middle-aged paid an unexpected dividend. When they moved to Ann Arbor, Rob had been unable to land a high school teaching job. "No one's going to touch a fifty-year-old with fourteen years of experience and a master's degree," he says. "I never even got an interview at a Michigan public school." The director of the adult education program where Rob teaches GED prep courses, social studies, and government values his knowledge and experience, offering flexibility to keep him. "I sent e-mails from Europe, left maps, and they did a 'Where in the world is Rob?' schtick until I got back and picked up the class," he says.

The barge trip was the toughest yet. "I was on duty from the time I got up until I went to bed, forty-four days nonstop." His company had never partnered with the barge operator before, which put Rob at the helm of a shakedown cruise. "There are sixty-seven locks between Budapest and Amsterdam," he says. "You'd better make your lock, or you find yourself traveling through the Danube's picturesque Wachau Valley in the middle of the night."

So far, Rob has averaged a trip a year and wouldn't mind doubling the schedule, especially if it could include some of his dream destinations. "I'd love to go to New Zealand or Southeast Asia. I've always wanted to see Angkor Wat. Antarctica? I'm there!" He knows his charmed life as someone who's paid to travel to some of the world's most alluring destinations could be cut short at any time. "If I ever have to take a nine-to-five job, that's it for the travel. The pay is so modest, I have to make sure I don't spend it all before I get home." But it's like the Master-Card commercial: salary: minuscule; experience: priceless. "All of this is possible because of Zelda, the big job she has, the money she earns," Rob says. Is she envious of Rob's travels?

"Not at all. She knows how tough it is. When she joined me for a week on the barge trip, I put her to work."

Zelda and Rob just sent their younger daughter off to college. Their long-range plan is to run a small business together, and they're still puzzling over what that enterprise should be. "One thing's for certain," Rob says. "I'd like to be busy at certain times of the year, free at others. Now that I've seen the world, I have to keep traveling."

Peak Experience

To celebrate her fiftieth birthday, Liz Bredeson climbed Africa's highest mountain.

Liz's Lesson: *Doing a hard and elemental thing, stripping your life down to what can be carried in a backpack, teaches you what's truly important.*

"I HADN'T GIVEN a lot of thought to my birthday," Liz Bredeson says, "and then one day I thought, *Ohmigod, I'm going to be fifty.* I remembered looking at my mom and dad at that age and thinking they seemed old." Liz came up with a unique way to celebrate, neatly proving that *old* is something no one can call her: She signed up for a trip to climb Kilimanjaro, Africa's tallest peak.

"My parents' life was hard," she says. "My mom grew up in Wisconsin and had to leave school in eighth grade to work on the family farm. She and my dad, who was a welder, struggled their whole lives. Then she was diagnosed with Alzheimer's in her late fifties." While Liz's mom lived another fourteen years, Liz's two daughters never knew their grandmother as a lively adult. "Part of me was thinking, *If I'm going to climb Kili, I need to do it now.*"

For most prospective climbers, the biggest hurdle is convincing themselves they can make it to the top. Not for Liz, who'd hiked above twelve thousand feet at Philmont Scout Ranch in New Mexico and to nearly ten thousand in the Tetons. "Climbing the mountain was not so much about the physical aspect. The hardest thing for me was looking at how much money I was spending—more than ten thousand dollars—that wasn't going into the house or my kids' education." Actually, it *was* contributing to the education of her daughter Chelsea, who would take two weeks off from college to make the trip to Tanzania with her mom. Putting hands on the money wasn't the issue. As a senior executive in a Midwest publishing company, Liz earned more than she ever dreamed she would. But all her life, like so many women in America, rich or poor, she'd worried about spending it. "Is this going to last? Or am I going to be a bag lady?" These questions ran through her mind. She knew they weren't rational concerns, but it was hard to break a lifetime habit of measuring every purchase.

Write a business plan. Itchy to launch a company? Put your dreams down on paper and see if the ink is red or black. The Small Business Administration's Web site (sba.gov) will give you the basics. SCORE (score.org), a resource partner of the SBA, offers an online template to use.

What convinced Liz to write the big check was remembering a similar decision she'd made in her midforties when she got an MBA in organizational leadership. Her company would pay 80 percent of the tuition, but she worried about taking so much time away from her family. "It was all about me, which made it hard to say yes. But everybody survived; we still made the mortgage payments." Liz's husband, Larry, who worked part-time in order to serve as the on-duty parent when the girls were growing up, was all for the Africa trip. "Go," he said. "Why else do you make all that money?"

"I always wanted to see Africa," says Liz, who grew up reading about anthropologists Louis and Mary Leakey's extraordinary finds in the Rift Valley and Olduvai Gorge. She wanted to give that experience to her daughter, who would be graduating from college soon. After that, Liz says, "I knew my opportunities to travel with her might disappear." Liz has always thrilled to the challenge of camping, going one-on-one with the elements. "It's not about your skill set at work. It's just you, your backpack, your boots. It's how you control your body and what you make it do. You can ignore pain, or let it overrun you. When I'm out in the Tetons, I totally forget about work, even about my husband and kids."

Kilimanjaro holds a special cachet among climbers as one of the fabled Seven Summits—the highest peak on each continent—yet it's one of the easiest to ascend. Technical climbing skills aren't required, as the route up is really just a very long hike—all the way to 19,340 feet. A couple of dozen people die on the mountain every year, mostly from pulmonary edema or cerebral swelling, both effects of altitude sickness, but weather on Kili doesn't carry the death-wielding force of an Everest snowstorm. It's not a mountain you're likely to lose your life trying to climb. Still, only half of all climbers make it to the top.

Before the trip, Liz wasn't worried about altitude sickness. "We'd both been up to twelve thousand and it didn't bother us." But the rarefied air on Kili proved to be a tougher challenge. On day three of the eight-day climb, at thirteen thousand feet, Chelsea was brought low with the nausea and pounding headache of altitude sickness. It was the toughest moment on the mountain for both daughter and mom, as Chelsea retreated to their tent, knowing there were more than six thousand feet to go. Liz remembers telling Chelsea, "If you wake up in the morning and are still this miserable, we cannot continue." Chelsea was horrified. "But Mom, you wanted to do this trip." "Yes," Liz said, "I wanted to do it with *you*." By the morning, Chelsea had rallied. "After that," Liz says, "I knew we were going all the way. Of course, nobody told us about the Western Breach, which was probably a good thing."

Two days later, amid the glaciers at 16,000 feet, they were staring upward at the formidable massif they'd have to tackle: the Western Breach, a wall of boulders that rises to 18,500 feet. For Liz, that was the most difficult day. "I wasn't scared, but I was so nauseous, just putting one foot in front of the other. I was so mad that I was missing the experience because I was sick." One of the guides wanted to take her pack, but Liz wouldn't give it up. "The whole idea was that I'd carry it to the top." After six hours of rock scrambling, she sat, exhausted and gray, at the top of the promontory. "Sure, I was relieved it was over," she says, "but never did I wish I hadn't come. It hit me every day on the mountain, how lucky I was to be strong enough to do this at this age, and to be there with my daughter."

After a bitter-cold night camping at 18,500 feet, where the water bottles froze inside the tent, it was only another 800 feet to the summit. "I was ready, I felt good," Liz says. By daybreak, she and Chelsea stood grinning into a camera in front of the SUMMIT sign.

Back in Iowa, Liz found herself missing the power of the experience. "I always have a letdown after a vacation, but especially this time. It's so stimulating living on your own, dealing with everything. You get back and you've got your car, your job, your refrigerator, everything's so easy." And nobody wants to hear as much about your adventure as you want to tell. "After the first hour, they start talking about mowing their lawns."

As she adjusted to her routine, Liz found that the trip to

Africa had changed her. "Little stresses eat up so much of your energy, your day, your thoughts. Now I always try to remember what's important," she says. "I am less hesitant about making decisions, and I'm not worried that I'm going to do everything 100 percent right." The other big lesson was to seize the moment. "I spent the money and it didn't hurt us. I did this very big thing, and it was for *me*." It's encouraged her to fulfill other dreams. "As I get older, spring comes around faster and faster, and I don't want to waste my time on anything that isn't important to me." She no longer goes to parties she doesn't want to attend, nor does she spend time with people whose company she doesn't enjoy. "Climbing Kili has allowed me to be more honest, and a little easier on myself."

Liz says their time on Kili fostered a strong sense of independence in her daughter. "She was encouraged by the African experience to move eight states and a thousand miles from home," Liz says. "Larry and I supported her decision and helped her move. Leaving Chelsea to start her new life wasn't as hard as I expected because we have so much to look forward to ourselves."

Saying Adios to the States

Her business closed, her marriage ended—it was the darkest time in Patrice Wynne's life. She reinvented herself by moving to a small city in Mexico.

Patrice's Lesson: *Sometimes, when things seem incurably black, focusing on the struggles and successes of a role model can keep you moving toward a happy new life.*

PATRICE WYNNE REMEMBERS the afternoon she arrived in the Mexican mountain town that would become her new home. "It was April Fools' Day, but I was clinically depressed." The preceding two years had been the toughest of her life. She and her husband ended a long marriage; she closed down Gaia, a bookstore and cultural center she had begun in Berkeley, California, twenty years earlier; and then her grandmother, who had been the lodestone of Patrice's life, died. "Everything I connected to as part of my identity was being snipped," she says. "I was in a state of shock."

With the shuttering of Gaia, the life force was being sucked out of her. For fifteen years, Patrice had been at work by seven every morning, often staying until ten or eleven at night, hosting authors' events. "The bookstore was my whole world—the people I went out with, the things I talked about." But with the advent of deep-discount mega-chains and online sellers, independent bookstores across the country were going out of business like so many dominoes tumbling down. It became more and more difficult for Patrice to keep her venture afloat. When she finally shut the door for the last time in the spring of 2000, it caused Patrice to question her life. "I'd hosted over three thousand author events, I was on the board of the American Booksellers Association," she says. "Who am I, if I'm not the owner of Gaia?"

For months, Patrice was immobilized by depression. Eventually, though, she began to recast misfortune as opportunity. "My life felt like a big, empty place, but then I found the freedom to reinvent myself. For better or for worse, I am not a dweller in the past." She credits two factors with giving her the courage, in her early fifties, to transcend her grief and move forward: a fundamental optimism and the inspiration of her grandmother. "She was fierce in her determination to imagine her life beyond the small world she was born into," Patrice remembers. The daughter of Welsh immigrants, she married into a Pennsylvania coal-mining family. "My grandfather wasn't interested in the world, so my grandmother would save money and take adventures. One day, he was watching TV. The pope had been shot, and a reporter was interviewing people outside St. Patrick's Cathedral. The next thing he knew, my grandmother was on camera." She'd told her husband she was going to nearby Reading, but had gotten on a bus to New York City. "This was a woman who savored life," Patrice says. "I try to model myself after her. I could feel her fierceness as I picked myself up and strived toward something new at the worst moment in my life."

As Patrice's spirit was mending, she met a kindred spirit, a woman who had grown up in Mexico and wanted to return. This reignited Patrice's childhood fantasy of living in another country. "I had always been attracted to Mexico. I studied Spanish in high school and college." Patrice had some money from the sale of the house in Berkeley where she and her husband had lived, and the two women decided to spend the winter of 2001 in Mexico. As they toured around, Patrice was drawn back again and again to San Miguel de Allende, a pretty colonial city in the mountains. It's a town with an active arts agenda that has lured the biggest community of Americans in Mexico. "The joke about San Miguel is that you show up on Monday and have bought a home by Tuesday," Patrice says. She took a little longer, house-sitting and renting in four different neighborhoods before purchasing a hilltop house on the outskirts of town. On holy days, she can watch the flickering candles as processions make their way to the chapel of San Juan de Dios. These days, Patrice lives to the backbeat of hammering. "I'm knocking out walls, lifting roofs. Colonial arches, richly colored walls, a huge Mexican-tiled tub—I'm letting my creativity soar."

Living an exciting life in a foreign city is easy; making a home there is the tricky part. "In San Miguel, you're living in two worlds," Patrice says. "You create a sense of home by surrounding yourself with a community of expats. But then, you realize you've separated yourself from the Mexican community you migrated to. You have to be very intentional about expanding your world beyond Americans."

While the relaxed rhythms of Mexican life appealed to this exhausted California workaholic, it took effort to adjust to a completely different pace. "I longed for a place where life was simple, sweet, sane, spirited, and sensual," Patrice says. "But it was hard to slow down." Over the five years Patrice has lived in San Miguel, that effort has resulted in a richness of leisure she never knew in those frantic years running the bookstore. "One of the insights at midlife for me is the relationship between being and doing." For all those years in America, she "did." "There's a drive in your twenties, thirties, and even forties to achieve, acquire, make a name for yourself. Now, here I am at fifty-three, living in Mexico, deliberately trying to be a different kind of person."

Plant a container garden. You can grow a surprising assortment of edible crops, including lettuce, tomatoes, peppers, and beans, without rototilling an acre of lawn. Extremists will want heirloom seeds, the old-fashioned nonhybridized, open-pollinated varieties. Heirloomseeds.com sells more than seven hundred kinds.

Here's the lesson she's learned at midlife: "We Americans spent all those years pushing, shoving, demanding success of ourselves, but when we look back, what was the quality of our days?" Now there is always time for friends. "In Berkeley, you had to plan for weeks. In San Miguel, when you run into people you know, it's not unusual to stop whatever you're doing, go into a café, and hang out for a few hours." Patrice hopes she's become a better listener, more interested in what others have to say, less preoccupied by her own interests, her own work. "The greatest gifts we have in life are love and time. Because San Miguel is small and because the Americans here have chosen to come, there's a spirit of goodwill I've never encountered before." Patrice notes the irony of being a bookstore owner who never had time to read a book. Now she reads constantly, and also makes time every day to work on a memoir she's writing, and to take photographs of the lives unfolding around her in San Miguel.

Yes, there are aspects of America she misses. "I miss *The New York Times*. I miss Tom's of Maine toothpaste, or driving across the Bay Bridge as the moon rises over the Berkeley hills. I miss eavesdropping about the latest book deals in line at Peet's Coffee." But, she says proudly, she's pared her life down to what's truly important to her. "I'm now content with books and movies that are three years past their prime, I wear clothes off the twenty-peso table at the Mercado, I have traded my Saab for my feet, and I have embraced a Mexican brand of Catholicism that is Aztecan at its core."

Two years after moving to Mexico, Patrice started a business, exporting clothing and housewares crafted from colorful Mexican fabrics—Day of the Dead aprons and camp shirts, Virgin of Guadalupe shower curtains. But this venture is very different from her Berkeley bookstore: This time, there's no workaholism allowed. Skilled seamstress Maria Dolores Hernandez Vilchez and her family make everything. "We started very small and it has been growing slowly, at a pace that gives me time for photography and writing, for three-hour lunches with my friends," Patrice says. "With the bookstore, I felt I was changing the world by selling books about psychological and spiritual development. Here I don't see my business transforming anyone." Though, in fact, the wages Dolores earns are putting her five daughters through college.

In California, Patrice called herself an activist. "Berkeley and activism are like peanut butter and jelly," she says with a laugh. She worked for Amnesty International, created libraries for women's shelters, and joined anti-nuclear-weapons campaigns. When people ask her to work on similar programs in Mexico now, she says, "I'm hesitant. My instinct is to keep that energy for myself. I don't even like hearing myself say that, but I need ten years just for me."

Patrice smiles to think of the new paths she and her ex-husband have taken at midlife. "I've always had a lot of energy, while he is more quiet and interior." When their marriage broke up, he intended to move to a cabin in Sonoma. "But he met a wonderful woman with two kids and now they have a third together. It's hilarious how our lives have switched. I've pared mine way down, and now he has a big job, much bigger responsibilities." They're both thriving in lives neither could have imagined.

CHAPTER 5

⌒⌒

Adding Meaning to Life

W E SAT CROSS-LEGGED in a circle, twenty-six women who had come from all over the country to Canyon Ranch spa in Tucson, Arizona, to explore what being middle-aged really means. As we went around the room introducing ourselves and explaining our reasons for enrolling in the week-long "Journey Through Midlife" program, women described difficult life experiences—evil bosses, unsatisfying marriages, serious illnesses, addiction. Some cited the rigors of menopause—hot flashes, memory loss, lowered libido. All mentioned their spiritual practices—yoga, meditation, Reiki, conventional religions. When it was my turn, I told the group that I was a magazine writer working on a story, then grinned ruefully and added, "And I still haven't located my spiritual side."

Making the Mind–Body Connection

That was six years ago, and I was convinced that I had no spiritual instincts at all. While I was a little abashed to be so out of step with the crowd at Canyon Ranch, I had always taken secret satisfaction in being emotionally self-sufficient, much the way New Yorkers pride themselves on their toughness and street-smarts. I didn't need the emotional crutch of spiritual practice, I told myself. I enjoyed the occasional yoga class for the challenges it set for my body, but I always unrolled my mat near the door so I could sneak out before the instructor made us lie down and close our eyes at the end.

When I left my job and began to write freelance, my schedule opened up, so I started taking yoga classes several times a week. Stretching my muscles regularly seemed a useful complement to the hours I spent building them in the weight room. I appreciated the new flexibility my hamstrings were gaining, however reluctantly, and the improved sense of balance that would become more and more valuable as I aged. I tolerated the breathing exercises that opened the classes, complaining to my daughter about all the potential workout time we were wasting doing something that comes naturally and that cornball Namaste bow at the end.

Then, over the course of a year attending classes regularly, something very strange happened: I began to enjoy yoga in a whole new way. As I became more skilled at marrying my breathing with the poses, I discovered that I was more in tune with my body here than anywhere else at my gym. And far from wishing to flee the room before we relaxed in shavasana, the corpse pose, I was savoring the minutes spent lying still, my mind untethered from the concerns of the day. At the close of class, my body and mind newly limbered, I was happy to bow to my fellow yoginis and wish them a Sanskrit g'day.

Good grief, I wondered, did I actually have a spiritual side, however embryonic? This was a surprising development indeed, a reinvention I hadn't sought out, but welcomed. Looking back, I think I needed to climb off the runaway train that was my former commuting/working life before I could even begin to relax enough to enjoy the mental benefits of yoga. While I was working in New York, every second counted, and every day was programmed. I used to joke that if you knew me, you could predict where I was every hour of every week. Six forty-five on a Tuesday morning? I'd be finding a seat on the commuter train. Ten AM on Saturday? I'd be leaving the gym to swing by the supermarket and the bank before heading home for a quick lunch, followed by an afternoon hike. And so on. The constant motion made me feel productive and efficient, but it never gave me a moment to think. Imagination and contemplation were relegated to monthly ideas meetings at the magazine. Think about my life? So sorry, too busy.

After I began working at home, pleasurable oases of quiet time began to appear in my life. Reading *The New York Times* and *Wall Street Journal* was no longer limited to a fifty-nine-minute ride on the commuter train. If Ellen DeGeneres had an interesting guest, I could knock off work and watch the interview. When the Perseid meteor shower was slated to light up the sky, I set the alarm for 3 AM, knowing I could sleep in the next morning. It took a while to unbend enough to enjoy all this new freedom, and the calming influence of a regular yoga practice helped me along.

Yoga's value was demonstrated rather dramatically after I'd been practicing about a year. On my way home from the gym one evening, while I was waiting to make a left turn, a big SUV rear-ended my tiny sports car, leaving me with a batch of broken ribs, a moderate concussion, and ten staples in the back of my head. After congratulating me on making an excellent recovery *for my age* (don't you love it?), my neurologist told me that I had escaped the most dire effects of having my head slammed against the rollbar hard enough to knock me out because I was ultra-relaxed from the yoga class I had just taken.

One of the first assignments I embarked on as a freelance writer took me deeper into the spirituality world, when I researched an article about the work of medical intuitives. I was fascinated by the concept that someone could actually see into your body, watch the blood rushing through your veins, examine the architecture of your bones, even detect illness. But to call me a skeptic is to put it mildly; I imagined I'd be talking to a lunatic band of charlatans and flakes. After all, wasn't *intuitive* merely the new marketing word for "psychic"? In the course of reporting the story, my attitude changed. I was impressed by the earnestness of the medical intuitives I talked to, who clearly believed in their powers, and who had an impressive knowledge of anatomy and physiology. Several were MDs. Even more, I was influenced by two well-known doctors whose work I respect. Christiane Northrup, MD, author of *The Wisdom of Menopause* and guru to midlife women across the country, believes there is a scientific explanation for medical intuition—we just don't know how to measure it yet. "If somebody had told you in 1890 that there were waves going through the air, and you could pick them up on a television set and see something happening in California, you would have thought he was completely crazy," Northrup pointed out. Yet we now routinely watch football games and rock concerts on live TV. Pamela Peeke, MD, who was the first senior research fellow at the National Institutes of Health's National Center for Complementary and Alternative Medicine, remarked that "There are savants everywhere, people who can do calculus in their heads, or the pianist playing Carnegie Hall at eleven." After being read by an intuitive, I can't say I came away a born-again believer. She said a few things that rang true, but other observations were off key. I was grateful, though, to have the opportunity to talk seriously with a group of people who had very different perceptions of the world from my own.

Opening Our Minds to a Bigger Picture

Whether or not I became a believer in medical intuition is not the point. I liked the idea that I was keeping my thinking flexible enough to examine a new idea, however outlandish it seemed. This is an important hallmark of a fertile midlife. We've all heard the cliché that as we age, our views solidify, even ossify, until we become the narrow-minded grumpy old men and women who are the butt of comedy. Clinging to what you've previously believed is the course of least resistance. It requires great heart to examine things that call your credos into question, but an explorer's nature is what it takes to be a successful Life Entrepreneur.

That's been my spiritual awakening, my reinvention at midlife—a tiny shift in thinking compared with the people I talked to for this book, but a sizable change to me. Midlife can be a fertile time for strengthening faith or testing its boundaries, finding religion for the first time or seeking out a new way of expressing it. There's no doubt that a heightened sense of our mortality is motivating some of the change.

This chapter explores various ways men and women have found profound meaning at midlife. Really, that could be the subtext for every profile in the book, because the right reinvention satisfies our psyches at the deepest level. Here, though, are people who've looked into their hearts and minds, examined their faith and values, and taken action in stirring ways, some by embracing religion or exploring their own spirituality, others by doing good works.

There's growing evidence that a rich spiritual life can actually keep us well. In 2005, a National Institutes of Health panel
reviewed studies that indicated that people who attended religious services regularly were healthier. Lynda Powell, a professor of preventive medicine at Rush University Medical Center in
Chicago, who led the panel, was a skeptic until the evidence
she found convinced her that, as she told a *Wall Street Journal*
reporter, "I should go to church." The mortality rate was reduced by 25 percent for people who attended religious services
at least once a week. Powell suggests that one powerful force
for healing may be the ability, when stress or anger strikes, to
calm your mind through prayer or meditation. Another recent
study at Massachusetts General Hospital suggests that meditation gives you a bigger brain. Researchers found more gray matter in the frontal cortexes of people who meditate regularly, a
change that was particularly dramatic in the older people they
studied, since it reversed the thinning of the cortex that occurs
with age.

Prime Time for Giving Back

Every Tuesday and Wednesday night, my husband sets the
alarm for 5:55 AM. When it rings, he pulls on a shirt and a pair
of pants—and climbs back into bed. That way he's ready if he
gets a call. For the past five years, Steve has been driving the
ambulance for our small town's volunteer corps.

How Steve has chosen to give back to our community is utterly surprising and completely predictable. In one respect, he's
a natural for the job. A former editor in chief of *Car and Driver,*
he's a skilled driver who has loved machines all his life. The
chance to pilot the big ambulance is every boy's dream, one
that still called to Steve at midlife. Before he'd even been fitted
for a uniform, he'd bought a revolving green light he could set

on the dash of our station wagon as he rushed down to the ambulance bays to answer a call.

On the other hand, this is the guy who said that much as he wanted to share the moment, he wasn't sure he could be present at our daughter's birth. Too much blood, too forceful a reminder of the many months he spent having surgeries as a child. When the time came, he was in the birthing room, but when the doctor asked him if he'd like to cut the umbilical cord, he almost knocked over his camera tripod backing away. Yet this uneventful delivery would be tame stuff compared with what he'd witness as the first responder to a highway crash.

Write a novel about yourself. Take a page from journal writers, and work on it the same time every day. Consider it your unpublished blog. Melding fact and fantasy, stretching your mind to imagine a different life for yourself, will feed your future.

Watching Steve meet the emotional challenge of dealing with carnage and vomit and death while reveling in the chance to drive the big truck, I've come to think that these two seemingly inconsistent impulses are a good model to follow for midlifers embarking on charitable work. There should be an aspect of volunteer work that is deeply satisfying, whether it's raising a guide dog for the blind or building houses for hurricane refugees. There should also be a challenge involved, which could be acquiring a new skill—say, learning to use a chain saw to clear brush off hiking trails—or overcoming a hesitation or fear, maybe by becoming a hospice volunteer. It's that second element, the one that demands mental or emotional growth, that will keep volunteer work compelling and fresh.

Steve has served as an officer of the Cornwall, New York, Volunteer Ambulance Corps, responded to almost a thousand calls, and has been voted Member of the Year twice. He's gotten to know the community where we live on a whole new level. This year, he wrote an official history of the organization, which is celebrating its fiftieth anniversary. His participation in the group has enriched his life. And that's the secret: finding volunteer work that works for you.

There are a multitude of options, as we discovered at *More* when we reported a story called "50 Ways to Give Back," profiling people who'd found important and satisfying volunteer work. Here's just a sampling of the surprising opportunities we uncovered: Some of the midlifers we interviewed formed charitable organizations. A breast cancer survivor and occupational therapist in Pittsburgh founded a nonprofit to provide other breast cancer patients with an exercise therapy routine. A retired police officer from Racine, Wisconsin, started a program that encouraged children to read. One mom in Greenwich, Connecticut, launched a charity to provide strollers and car seats to pregnant women in need, and another in Huntington Woods, Michigan, honored her son, who died in a car accident, by establishing a scholarship fund in his name. A speech pathologist in Sonora, California, who's a private pilot flies needy patients for medical treatment. A Boston business owner does repair and restoration work in the homes of the inner-city elderly. A marketing executive in Hartford, Connecticut, volunteers every week at a local homeless shelter.

This is just a sampling of the ways that boomers can harness their skills and experiences for a cause, or choose a charity that helps them learn new skills.

Leaving a Legacy

Americans donated $250 billion to charity in 2004, 5 percent more than the previous year and a new record, according to the

Giving USA Foundation. Boomers, who contributed a healthy share of that total, are in a unique position to flex their philanthropic muscles. By our fifties, most of us have experienced the darker realities of life, maybe losing a loved one to a car crash or watching a relative or friend battle a terminal illness. We may still feel healthy and vigorous ourselves, but we have a new appreciation of our vulnerability. Often this gets us to thinking about putting our money to good work, now and in the future.

Our generation has not just the will but also the way to leave a legacy. We stand to inherit an unprecedented amount of money from our parents—an estimate published in *American Demographics* magazine put the number at an astonishing forty-one trillion dollars.

Over the years at *More,* we wrote about various ways boomers were leaving a legacy. For some, who had significant financial resources, it meant setting up a foundation that would live on after they died. For others, it was making careful choices about where their charitable dollars went. For both groups, setting an example for their kids was an important motivation.

At forty-six, Melissa Berman launched a second career helping people become better philanthropists. Director of Rockefeller Philanthropy Advisors, which helps wealthy clients direct their charitable dollars, she promotes a credo that is twofold: Know your charity and know yourself. She encourages people to think hard about what is truly fulfilling: Do they want to fund a cure someday by donating to cancer research, or would they prefer to ease the suffering of today's patients by contributing to a hospice? "Sure, it is important to stamp out world hunger and to cure AIDS—but it's also important to help hungry people and AIDS sufferers now," she told *The New York Times*. And she emphasizes the importance of doing it in a way that is gratifying to you. "Don't feel bad if your motivation for giving includes personal recognition. If you're getting something out of it, chances are you'll give more, and more often," So if you yearn to see your name on the back of a chair at the opera, or serve on the board of a local YMCA, that's a perfectly commendable reason to give.

We're a generation that's worn the label "history's most self-centered." Sometimes it fits all too well. Here's a chance for us to turn that description on its head.

The Life Entrepreneurs

Hearing a Higher Calling

Attending a spiritual retreat at forty-one spurred Alan Graham to remake his life doing God's work by feeding Austin's homeless.

Alan's Lesson: *There's a deeper satisfaction in doing good work than making good money—a simple lesson that's tough to learn in your twenties and thirties.*

ALAN GRAHAM WAS living a typical American life, albeit a quite enviable one. A real estate business he'd started in his twenties had made him and his wife wealthy enough to buy a home in Austin's toniest suburb with their four children. In his mid-thirties, he'd returned to the Roman Catholic faith of his childhood and begun attending church regularly. Now he truly seemed to have it all, a life rich in both spirituality and material things.

That would have been Alan's life story if he hadn't attended a spiritual renewal retreat the year he turned forty-one. He very nearly didn't go. "Had I known it would be a bunch of guys holding hands and praying, no way I would have signed up," he says. And at first he was embarrassed as the men began to talk about their emotions and their interior lives, hugging each other and crying. "My intimacy with men had been limited to hunting and fishing, talking trash about girls, and sports." To his surprise, he found the retreat liberating, and he signed up to lead the next one. During that second weekend, the idea was born that would turn his life inside out.

"At this point in my career, I was developing air cargo facilities at airports across the US. Things were going pretty doggone good." At the second retreat, he had the vision for a very different venture for which he would ultimately abandon his thriving real estate business. "I had this image in my mind of a catering truck delivering meals to the homeless," Alan says. "It just wouldn't go away." When he mentioned the idea to friends, they offered to help, and a plan started to take shape. "But we wondered, *Can a bunch of white guys from West Lake Hills, the highest-income zip code in Austin, feed the homeless?*" Then Alan met a real expert, someone who would prove indispensable to launching the new organization. Houston Flake was a homeless man who'd begun to work as a janitor at Alan's church. "Befriending Houston was a godsend," Alan recalls.

At a planning meeting at the law office of one of Alan's friends, Houston shook his head at the finery, saying, "After we eat, I want to take you to *my* conference room." They drove to a downtrodden part of town where a sixty-year-old woman sat on a patch of dirt, smoking and drinking a beer. "The closer we got, the uglier and more homeless this woman looked," Alan says. "But Houston walked right up and gave her a hug. I'm thinking she's full of cooties. And I realized that Houston represents everything I pretend to be but know I'm not. He took my hand and walked me through a wall of prejudice."

Houston was also with Alan on the September evening in 1998 that Mobile Loaves & Fishes was born, when they took a carload of sack lunches to homeless people in downtown Austin. Soon they'd raised twenty-five thousand dollars from friends and fellow churchgoers, enough to buy a used truck and have a catering bed built on the back. Mobile Loaves & Fishes provisions are purchased from wholesale suppliers with donated money. Alan avoids leftovers. "Fruit? Milk? Fritos? When our truck pulls up, people can choose. It's a matter of dignity."

The concept took off. Alan trolled for volunteers at Mass one Sunday, expecting to interest ten or twenty people. A hundred fifty signed up. Six years later, Mobile Loaves & Fishes has five thousand volunteers running six trucks, delivering 140,000 meals a year. "You would never pick me out of a lineup and say, 'This is the guy to start a nonprofit to feed the homeless,'" Alan says. "But I was chosen by God to do this because I had good skills—marketing, raising money, managing projects." One crucial ability was knowing his way around a desktop. "I got some technical help and developed a Web site with database tools that manage the operation so well, I'm the only full-time employee."

Leaving the real estate business three years ago has drastically changed the Grahams' finances. They still live in the fancy zip code, but "My family now lives on the modest salary I take. We have no savings." The whole household pitches in at Mobile Loaves & Fishes, and his kids are okay with their leaner, more spiritual life. "My sixteen-year-old daughter probably struggles with it the most," Alan says. "She'd like to have a fancy car." His oldest son is in Germany, helping plan World Youth Day, a Roman Catholic convocation. "He's very spiritual. When I was eighteen, I wasn't even talking to my father."

Alan and his son recently spent three nights together on a program Alan launched called Street Retreats. "We drop people downtown with no credit cards, no money, no phone. It's just you and God." The first night, a homeless friend took the two Dumpster diving. They slept in alleys and parks, on bridges and sidewalks. "Strip yourself of all the material stuff, and you'll be taken care of. That's the message."

It's one that Alan himself has heeded with a vengeance. "Lately, I've been on a quest to get rid of all the crap I spent the previous twenty years surrounding myself with." From his massive collection, he sold all but a few guns that he and his sons use to hunt. His fountain pens, original art, and leather-bound books ("the ones you put on the shelves to say, *Look how smart I am*") have all made their way onto eBay. "Sure," he says, "I've had my flashes of wanting a Harley, but I'm over that."

Mobile Loaves & Fishes has also taken Alan back into real estate with a new program, Habitat on Wheels, which furnishes homeless people with used travel trailers. "It's affordable housing, and it's kicking butt right now," he says proudly.

Take a flying lesson. Check out the Aircraft Owners and Pilots Association Web site, aopa.org/learntofly, for the basics and a directory of flight schools nationwide. An introductory hour in the air could be the most fascinating hundred dollars you've ever spent.

What's sent Alan on this extreme journey of caring? His difficult childhood may hold a clue. "I grew up in a pretty dysfunctional family. My mother had serious mental health problems, and my father divorced her when I was four. I lived with my mom, moving to my dad's whenever she was hospitalized. She was nurturing, and Dad was the disciplinarian. Together, they would have been great, but separately it was a disaster." Alan ran away when he was seventeen, and by eleventh grade had a part-time job and his own apartment. Ultimately, he reconciled with his father, but the years alone made him independent and gave him compassion for people who draw the short straw in life.

In his go-go real estate years, he'd done volunteer work, but in those days there was an agenda. "I was always networking, looking to meet people who could advance my business, always asking 'How could this benefit me?'" Now he feels a moral imperative to help—especially as a boomer. "I'm not proud of our generation. A lot of us walked away from core ethical and moral values. Look at the Enron and MCI scandals, the abject cheating in high school and college." And, he says, midlife was absolutely the right time to turn this corner in his life. "I can't see it happening to me any sooner. I don't look back and say, 'Boy, I wish I had a do-over.' I had a great time at eighteen. That's the direction in which God took my life, and those experiences formed me into the person I am today." You can cruise the Mobile Loaves & Fishes Web site without spotting his name, and that's intentional. "I spent most of my life trying to get people to look at me. Now I want people to see the work Christ is doing through me.

"I don't know if this is my midlife crisis, but I love what I'm doing and I don't miss my real estate career."

Putting Menopause Center Stage

Jeanie Linders wrote a musical about hot flashes that took America by storm. She's using the profits to help other women.

Jeanie's Lesson: *No matter how many people tell you no, if you have an idea you believe in, keep going. And never look down the road too far. Instead, make sure what you're doing today is important.*

"IT'S TAKEN OVER my life," Jeanie Linders says, laughing. Did this former Florida-based ad agency owner have any inkling that the lyrics she wrote poking fun at hot flashes would generate a theatrical empire? "Not a clue." Yet now, four years after it opened on a small stage in central Florida, more than a hundred thousand people—mostly women in their forties and fifties—are seeing *Menopause The Musical* every month, worldwide. And it's changed women's lives on both sides of the footlights.

It all started one evening ten years ago when Jeanie was about to attend an NAACP ball in Orlando. "There I was in my gown, ready to leave, when I had a ferocious hot flash. I was standing in front of the refrigerator, fanning myself with both doors, singing Rod Stewart's 'Hot Legs,' only I was singing 'hot flashes.'" Though she'd never written a play, the idea of creating a musical based on menopause just clicked. Jeanie pinned cards listing menopause symptoms on a bulletin board, bought a pawnshop record player for ten dollars, got out her old 45s, and starting writing new lyrics for old favorites. "Chain, Chain, Chain, Chain of Fools" became "Change, Change, Change, Change of Life." "Staying Alive" became an insomnia lament, "Staying Awake." "I would e-mail the lyrics to friends, and they'd write back, 'That's funny, send more.'" When she had enough material, she sent her play, featuring four women shopping at Bloomingdale's and singing about hot flashes, mood swings, and weight gain, to a theatrical lawyer, who told her that nobody would produce it.

But she couldn't let go of the idea. "I just knew it would work," she says, and so she produced the play herself. It opened on March 28, 2001, in a seventy-six-seat theater she built in a former Orlando perfume shop. "The actors had to climb through a hole in the wall to their dressing rooms in the shoe store next door." The show is lovably dorky, with the four actors wearing goofy outfits and doing 1970s disco moves; critics sneered but audiences ate it up. Women flocked to the show, they brought their friends, and everybody howled. The musical moved to West Palm Beach, then opened off-Broadway, where it's still running three years later. The cast members are all over forty, all over size 10. This brand of reality theater really strikes a chord with midlife women. "Walk down any street in America and you will not find four desperate housewives who look like those women on TV," Jeanie notes. "Hollywood says you're young, you're thin, you're hip. My audience is not. I always say, there are five girlfriends at the show—four on stage and one in the audience. If she gets up and dances at the end, we've done our job."

Jeanie receives a constant flow of e-mails from women thanking her for taking menopause out of the closet. "Most of our parents went through the change, retired from their jobs, had grandkids, and waited to die. It's not like they started whole new lives." Not so for us boomers. "Our generation had a president killed, a war in which the guys we were engaged to were dying, our parents were divorcing—all of a sudden, things were upside down. With nothing to hold on to, we've been reinventing our lives all along.

"Menopause is not just a physical change," she continues. "Not only can we no longer reproduce, but our parents are passing away and suddenly there's this reality that we're not going to live forever. What happens then is that all the people we've paid attention to our whole lives—husbands, children, bosses—take a backseat. Our inner voice is saying, *Excuse me, it's my turn.*"

As she rode the crest of seemingly unstoppable success, and her ad agency morphed into a single-show theater production company, Jeanie's inner voice told her to take the money and do some good. She launched a nonprofit called Women For Women Foundation that makes grants to women over forty. W4W provides mentoring and financial support to women's service organizations, grants scholarships in the arts, and serves as a clearinghouse for information on issues that affect women at midlife. She's also launched the If Only Award. "I call it the Make a Wish Foundation for living women with dying dreams," Jeanie says. "This is not 'I want to meet Brad Pitt.'" These wishes are the stuff of life reinvention—going back to school, starting businesses, seeing the world.

Jeanie may have a soft spot for struggling women because she's known failure herself. "In 1986, I tanked totally," she says, with typical candor. "It rained and nobody came to a jazz festival I created." She was on the line financially, and when she lost her business, she lost her identity, too. Suddenly, she was no longer "Jeanie Ad Agency"; as just plain Jeanie Linders, "I spent five years trying to figure out who the hell that was." She had produced events her whole life, from a fine arts mall in a derelict shopping center to multistage music festivals. "I've done all these bizarre things—worked for Michael Jackson, ran Francis Ford Coppola's resort in Belize, taught high school in Jamaica." But now she wanted to do work that was truly meaningful.

When she saw three hundred women in an off-Broadway theater standing and clapping, shouting, "That's me, that's me," she knew she'd found the vehicle to change people's lives. She's grown her company by extending opportunities to the women around her. "At first, I was running this whole production out of my back bedroom," she says. "The phone would ring at two in the morning with people reserving tickets. Menopausal women don't sleep." Now she has twenty people working at an office in Orlando, and additional staffers in each of the thirteen cities with long-running productions. One is her former cleaning lady. "She's my production manager and she's fabulous. She just needed that hand up." Another is a friend of twenty-five years, who advised Jeanie to forget about producing this show. "She's now my advertising director," Jeanie says.

Getting rich isn't the plan; adding richness to life is. "Somebody wrote a newspaper article saying that Jeanie Linders is making a mint. That's not true. I finance all my own shows, and when we make enough money, we open in another city. Souvenir sales benefit the foundation." Jeanie, who is single, adds, "I can only spend so much money. For the first fifty years of my life, I lived on thirty-five thousand a year."

Enter a model contest. *More* magazine runs an annual search for over-forty models, offering contracts with Wilhelmina Models; one grand-prize winner has parlayed it into a hundred-thousand-dollar career. You'll find an entry form on more.com. Sorry, women only.

When she went through those tough times, her friends told her, "You're a survivor, you'll make it." And despite raging arthritis that has already meant multiple operations, including two knee replacements, Jeanie is optimistic. "Sometimes I feel like C-3PO. But no matter how much metal they put in your body, you have to choose life. When I was sixteen, I wrote Jeanie's Beatitude: *Cursed are they who live to exist but fail to live while existing.* I never want to just take up space."

Where will she be in five years? "No idea," Jeanie, who's now fifty-six, says. "I never look down the road that far. My biggest concerns are taking care of my employees, and getting the show in front of as many women as I can."

Finding God at Fifty-one

Diagnosed with a life-threatening cancer, Gary Regan got a wake-up call from God, and a new outlook on life.

Gary's Lesson: *Listen hard. Even the worst thing that's ever happened to you can have a silver lining that shines beyond the shock of the original event.*

"IT STARTED WITH the cancer," Gary Regan says. As with so many other people, having a mortal disease proved to be a transforming experience. At first, he thought, "No big deal. They'll cut the cancer out of my tongue and that will be it." But it turned out to be a very big deal indeed. Gary was thrown into four months of debilitating treatments. First up was an eighteen-hour surgery in which the left side of his tongue was removed and replaced by a muscle graft from his forearm. He recovered quickly, only to face an even more brutal regimen: six weeks of radiation, which stopped saliva production and created mouth sores so painful he couldn't eat. By the last treatment, he'd lost fifty pounds, a quarter of his body weight.

Gary, who grew up in a small town in Lancashire, England, living over the pub his parents ran, became a bartender himself, and then a spirits writer who's authored and coauthored half a dozen books, including the *New York Times*–acclaimed *Joy of Mixology*. He knew the cancer treatment could jeopardize, even end, his career. After radiation treatment, many patients lose their sense of taste, which is critical for judging liquors and developing cocktail recipes. Furthermore, surgery can leave their speech unintelligible. For Gary, who teaches a lively weekend bartending course, "Cocktails in the Country," at an inn near his Hudson Valley, New York, home, this would be a blow to his career—and his family's finances. Luckily, Gary's taste buds survived the assault, and his friends joke that his British accent is just as opaque as ever.

The unkindest cut was loss of his bushy beard, which never grew back after the radiation. "My beard was my trademark," says Gary, who hadn't shaved in thirty years. "The cancer attacked my tongue. I think of myself as a storyteller, so my whole being was threatened. Night after night I wondered why this was happening to me." Physically, he could attribute the cancer to being a smoker, but he felt there was something else going on.

Without realizing that he was launching a life-changing exploration of spirituality, he consulted a Roman Catholic healer recommended by a friend. "I was brought up Congregationalist, but had no belief in God. I thought, *This black-belt Catholic and me—no way*. But with cancer, I was open to anything." When Paul blessed Gary, it changed his life. "Paul put his hands on my shoulders, and I felt a breeze on my face. The next thing I knew, I was lying on the floor sobbing." A lifelong skeptic, Gary drove home amazed and puzzled. "This didn't happen to somebody's aunt in Australia. It happened to me."

He visited Paul again the day before the surgery, and again he was literally knocked down by the power of the experience. Now Gary was questioning his deepest beliefs: *Maybe, just maybe, there is a God*. Around this time, a friend gave him a book by Deepak Chopra, who writes that there are no coincidences. Every tiny act ripples outward to affect people's lives in astonishing ways. The concept made sense to Gary, bolstering his belief that his beard and tongue were attacked for a reason. But he still didn't know what it was.

One morning, he spotted an ad in the local newspaper: "Is normal healing not doing everything for you? Shamanic healing can help." The following week, the ad caught his attention again. The fourth time this happened, Gary says, "I figured I was supposed to call." At his first session, he and the healer, Xuni, spent an hour talking about what his cancer meant, followed by an hour of shamanic massage. "While I was on the table, I had visions of friends and family members who had passed away. They were telling me that I was in the right place." Gary continued to go once a week, and he realized the visions had to do with God.

Gary was becoming a believer, but it wasn't an easy road. "The whole God thing is difficult because I have no idea who or what God is," he says. "*God* is a word we use to describe something we can't describe." So Gary, who's known for his sense of humor, figures the Almighty must have one, too: "I conjured up my own vision, of a woman with great tits. She's God and she's good to look at, too."

As his shamanic treatments progressed, he came to believe that God wanted him to help other people. Within two weeks of this epiphany, four people called asking for advice on how to handle the death of a parent, reminding Gary what a crucial role hospice had played when his mother had died. "Bear in mind," he says, "I was now thinking there are no coincidences." He called hospice to volunteer, but he'd just missed the bi-annual orientation. Reading a book by a fellow spirits writer about what it's like to be behind a bar on a busy night, he decided he wanted to bartend again. "That book was sent to me by God," he says. Within a week, he had a plan: He would tend bar every Wednesday night at Painter's Tavern in Cornwall-on-Hudson, New York, where he holds "Cocktails in the Country," and donate his tips to the local hospice. In a sly nod to the power of coincidence, he called these weekly sessions "organized chaos." His first year, Gary raised more than four thousand dollars.

Finding God has revamped how Gary approaches life. "Now that I know everything happens for a reason, I can go with the flow," he says. "I used to drive down Main Street thinking, *Why is this asshole in front of me doing eighteen miles an hour?* Now I wonder why God wants me to be late." His spiritual awakening has damped down his stress level and softened his attitude. "I rarely get upset with anybody anymore. I know other people will do whatever they want, that I don't have any control."

Even more important, spirituality has given Gary a new feeling of belonging in the world. "Before my cancer, I'd have said the one common thing among all humankind is loneliness. Now I feel a part of everything rather than apart from everything," he says. "I don't feel lonely at all."

Gary, who has not been able to stop smoking, faces an increased risk of a recurrence of his cancer. "Since I found God, I'm no longer afraid of death," he says. "I understand that I'll be okay whether my body lives or not; it's just the vehicle I happen to be using right now."

Try a tattoo. Go ahead, release the rebel in you. My daughter, my high school buddy John, and I all got the same image of a glacier-capped peak to commemorate scaling Kilimanjaro. Mine's on my hip, where it peeks out only when I wear a tankini. John, the same age but more adventurous, got his on his forearm, as did Brook. TattooNOW.com has a gallery of designs to start you thinking.

Meantime, life isn't easy. Gary still can't eat many foods comfortably and consequently remains rail thin. He carries bottled water as a necessity, not a status symbol, to compensate for the saliva production he has lost. But his new spirit is accepting of these inconveniences. He's a born-again jock, a regular at the local gym, and is reveling in a revitalized relationship with his wife of twenty-five years, after a short separation following his illness.

Gary says there's a reason spirituality came to him at midlife. "I could not have had this experience without all the others that went before. When I was thirty and struggling financially, I wouldn't have had time to do volunteer work or the money to pay for Xuni's sessions. She was a conduit to the universe for me. She helped me get in touch with what's really important."

Gary's beard is memorialized on the label of Regan's Orange Bitters, from a recipe he developed. He still misses it, but is grateful for the rich new attitude toward life that has been its legacy.

Becoming a Pastor

Susanna Margaret Goulder gave up a glamorous career as set designer for movies and TV to find more meaningful work.

Susanna's Lesson: *Respect the challenges and difficulties you face in life. Pay attention to them, and they can guide you to the right path.*

"I WAS ALWAYS a little actress," Susanna Margaret Goulder tells me. "My parents used to call me Sarah Bernhardt." She thought she was headed toward a career on the stage until she got to college and faced a crisis of confidence. "My best friend was an actress, too, and competing against her was troubling. Besides, I didn't feel secure that my talents were that great." So she left school to hitchhike around the country and figure out a life plan. "I still don't know why my parents said yes to this," she says, laughing. Susanna only got as far as Florida when a friend of a friend hired her to make sandbags to weigh down the lights on movie shoots. From this humble beginning—"Eventually I made about two-thirds of all the sandbags used on location in the Southeast"—she developed a successful movie and TV career, progressing from sandbag seamstress to motor-home driver to set decorator, ultimately moving to New York. It was a job she was good at, and she expected it would be a lifelong career.

But at the age of forty-one, after a long, wearing decade of discontent, she found her life blossoming in ways she had never imagined. "I'm a Jewish girl from Shaker Heights, Ohio. Who would guess I'd be a minister to Christians in Yonkers, New York?"

There were many things Susanna loved about working behind the camera. "It was glamorous, exciting. The sets were my canvas—how I'd represent a character through his things." But while she thrived on the work, she hated the politics. She worked on *Disappearing Acts* with Wesley Snipes, *Stir of Echoes* with Kevin Bacon, and *The Big Kahuna* with Kevin Spacey, and was the original set decorator on *Sex and the City*. But the work was so grueling that she'd have to hibernate for a month or more after every job—eating well and resting up before diving back in. And she never reached the pinnacle she craved: "I wanted to be on the A list, I wanted to win an Oscar." As she moved into her thirties, Susanna says, "Nothing in my life was taking off." She'd just ended a six-year relationship with another set decorator. "Breaking up with him was like pulling apart Velcro."

After they split, she began a decade of spiritual questioning, studying Reiki and trying to figure out how to make a more satisfying life for herself. When a new relationship foundered after three years, she fell into deep despair, a hopeless time she calls "the dark night of the soul."

"As the years went by, I was working purely for the money and taking more and more time off to recover. I tried everything. I was using Buddhist meditation techniques and jogging every day." She began to study with well-known healer Rosalyn Bruyere. "One night Rosalyn channeled a four-thousand-year-old Tibetan man. I asked Master Chang what I should do with my life—stay with set decorating or pursue energy healing—and he said, 'For seven months prepare, and in seven months you'll know the answer.'"

As Susanna took the advice to heart, an eviction notice was

slid under her door. Her shepherd-terrier mix, Sienna, was no longer welcome in the building.

In great distress, she phoned her spiritual adviser and made an emergency appointment. "She did something called soul work, a very simple process of meditation, which indicated I should move to nature." Susanna didn't know what to do with this information. "Do I really believe this?" she wondered. "Is it crazy?" But her life was at a standstill and she was willing to take a leap; she contacted Realtors outside the city and threw herself into the search for a new home. Four months later she was still looking for a place that would accept Sienna, now panicky because she had to be out of her apartment in a matter of weeks. "I'd walk across 15th Street and say to myself, *Why am I trusting this voice that's saying, 'You will live in lots of light on the water'?*" Desperate, she called the original real estate agent she'd worked with, who showed her three lovely apartments in a historic Hudson River town, all in her price range. The next day, at a nondenominational church in Manhattan, she asked God which one she should take. The first person she saw walking out of the service was one of the landlords. "I'd never seen her before at church, so I took this as a sign. Now I live in this beautiful place overlooking the Hudson River."

One problem in her life was solved. And she had just begun work on a TV courtroom drama. "Then out of the blue the production designer told me she'd decided to bring in her own decorator." Susanna drove home in shock. The next morning, waking up in her sun-filled apartment, she knew it was time to leave the film business. "I decided I would do energy healing professionally." A couple of days later, she realized she'd made her decision seven months, to the day, after Master Chang's prediction. "I knew it was preordained. When I learned to trust the voice within me, I found a wonderful community of friends, a beautiful place to live, and a new career."

But there were still some kinks to iron out. "In New York State, you can't legally touch someone as an energy healer. I decided to become a minister, so I could." She embarked on a two-year ordination program at One Spirit Interfaith Seminary in Manhattan purely to allow her to practice energy healing—and stumbled into a career she adores. "When I entered seminary, I found the place I should be." But she still never envisioned herself before a congregation. "The last class was on how to open a church. I closed my notebook. I knew I'd never be doing that." But a week before her ordination, she was offered a job as a pastoral counselor at Greyston Foundation, a former convent that is now a health services organization, where she had been volunteering. "I was terrified, but I knew I should take the job." To her surprise, the ministry was a perfect fit. "I do Sunday service every week. I love it. It may sound airy-fairy, but I really feel I'm getting teaching direct from the spirit." She still appreciates her Jewish heritage but has opened her faith to embrace many paths. "Can you imagine me creating a church with an African American fundamentalist Christian and a former Roman Catholic who now practices Buddhism? Somehow the three of us have come together with respect for one another's beliefs."

Mentor a business overseas. The International Executive Service Corps dispatches volunteers with applicable career experience to advise business ventures in dozens of nations worldwide (iesc.org).

Once one pathway opened up, the underbrush in other parts of her life began to fall away. "For years, I'd been working with my spiritual adviser on an intention to have a man in my life. I always thought I'd marry, have kids." She tried dating services—nothing. But within a year of moving to her river-view apartment, she met a man at an energy healing workshop and fell in love. Now Susanna is moving to Cleveland to build a new life with him.

Susanna feels that her life has really come together in her forties. She is grateful, but she doesn't look back at the hard years with regret. "All the pain and struggles in my life propelled me into something wonderful," she says. "Once I let go of all the things that were preventing me from being who I truly am, the rewards have been fantastic." And she knows how hard she worked to gain the wisdom and maturity to have the life she wanted. "I dove into different therapies, programs, workshops. It took a long time, but my life has blossomed because of the hard work I did. All that came before prepared me for my life today."

Hat Trick

When Carol Galland beat the odds and survived breast cancer, it changed her line of work. She now runs a business dedicated to filling the needs of other cancer patients.

Carol's Lesson: *Take a cue from the little engine that could. When you're doing something you believe in, whether it's launching a business or treating your cancer, just keep plugging away through the hard times until you succeed.*

WHEN CAROL GALLAND was forty-one, she had a vision. "I dreamed there was a lady standing at the foot of my bed. She told me I had a lump under my arm and needed to see a doctor." The next morning, in the shower, Carol remembered the dream. "I'm not a religious person," she says. "I was raised Catholic, but I am not devout." Still, feeling the lady was a messenger, she checked under her arm. Carol was horrified to feel something there. "The lump was huge, the size of the big marble you knock the little ones with. My heart just sank."

It was the beginning of the most painful period in Carol's life, but her troubles pointed her toward a new career, founded on a pledge to help other women like her.

Carol wasted no time getting to the doctor, and was relieved to hear the initial diagnosis: cat scratch fever. *"Why, oh why did we adopt that stray?* I thought to myself." But when the lump didn't disappear after a course of antibiotics, her doctor sent her to a surgeon, who performed a biopsy. The lump was malignant, and the news got even worse: This was a secondary site, which meant that the disease had already spread. Breast cancer was the most likely culprit, but four different doctors were unable to locate the primary site. It was terrifying for Carol to realize there was cancer in her body, but nobody could tell her where. Finally, she made a decision that saved her life, traveling from Ardmore, the small town in Oklahoma where she lived with her husband and three children, to Houston's famed M. D. Anderson Cancer Center, where she consulted a specialist in unknown primary tumors. He found ground zero for Carol's malignancy in her left breast. "He told me my condition was grave; I needed chemotherapy before they could even remove the cancer in my breast," Carol says. She endured a mastectomy and month after brutal month of chemo. "Twice I was in the hospital for five days with fever," she remembers. "But my youngest child was only in first grade. I knew I had to give it my very best shot."

Carol, who is a hairdresser, was bald from the treatments for a year and a half. "It was pitiful," she says. "I survived in a granny bonnet the Pink Ladies Auxiliary gave me at M. D. Anderson." She also bought a wig, but there was no way to strike the right balance between comfort and looks. "Those wigs are miserable to wear. I just put mine on the stand and went bald at home."

During chemo, Carol's whole mission was to get well for her kids; she had a daughter in college and another in high school. Her first-grader would travel with Carol and her husband to Houston for treatment. "When your six-year-old says to you, 'Mommy, are you going to die?' and you can't honestly say no, it is tough. When you're as sick as I was, you get through it and finally are at peace with the fact that you're mortal. And then you go on." All the while, she couldn't stop thinking about those awful bonnets and wigs. "People who don't know how to fix their makeup are walking around with no eyebrows, no eyelashes, no hair. Not only do you have to worry about dying, it's undignified." As a cosmetologist and a cancer patient, Carol was uniquely qualified to develop products that would make chemotherapy patients feel whole. But first, she had to believe that she was going to live.

On her five-year anniversary of being cancer-free, Carol launched a business to help other women like her. She says, quite simply: "When you face death head-on, you seek out meaning in life." Carol figured that given her background, she'd be able to find high-quality head coverings. With her cancer in remission, she began to search, but there was almost nothing out there. "I started with wigs," she remembers. "I ordered a thousand dollars' worth on my credit card and sold them at the salon where I worked." Gradually, she made contact with fashion merchandisers who could help her design hats specially attuned to the needs of cancer patients, and her stock of merchandise grew. She wasn't making any money, but the work felt too good to quit. "I supported Headcovers Unlimited by working two jobs. I just kept plowing money into the company." Carol built a network of seamstresses around the country who fashion turbans and hats to her specifications. "A lady in Michigan whose husband had cancer makes several of the hats we sell," she notes. "Eight friends come to her barn to sew." And every week, she'd hear the kind of feedback from clients that makes you never want to quit. "One woman wrote how much it meant, as a single woman, that she could feel desirable to a man. Another woman described how awful it was when her eyelashes fell off on a date."

Carol's Web site offers a cheering array of products to people at a time when they've never felt worse about their looks. There's photo after photo of hats and turbans in a flattering array of colors, plus wigs and eyebrows and eyelashes. The prices are surprisingly low; there are cotton turbans for less than twenty dollars, a handsome broad-brimmed linen hat for forty. Carol is committed to keeping costs low for an audience that is already overextended by skyrocketing medical bills.

The site also encourages shoppers to make a donation that will buy a hat for a child who is being treated at St. Jude Children's Research Hospital. In the first eight months of the program, Headcovers Unlimited provided more than two hundred hats. Carol's goal is a care package of headcovers for every child at St. Jude.

Measured in happy customers, the business was an instant success. But it has been a long, hard road to black ink. Carol crossed a big threshold in 2002, when she was finally able to leave hairdressing and devote herself to Headcovers Unlimited full time. "I never borrowed a dime," she says proudly. "I just built the inventory by plugging away."

Six months ago, Carol finally started paying herself a salary. But of course, money has never been the driving force; helping people is what keeps her going to work each day.

Fifteen years after her diagnosis, Carol still experiences fallout from her battle with cancer. "I have hot flashes constantly because the chemo put me into menopause," she says. "I can't take hormones because my receptors were positive for both estrogen and progesterone. And I have 'chemo brain'—my mind is scattered, going in ten directions at once, getting sidetracked." She laughs and adds, "My staff of five just puts up with me." But these little travails are also reminders of how lucky she feels to be alive.

Midlife crisis? Carol doesn't have time. And her health crisis has taught her a very basic lesson: that every day is a gift. "I'm at peace now. I have three grandchildren, who model hats on the Web site. My daughter Danielle runs the business with me. My son, who was only six when I was diagnosed, is away at college now. It's all about making people look good and feel better, and after all, that's what I've done for thirty years."

CHAPTER 6

~⌐~

Continuing Education

W E BOOMERS WENT to college in record numbers, and we relished the experience like no generation before. I started at Middlebury, a small liberal arts college in an adorable Vermont town, in 1969. It was an extraordinary year of triumph and tragedy. Neil Armstrong walked on the moon, the Stonewall riots in New York City sparked the movement for gay rights, and teenagers whose parents were more liberal than mine journeyed to Woodstock, New York, to attend the world's most famous rock concert. While I was in college, *Midnight Cowboy* debuted (the only X-rated movie ever to win the Best Picture Oscar). So did *Ms.* magazine. Four students were killed by National Guardsmen at Kent State University in Ohio, and a team of burglars bungled a break-in at Washington's Watergate Hotel. The Beatles split up, and Idi Amin took over Uganda. The Twenty-sixth Amendment lowered the voting age to eighteen, allowing my class to vote in our first presidential election in

1972. A year later, a peace agreement was signed and US troops came home from Vietnam. It was a wild and woolly four years.

The social revolutions of the 1960s were rippling across campuses, forming us politically and transforming our college experience. My first year, I lived in an all-women dorm watched over by a house mother. Men were allowed to visit only at certain times, during which our conduct was governed by a set of arcane rules that, among other things, required three feet on the floor at all times. By my junior year, Middlebury dorms had gone coed, and sprays of plastic flowers sprouted from urinals in bathrooms that had switched signs from MEN to WOMEN. I remember the tension-filled day each year when draft lottery numbers were drawn. One glance at the face of any guy on campus would tell you whether or not he was nestled safely up in triple-digit territory.

It was a tragic time, but tremendously exciting, too. There's little wonder that so many of my cohorts, boomers now in their fifties, were inspired to go back to school, to relive those days of extraordinary freedom, extraordinary challenges, extraordinary opportunities.

Fast-forward to 1979 when my friend Sarah was a sophomore at the University of Michigan, a campus famous back in my day for educating radical/visionary Tom Hayden, a co-founder of Students for a Democratic Society. But in 1979, no one was demanding social change. Detroit was reeling from a recession, and Chrysler had just told an entire shift they were out of work. Unemployment in some Michigan communities soared to 40 percent, and Sarah's classmates worried about their factory-worker family members committing suicide. Students still protested world events, Sarah says, but the tone wasn't peaceful. "Bomb, bomb, bomb, bomb, bomb Iran" reverberated across campuses to the tune of the Beach Boys hit "Barbara Ann," and students denounced college administrators not for supporting the nation's military-industrial complex, but for offering too few computer and business classes, too little career advice. These kids didn't want change, they wanted jobs.

It was a totally different mind-set reflecting wildly different times from the years I spent at college, but Sarah and I had one thing in common: Two decades later, we both craved a do-over. So do lots of other men and women in our generation. Some, like me, didn't pay enough attention the first time around and now want to savor the academic rather than the social experience. Others, like Sarah, yearn to enroll in the courses they always wanted to take. In fact, Sarah says, once she gets her kids off to college she's going to study astronomy and ancient poetry—not for career advancement, but for the sheer love of it. This latter-day thirst for learning has created a big back-to-school trend. The number of students over thirty-five at degree-granting institutions has more than tripled in recent decades, from 823,000 in 1970 to 2.9 million in 2001, according to the National Center for Education Statistics. Graying sophomores are no longer even a curiosity in class, since they now account for one in five students. In 2006, the Oxygen TV network launched *Campus Ladies,* a comedy about two midlife women who go back to school with a signature boomer attitude—"What? Me, old? No way!"—dating undergraduates and diving wholeheartedly into twentysomething campus life.

Learning Every Which Way

The people profiled in this chapter returned to education in the traditional way—pursuing undergraduate and graduate degrees—most of them for the classic reason of reinventing their professional lives. But going back to college is just the tip of the iceberg when it comes to supplementing your education at midlife. Learning is a fundamental way to grow and stretch, and the variety of methods to accomplish it is limited only by our imagination.

My husband and I recently went back to school in an off-beat way—taking a weekend course in Thai massage at a Miami hotel. It seemed like a fun, romantic adventure. The reward it delivered was quite different from what we'd expected. Six months later, neither of us can give a decent massage, but we still remember the fascinating life story of our teacher, who grew up in a small village in northern Thailand without running water or electricity and now runs the Thai massage program for the Mandarin Oriental Hotel Group. It was a stirring cross-cultural experience that neither of us would have missed.

Give a speech. Get on the program at a local club lunch, or simply stand up and express your opinion at a community meeting. Conquer your fear, then unleash your new confidence elsewhere in life. Too terrifying? Cruise the Toastmasters International Web site (toastmasters.org) and look for a local meeting where you'll practice getting up on stage. A friend who had to get up to speed fast swears by this corny but effective method.

A few years back, a friend of mine took an inventive tack on continuing her education. Wishing she'd studied more literature back-when but unable to find a great-books course to her liking, she hired a tutor—an English professor who drew up a custom reading list and then discussed each book with her. Anybody who lives in a college town could follow her lead, employing a historian, physicist, psychologist, or Chinese-language prof. If the budget's tight, a graduate student could be just the ticket.

A forty-nine-year-old woman in New Mexico is taking a different do-it-yourself approach to continuing education. A year ago, her husband bought her the complete collection of the Penguin Classics Library (1,062 paperbacks, $7,989.50 from Amazon.com) to replace their library, which had burned in a forest fire. She is now reading them all, at quite an impressive clip—one every two or three days.

Though I daydream about winning a Nieman Fellowship— offered to just a dozen lucky journalists annually, who spend an academically idyllic year at Harvard auditing classes in any subject they choose—I haven't made the move back to school yet. So far, I've been satisfied with the learning that comes as part of my job as a magazine writer. When I'm asked to write about India's ancient system of ayurvedic healing or wooden kayaks or mountain gorillas, it immerses me in new and fascinating subjects. Right now my personal education campaign is a lot less sophisticated—I'm teaching myself to stand on my head.

Dipping a Toe In

Going back to school can be scary, particularly if, like me, you weren't a stellar student the last time around. (I recently learned that you have to pay to join the academic honor society Phi Beta Kappa, a fact that escaped my attention three decades ago, no doubt because no one invited me.) Many of the midlife scholars I've talked to started small, taking a single course before committing to a degree program or interviewing people in their chosen field of study to figure out if it's really what they want. In short, they approach going back to school with all the skills and contacts and experience of a seasoned adult.

There's a compelling reason to keep learning, whatever way we can: We'll reap significant health benefits. Scientists have documented that when we challenge our brains, they construct new intercellular connections. And the universe of researcher-recommended adult learning experiences is broad: taking college courses, learning a foreign language, attending lectures, among other things. Japanese neurologist Ryuta Kawashima, author of *Train Your Brain,* says we should work out our brains just as we do our bodies. What better way than back at school?

The Life Entrepreneurs

College at Forty-four

Holly McCamant missed a chance to go to college in her teens. After two failed marriages and raising six children, she finally got her bachelor's degree—after she created the opportunity for herself by writing a new life plan and working her way through college in her forties.

Holly's Lesson: *Being adaptable isn't always an asset. You have to do more than make the best of the situation in which you find yourself. Sometimes you have to reinvent your world.*

"I ALWAYS WANTED to go to college," Holly McCamant says. But life kept getting in the way. It wasn't until she'd sent two of her six children off to top universities that she finally became a coed herself, at forty-four. After living her life for everybody else, she finally did something just for her.

Holly was the third child in a big, unwieldy family. "My parents had seven children. They got divorced when I was in seventh grade, and after that my dad had another child and my mom had two more." When Holly graduated from high school at seventeen, there was no money for college. Instead, she went to work in a law office, a career she'd continue for the next twelve years. At eighteen, she became pregnant. Two years later, raising her daughter alone, she fell in love and married a man nineteen years older. They had three children and a marriage that lasted thirteen years.

When they divorced, Holly moved directly into the arms of another man, which she says "was really stupid. You should take some time to get yourself together. You can't always see the big picture when you're in the middle of things." She and her second husband were married for ten years. When their first child, Heather, was born with Down's syndrome, Holly quit work to care for her. Heather needed open-heart surgery at two, resulting in one of the most difficult times of Holly's never-easy life. Still, she found time to volunteer at the YMCA in Butte, Montana, as a fitness instructor. When Heather was five and her younger brother, Tommy, was three, Holly went to work at the Y part-time. Unlike her legal secretary job, this was work she loved, and she earned a promotion to program director, a full-time job.

This marriage wasn't happy, either, and Holly calls her second divorce "the biggest transition in my life." In an attempt to figure out why she'd gone off course again, she dove into self-help books and went to counseling. "When we separated, I was determined to have my own goals and make things happen." Holly felt that she'd always been good at making the best of whatever situation she found herself in. Now she wanted to do more. "I don't know that being adaptable is an asset," she says. "People who are impatient make their lives what they want them to be, while I saw myself as floundering. Sure, I was holding my chin up, keeping my sense of humor, but I never made anything *I* wanted happen." She sat down and wrote out her goals. Getting a college degree was number one. Number two was quelling the stress of an overloaded life. Number three was getting some housecleaning help, and the fourth was finding a long-term relationship.

Holly didn't waste any time getting started on item number

one. She enrolled in college. Luckily, Montana Tech, an engineering division of the University of Montana, offered an exercise science degree, just what Holly was looking for, right in Butte.

Holly threw herself into college with her customary ambition and enthusiasm. "For the first two and a half years, I took twelve to fourteen credits a semester and worked full-time. It was crazy," she admits, with two children still at home, but she's never lived her life at a leisurely pace. "How did I do it? I don't really know. You just go through each day, do everything you have to, don't sleep as much as you're supposed to." She'd drop Heather and Tommy at the Y's day-care program while she worked and took classes, then put them to bed and study late into the night. "I function better that way. When I don't have a lot to do, I waste time."

But eventually, the pace became too much even for Holly, and she throttled back to part-time work for the final year and a half. "I took more credits, so it was still nuts, but at least I could study during the day." Holly never worried about being able to make the grade academically. "I was a really good student in high school. I graduated college with a 3.7. If I'd had the luxury of having somebody support me while I spent my days studying and going to class, I bet I could have pulled a 4.0." The only C's she got were in chemistry, the subject in which her son Jerry is now getting a PhD.

In college classes, she found herself surrounded by her son Howie's high school friends. This was nothing new for Holly, who was the neighborhood mother hen, taking in her kids' friends to live with them for weeks at a time. "It was funny to be in the same boat," she says. There were also a number of "nontraditional" students Holly's age, one of whom said in awe, "You do more in a day than the rest of us do in a week." She had lots of real-life experience to contribute to the classes in exercise physiology, which made her feel less like a student, more like her professors' peer.

There was just one time her oversubscribed schedule almost did her in. The volunteer work she does every year on a Youth in Government program for high school students coincided with finals. She had a big paper due for a literature class, so she borrowed a laptop, wrote the paper one night after the program, and saved it onto a disk. "When I got home, I was so tired. And the file just wouldn't open." The paper was due at ten o'clock the next morning. Holly got up at five and rewrote it, from notes and memory. "No way was I going in at ten and asking for more time," she said. She got an A.

Take ten shots a day. Use a digital camera to record images of what really matters to you, ten photographs—no more, no less—every day for a month. Don't peek, just keep clicking away. At the end of a month, look at the three hundred photographs you've taken and see your life from an entirely new angle.

Holly has almost twenty thousand dollars in loans to repay, but no regrets. Her salary more than doubled with her first job after graduation. College has also brought her a new career direction. "The more classes I took, the more corporate wellness—setting up health screenings, developing exercise and diet programs—grew on me. My last year at school, I had a part-time job in the field." Right now, she's the program director at a fitness center in Great Falls, Montana, but she still has her eye on this ultimate prize. "I toy with the idea of getting my master's," she says. "It'd really help in landing a corporate wellness job."

Holly is both determined and patient. "I'm more confident at midlife. I was always better at standing up for myself in a work environment than in my personal life. Now it's across the board." And with her newfound assertiveness has come a new love. "The type of man I was attracted to when I was younger— very aggressive, sweeps you off your feet, won't let you alone until you're married—ended up not being very good for me," she admits. She met Mike in a class for fitness instructors at the Y. Mike had been divorced twice and was wary of committing for a third time. "He didn't even like doing the 'I love you' thing," Holly says. "When I moved to Great Falls for my job and he didn't follow me, I said, 'Let's call it off.'" What ensued was a standoff in which Mike refused to accept that their relationship was over. "He kept asking to see me, and I kept saying 'We're broken up.' One day he called and said, 'If you don't want to see me, I'm going to ship your things that are at my house to you.' I said okay." Five minutes later he called back and asked her to marry him. It took her three weeks to agree. "He had to woo me," she says, noting, "We wouldn't have had as good a relationship if he didn't realize how much he really does want to be with me."

This summer they'll be married in Holly's first big wedding. Their eight kids, four boys and four girls, will be the wedding party. She's already found a beautiful gown, ivory with ruby accents. Once they're settled into married life, Holly may just check off number five on her list: graduate school. "If Mike got a good job opportunity in Missoula, where the university has a great master's program, I'd be inclined to go back to school. I have some good ideas for a thesis."

Singing the Praises of Healthy Eating

Helen Butleroff had a rewarding career as a Broadway dancer and choreographer. At fifty-four, she began a graduate program in a completely different field—nutrition.

Ultimately, she found a way to marry her past and future professions.

Helen's Lesson: *There's no point in being bitter if you age out of your first career. Don't dwell on the fact that life can be unfair. Dwell on a solution.*

ONE OF HELEN Butleroff's earliest memories is being carried around by Sid Caesar. "My mom choreographed *The Children's Hour* on NBC, and I was a regular on the show," she says. "I loved it." From the age of four until she was twelve, Helen sang and danced on live TV every week. At seventeen, her Broadway career was launched when she auditioned for the June Taylor Dancers, famous for performing on *The Jackie Gleason Show*. "Back then, June Taylor staged huge extravaganzas at the Jones Beach Theater. It was a Broadway contract, Broadway pay, and I thought I was really hot stuff."

Helen thrived in the footlights' glare, first on stage, then off. "It's very unusual for a Broadway dancer not to wait tables, too, but I never had to." She worked as a Radio City Rockette summers while she was getting her BA in theater at Queens College. "It's fun the first time you're in the line of girls. But it's not rocket science. After three or four weeks, I was bored." When dancing wasn't thrilling enough anymore, she began to choreograph and ultimately to direct. "I danced in my twenties, choreographed in my thirties, and in my forties, I created, produced, and directed musicals." Over thirty years, she worked on more than fifty musicals, on and off Broadway. One of the first shows she created, *That's Life!*—about contemporary Jewish culture in America—opened to rave reviews. "I said to myself, *Now I've done everything I wanted to do in my life. I have a great review in* The New York Times."

It was a full and happy life, but Helen knew it couldn't be forever. "In my career, unless you're Bob Fosse, you age out, even if you're a choreographer or director. You don't have the same vision that younger people do."

In her early fifties, when she stopped getting the kinds of jobs she wanted, Helen was crestfallen. But not for long. "You can dwell on the fact that life has not been fair, or you can figure out a solution. I'm the type of person who takes action." And she knew what her second career would be. All those years in off-Broadway dressing rooms, the other dancers would be reading *Glamour* or *Vogue,* and Helen would have her nose in a medical journal. "In another life, I would have been a doctor," she says. "But at fifty-four, I felt I was too old. What, I'd start practicing at sixty-seven?" Her husband, Robert Leahy, a psychologist and director of the American Institute for Cognitive Therapy, applauded Helen's decision to go back to school to study nutrition.

Even in the notoriously undernourished world of professional dancers, Helen had always been a healthy eater. "Ballerinas tend to have dysmorphic views of their bodies, a lot of which comes from crazy-ass teachers who tell them they have to be pencil thin." Helen escaped the surge toward anorexia because she studied with her mom, a strong proponent of healthy eating, healthy weight. "Even way back then, I was eating soy, bran, fiber."

Before plunging into graduate school, Helen enrolled in a nutrition course at NYU to make sure she was on the right track. She took to the subject matter immediately and decided to tackle the three-year program to become a registered dietitian. A professor encouraged her to develop an idea she had for a musical that would teach kids about the food pyramid. She started NYU's RD program at age fifty-four. "Most of my fellow students were thirty years younger. They probably thought I was their mother, but when you're around young people, you think you're twenty-five again." Helen loved studying but found it wasn't easy to reincarnate math and science courses after decades away. So when victory came, it was especially sweet. "The first course in chemistry, I had a teacher who didn't care if he failed all of New York. I got an A. It was unbelievable." Math, with all the memorization, was just as tough. "The professors thought of me as a peer in life experience, which was good since I was a complete novice in everything else." She graduated with a 3.975 average—"not because I'm that smart, but because when you're older you work harder." In her undergrad days, juggling college and dancing gigs, she'd been content with pulling B's.

The other critical factor to her success was her marriage. "My ability to concentrate was there because I had a stable relationship at home." While she was working on her RD, Helen developed her show, *The Food Guide Pyramid Musical*. As the children on stage dance their way through numbers like "Veggie Rock" and "Pasta Rasta Man," classrooms absorb Helen's *Eat well, play hard* message. "I bring in Broadway actors for a couple of the parts, which the kids just love. The show is really active, so at the same time they're learning about nutrition, they're also exercising." A performance at PS 1 in Brooklyn led to funding to stage the musical in five more schools.

Throw a reinvention party. Celebrate a friend's big life change, or launch your own with appropriate fanfare.

Her GPA and *Pyramid* helped Helen win a coveted position as one of fourteen students in a New York/Cornell/Columbia University internship, a yearlong program in which she rotates through the various services in the hospital, from pediatrics to geriatrics, from oncology to neurology. This summer, she'll take the exam to become a registered dietitian.

Next year, Helen plans to set up a nutrition counseling business for private clients. "I'd like to see patients four days a week and have a nice, long weekend." She's converting her theater production office to a place where she can meet with clients, taking down the Broadway show posters and hanging her diplomas. "I'm going to build a Web site and market myself. I'm very interested in geriatrics."

She's thrilled to have added the dietitian's credentials at this time. "I'm fifty-eight, and I understand the concerns of people at midlife." It's a critical transition time nutritionally. "I know about menopause, I understand the dietary issues, the problems with weight gain, calcium loss. Diabetes can arise. I cannot tell you how many people I see in the hospital with cardiac disease who are my age." And she's just gotten funding to bring *Pyramid* to ten more New York City schools; an additional grant will extend her reach to schools across the state.

Does she miss performing? "I feel happy when young people are on the stage. What does Erik Erikson call it?—generativity. When you're older, you've done it, you're ready to move on."

It would be hard to imagine two less likely careers to combine than nutritionist and Rockette. But that's just what Helen has done.

The Music Woman

Barbara Wild always wanted a graduate degree in music. But family concerns kept her from enrolling. When she turned fifty, she knew it was now or never.

Barbara's Lesson: *It's useful to look at our lives in three stages. The first twenty-five years are spent growing up. The second twenty-five are devoted to raising a family. The third twenty-five have to be for ourselves.*

THERE'S NO SINGLE moment, no grand epiphany that Barbara Wild can point to and say, "That's when I decided to go for my doctorate." She'd always wanted to teach college, and so a doctorate of musical arts was a logical "get." But that ambition would remain back-burnered for several decades. After college, she conducted choirs in California, then moved to New York City, where she "flirted with acting," appearing in plays and working the teleprompter for Walter Cronkite and Dan Rather. She and her husband, Mike Nelson, a commercial photographer, moved upstate, where they raised their two girls. She gave music lessons, led the choir at a Methodist church, and formed an experimental vocal group. When her older daughter, Emily, was seven, Barbara went back to work. "Teaching high school wasn't something I'd planned to do, but it was great. At one school, the choir grew from 38 singers to 108." The DMA was still on simmer, and her success at teaching only fed the flames. "I have a recording from a concert I conducted back then labeled TAPE FOR APPLICATION FOR DOCTORATE." But when their younger daughter was unhappy in their town's notoriously inadequate middle school, Barbara and Mike took the money that could have paid for Barbara's courses and transferred Becca to private school. "There was no question," Barbara says. "I'm a mom and I had to put her first."

Then came what Barbara calls the big detour. She accepted a job teaching theater, believing there would be an opportunity to move into conducting. It never happened, but once again, with Barbara's touch the theater program doubled, then tripled. "The job was huge," she remembers. "My first class was at seven fifty, and often I wouldn't leave until nine thirty at night."

Meantime the girls were growing up, and two events in Barbara's life convinced her the DMA was now or never. Her father died when he was only sixty-eight, and then her mother succumbed to a long illness. As Barbara turned fifty, it triggered a reevaluation of her own life. She knew it was time to go for the degree.

"To be certain I did need that DMA, I investigated college teaching positions around the country," she recalls. Sure enough, they all came back saying "doctorate required." But there were other factors pushing Barbara toward the advanced degree. For one thing, she wanted to get back into music. "It's easier to access the spiritual through music, and I wanted to spend more time in a spiritual zone."

Barbara knew it would be her last year teaching high school, so she staged her favorite show. *Into the Woods* is a metaphor for Barbara's own life. "It's based on fairy tales, and the first act is happily ever after. Then the second act becomes very dark. A giant terrorizes everyone, and happily ever after is more complicated than anyone thought." Barbara needed to find her way out of her own dark time, when her kids were leaving home and her job was eating her life. As she prepared an audition performance, she felt she was on the brink of a big, intimidating change. "Teaching high school represented control: I knew where the money was coming from, I knew I could do it well. Did I have the courage to step out into the unknown, maybe fall on my face?"

As Barbara sent off applications, her family seemed oblivious. "I was doing it right in front of them, and they didn't notice, or they didn't believe it. One of my girls laughed and said it was a midlife crisis." The two people who did believe it were her therapist and her best friend. "My buddy Lesley and I would go on long walks, talking it through over and over again." It was an insanely busy time, but Barbara remembers being strangely calm. "I was doing lots of yoga. I was very prayerful about it."

When the fat envelope from Boston University arrived, the reality finally hit Mike: Barbara was going to school in a city two hundred miles from their home. "It was really the timing that surprised me," he says. "I thought it was a little premature with our daughters still in college, but Barbara was hot to go, and there are two of you in a marriage." Barbara's new plan sent shock waves through the family: Mike had to decide whether he would follow her to Boston or stay in New York, where his photography clients were. "To keep the house seemed impossible financially," Barbara says. Mike agreed; he'd move to Boston. "I saw it as an opportunity, my chance to plunge into shooting digital video."

"It was not a popular decision with the girls," Barbara admits. They wanted to be able to keep coming home to the house they'd grown up in. "You know the expression, *Children would rather have their mother unhappy at home than happy anywhere else.* My girls aren't like that, but there was a feeling that if I'd stayed with my teaching job, and somehow made it work for me, it would have been easier for everybody else." It wasn't easy for Barbara to uproot her family and follow her vision. She felt guilty that in order to move forward she had to cause her family pain. But she also knew that this time, she had to think of herself and hope that all would benefit.

Barbara found a sunny two-bedroom apartment in a neighborhood of graduate students and young families. "The move was horrible, just horrible." The lowest moment came when the movers couldn't fit her Baldwin grand piano up the stairs, but losing the piano turned out to be a blessing in disguise. "Every time I changed apartments, moving it would be a huge expense," she says. "I've bought a digital keyboard I can patch into my computer. I practice with headphones late into the night. It's a much better system.

"School was scary at the get-go," Barbara continues. "I worried whether I was up to the work. I had not been at school since my master's, in 1976." But she can pinpoint the moment she knew it would all be not just okay, but transcendent. "At the first convocation, a violinist played a Bach concerto and I burst into tears, thinking *Ohmigod, I've made it. I'm really here.*" She appreciates school much more than she did in her twenties. Now it's all about the work. "I know what's important," she says. "I watch the people who are competitively climbing and clawing, and it's humorous, because I don't care about that. For me, the music is everything." And she has a breadth of knowledge that she lacked when she was younger. "At the same time Handel was composing, Hogarth was doing engravings and Fielding was writing. I wondered how this informed Handel's work," Barbara says. "I'm puzzling out connections, while many of the younger students are just looking at the music itself."

Read *When Trumpets Call.* Nobody faced a bigger midlife crisis than Teddy Roosevelt, who was only fifty when he left the presidency. Pulitzer finalist Patricia O'Toole's biography details how he reinvented his life, going on safari in Africa and exploring the Amazon, even running for the White House again.

Barbara has finished her first year, and the only cloud on the horizon concerns the family's finances. "I'm not making money anymore, I'm spending it, investing in myself, and that can be scary." If she's able to finish the program in four years, she'll be fifty-five, the classic age for early retirement. She hopes a hiring dean won't hold that against her. "I just have to have confidence that with my skills, my experience, and the doctorate, I'll be fine."

Mike, meanwhile, has found studio space in Boston, and is struggling to manage a two-city career. He's joined several professional associations in Boston, making contacts to launch his business there. "It's a tough market to break into," he says. And there's not as much work as in New York. He's been taking courses in digital editing, screenwriting, and audio work. It's not easy, but Barbara and Mike are managing.

"I've had enough experience in life to know that you don't necessarily get to a spot where you're gliding," Barbara says. "It's a matter of keeping your inner peace while things are changing around you. I really don't want to live a fear-based existence anymore. Like, *I have to work this job because if I don't we won't have enough money.* I'm tired of that. I told my family, I don't want to complain anymore, I want to be happy. The phrase I used is *happy, joyous, and free.* And I am moving toward it."

Early Retirement—Not!

When Pam Crowe-Weisberg went back to school, she did it for the joy of learning, never suspecting that in her fifties she'd be able to find a job as a museum head. Her husband, Jon Weisberg, is enjoying college from the flip side, teaching marketing and public relations.

Barbara and Jon's Lesson: *Their reinventions were sparked by an ill-fated early retirement that, by providing a reflective period, led them to appealing new jobs. Sometimes you have to quiet your life down so you can really listen to your heart.*

PAM CROWE-WEISBERG and Jon Weisberg earned the envy of their colleagues and friends when he took early retirement from his job as a senior public relations executive at Bristol-Myers Squibb, Pam quit her job, and they moved out to Park City, Utah, when Jon was fifty-five and Pam, fifty-two. Pam had grown up in Salt Lake City, and she and Jon both loved to ski, so the location was ideal. But retiring didn't work out. Jon quickly decided to establish a freelance PR business, but Pam had a harder time finding her way. "We moved in 2000, and then 9/11 happened. The stock market crash that followed definitely had an impact on our savings," Pam says. "Even more than that, I realized I wasn't ready to retire emotionally. It's hard to get off the fast track when you're a type-A personality who thrives on routine and challenges."

Back in the New York area, where they lived and worked for thirty years, Pam had enjoyed a glamorous career as a buyer at Bloomingdale's, and later launched her own buying office, which allowed her to control her schedule and spend more time at home with the couple's two girls.

In her fifties, Pam left a job at Christian Dior to return to school full-time. "I was burned out, and fashion is a young person's industry." She'd always wanted to go to graduate school, and she found a program at the Fashion Institute of Technology in museum studies, where she could major in costumes and textiles. Pam took courses full-time for a year, then got an offer she couldn't refuse to run a fashion business in New York City. She plunged back into work, taking grad school classes at night.

As if that wasn't enough to juggle, Pam and Jon decided to move into Manhattan from the Westchester suburb where they'd raised their girls. Neither of them had ever lived in an apartment before. It was a brutally hot summer, the city was dirty and smelly, and it cost $450 a month just to park their car.

Without regret, they decided to move on. Enter Park City and the ill-fated retirement plan. "I was really depressed," Pam says. "I had no clue what to do with myself. I played for almost two years, skiing fifty days the first winter, sixty days the second, but feeling very unfulfilled."

Pam had taken yoga classes for years, and when one of her daughters suggested she try Bikram (a type of yoga that's practiced in a very hot room to allow the body to go more deeply into the poses) it really clicked with her. Deciding to earn certification to teach Bikram, she enrolled in a nine-week course in Beverly Hills. It was one of the hardest, most rewarding experiences of her life. "It was nine weeks of torture—twenty-two hours of yoga a week, plus learning twenty-six pages of teaching dialogue verbatim." Of the 270 students, only 5 were over fifty, and two of them dropped out. "I thought about leaving, too," she says, "but every time I finished a day, I would think, *Wow, I really accomplished something.*" Back in Park City, though, she never opened a yoga studio. "I didn't feel teaching Bikram was creative enough. There were twenty-six postures, and you had to do them the same way, using exactly the same dialogue, every time."

Then came a fateful phone call. "I knew a man on the board of the Kimball Art Center here in Park City. He asked if I'd be interested in the director's job." It was a dream come true—a job in her field, museum studies, with a heaping serving of that challenge she so craved. Pam had never run an institution before and, she says, "I inherited a real disaster. When I came in, they were almost ready to close the doors." She reduced payroll costs, hired an enthusiastic new staff, and got lots of exposure for the crowd-pleaser exhibits she was mounting. Last Christmas, the center exhibited work by a world-renowned glass artist, William Morris, and this spring the museum staged a six-week celebration of Latino art, the first such program to recognize this growing segment of Utah's population.

"We're working our butts off," Pam says, "but I don't have the added pressure of making an early train to put the kids to bed. I'm fifteen minutes from the office, and I don't work most Fridays, which I negotiated."

While Pam was struggling to find a new direction, Jon was going through a more evolutionary change. He left Bristol-Myers with a continuing consulting role on his favorite project, an AIDS relief effort in southern Africa. Adding other clients, this longtime Fortune 100 company employee figured out how to run his own business from an office in their Park City home.

When the head of the communications department at a local college took him to lunch and asked for some ideas on how to teach public relations, Jon walked out of the restaurant with a new job. He now teaches four classes, which he loves. And for a few years, he worked part-time as a ski instructor.

"My life has been on boil since I was a little kid," Jon, who's now sixty-one, says. "When you dial the heat back to simmer, things happen. When you're not waking up at five thirty, race-walking for forty-five minutes, getting the suit on and catching the commuter train, you find out things about yourself." At Bristol-Myers, he'd while away the hours in long, dreary meetings sketching caricatures of his co-workers. "I've always liked to draw, but never took the time to do it," he notes. "A few years ago I met a painter here who invited me to a figure drawing class. Now wherever I go, I take my sketchbook and pencils."

Pam says she's always been brave about making changes in her life. "It's a credit to my father, who says, 'Don't give up, try something else, move forward.' I can't sit back and tell myself, *Okay, that's the way it is*. Some days I wish I were more laid-back, but Jon and I are both doers." Jon quarrels with the idea of ever getting it absolutely and finally right. "Our lives have never been perfect. There's always been a little edge. It's not tidy and it can be frustrating, but it works because we're always in the process of learning and becoming."

CHAPTER 7

⌒⌒

The Power of a Passion

I DON'T KNOW WHO invented the word *hobby,* but they ought to be punished. It is so inadequate to the activity it defines. Blame it on the hobbyhorse. The word *hobby,* which originally referred to a pony, was first used to suggest a pastime in the seventeenth century because it was considered to be an activity that, like the childhood toy, doesn't go anywhere. What a bum rap. *Hobby* should in fact be one of the grandest words in the language. A well-chosen pastime can be a miracle worker, transforming a humdrum life into an exciting one. The trick is to find one that touches your heart and challenges your body or your mind. Let's call it a passion, which sums up the emotional power of the activity.

Passions are the quick-change artists of reinvention. You can take up a new one without switching spouses, ditching a career, or otherwise disturbing the bedrock of your life. A passion can be a way to recharge your psyche with new enthusiasm or to take on a new challenge. The best ones address something that's been lacking, or stake a claim in new territory that you've always wanted to explore. The wild growth in knitting and crocheting since September 11 is a good example of how a passion can satisfy in multiple ways: It's given people the emotional reward of a soothing activity, a traditional pastime that echoes back to simpler, saner times, and it offers the satisfaction of engaging in a creative act, matching pattern and yarn, and producing a handsome product. The yoga craze has answered people's need for spirituality in troubled times, with the added benefits of strengthening and limbering our aging bodies.

Reading, walking, playing golf—the most common hobbies sound so humdrum. But in truth, the quality of a pastime is in the beholder's eye. Any of these activities can rise to the level of a passion, ignited by delight, enthusiasm, and ardor. A hobby is something you do to pass the time; a passion is something that fulfills you.

> **Fly a trapeze.** Just a little scary, just a little insane. Google "trapeze schools" to find one near you. The night before the big day, rent the DVD of *Sex and the City* Episode 82, "The Catch," where Carrie takes to the air at a trapeze school in New York.

Walking sounds dull, but if you set out into the neighborhood every morning with a good friend, it can be a soul-nourishing time as well as good exercise. Playing a tricky hole well can give a golfer a sense of purpose and satisfaction. These are passions, not just time fillers. Often they can introduce us to a new community of like-minded people.

A pastime we're passionate about can spill over into the rest of our lives, keeping us happy and fulfilled despite a less-than-satisfying job that we cannot change, or even a humdrum marriage. Recent research suggests the power of a passion is considerable. Positive psychology is a relatively new discipline that studies happiness. These social scientists say that one of the most powerful tools toward happiness is a great hobby.

Having a passion can even give us an identity. For people whose jobs are unexciting or even unpleasant, the passion they pursue can offer a more satisfying way to define themselves. When the classic cocktail-party question comes up—"So, what do you do?"—they don't have to admit they're accountants. Instead they can segue gracefully into their enthusiasm for their pastime. Whether it's building scale-model boats, playing the piano, or throwing pots, the activity gives them a way to convey their essence, to say, in effect, *This is who I am.*

There's no better moment to find the right hobby than midlife. By the time we celebrate our fortieth birthday, we know what's fulfilling, what makes us tick. In addition, with our career well in hand and our children becoming more independent, we have the time and money to really pursue a pastime. Such passions do have a potent new enemy: technology. We are fast becoming a plugged-in society, and we need to remember that assembling an iPod playlist is not a hobby; composing our own music and burning a CD is. Neither is watching a movie on our laptop as we ride the train home from work; creating a video scrapbook from all those home movies of the kids is. Modern technology is the enemy of hobbies. With five hundred channels to choose from, it's all too easy to relax in front of the TV. We're tired from a hard day, and it's tempting to sink into the nearest comfy chair. But it's worth the effort to find a passion. Once you do, it'll call for your attention much more loudly than the latest episode of *Lost.*

The Life Entrepreneurs

All That Jazz

When her son left for college, Jil Eaton took up a new pursuit—playing bass guitar. Now she performs with a jazz group.

Jil's Lesson: *The empty nest can be a fertile place, the ideal incubator for a new passion, offering enough free time to pursue it.*

"I'M VERY CLOSE to my son, and everybody thought I was going to fall apart when he went off to college last year," Jil Eaton, who's fifty-five, says. "I was worried, too, but I did most of my grieving before he left, standing in the basement organizing his clothes and weeping." When Alexander headed south to Skidmore College, in Saratoga Springs, New York, from their home in Portland, Maine, he left behind something that launched a new chapter in his mom's life. "Alexander is a drummer, and he'd heard that if you can also play bass, every band wants you, so while he was in high school he bought himself a bass." When Jil saw the instrument sitting in his room, she was inspired to try playing it. "I was a classically trained pianist and had sung in a cappella jazz groups. I figured I'd learn to play the bass and then teach him. I had no idea I was going to fall madly in love with it."

She took some lessons from a friend who plays string bass. Jil was a fast learner, and soon they'd formed a jazz group with another friend who plays keyboard. "I dragged her kicking and screaming into the group," Jil remembers, laughing. "She's a great musician, but when you're playing jazz, you're out on a limb, improvising. She said, 'I couldn't do that.' Now she's pretty excited about it."

Before the jazz combo had even found a name—the group ultimately went with Toast—they'd already booked a number of engagements. "We're playing at a coffee and wine bar, among other places," Jil says. "Music has always been a big part of my life, but I'm really branching out and doing things in my fifties I haven't done since I was a wandering minstrel, a folksinger, in college. I was clueless that I'd have so much time when Alexander went away."

Now she's making the most of it, broadening her horizons in all kinds of ways. The new freedom she's feeling in her fifties has led to a fertile burst of composing, too. "I just wrote a salsa waltz, called 'If I'm Still Here in the Morning,' and a country-western piece in French. I'm all over the place, and it's all good."

Meantime her house is filling up with the elements of her passion—instruments and microphones and amplifiers and feedback monitors. Her son likes to tease her about her new passion, calling her Mom.2. When he came home for the summer after freshman year, one of his friends asked Jil to jam with him, she proudly reports. "It was the ultimate compliment to have a twenty-year-old want to come and make music." Now Alexander is making a CD of her music that he'll play on his college radio show.

Her husband, David, who's a mortgage banker, doesn't share her passion for performing—"He's a linear thinker, a great fisherman and hockey player"—but he goes to her gigs whenever he can, and says he's all for the happy clutter and sound. "He told me the other day that it's like I'm in love. And that's really true. I feel transformed. I had a certain heaviness about my life, even though I was designing knitting patterns and running my own company. There was something missing. It was the music."

Meantime the new enthusiasm Jil is feeling because of her

music is cross-pollinating across her life. Her knitting pattern business, MinnowKnits, which she started in 1990 when her son was small, is humming along. "There are five million new knitters in the US since 9/11," Jil says. "It's getting back to basics, a little Zen, and you end up with something you can wear. It spreads around good feelings. It's addictive." She's just published her seventh pattern book, a handsomely photographed collection of knitted evening wear—gloves, halters, even clutch bags. But even here she's branching out: The venture she's most excited about is a children's book, her first, called *Yarn Soup*. "It's an *Eloise at the Plaza* kind of story about two little girls from different cultures. A family from Africa moves to town, and they sing and drum and knit." Jil not only wrote the liltingly told story but also painted the vibrant watercolor illustrations. "I thought I didn't know how to do that, but it turns out I actually do," she says, underscoring her can-do theory of life. "I'm an alto, but if I can't see what notes are being played, I can sing way high. This applies to my writing, to everything."

She's found a fertile new nest in a building that bubbles with creativity. "I rented space at Bakery Studios, a building two painters bought and run as a nonprofit, so you can actually afford to work there. There's a photographer, painting studios, a dance collaborative. The place is full of interesting people, and it's so great to be out in the world with other creative minds."

A recent concert at a senior citizen housing project triggered yet another reinvention in Jil's life. "After we played, this old geezer came up to me and said, 'You're Gertrude Stein.' I Googled her at home, and she's a mountain of a woman. The next morning, I was out at six, running. I've run every day since." Jil has lost twenty-five pounds, and her husband, whose blood pressure was rising, has lost forty. Her new physique is paying dividends across the board. "The running is good for singing. An electric bass is heavy and I'm five foot two, so it helps me there, too."

Building on the fun the jazz combo has brought her, Jil has embarked on a second new hobby: gardening. "I'd always dreaded the heat and humidity of summer," she says. "It gets so bad that David wants to offer me up to Harvard as an example of reverse seasonal affective disorder." Last summer, she embraced the season by planting a garden around her urban Portland home. "I hooked up with a friend who's a landscaper, and we tore out hedges and planted flowering beds. We've now got a double pond with a bridge and waterfall. It made me feel strong and happy and vibrant." Her design was so attractive, she got a commission to create another garden. "The ideal world would be design and knitting in the winter, garden design in the summer, and music all the time.

> **Make a firsts pledge.** Promise yourself a new experience every three months—your first massage, your first opera, your first night sleeping under the stars. Shake life up a little by getting out of your comfort zone.

"You really have to be brave or you don't get anywhere," Jil continues, pointing to a stressful time earlier in her life when the art gallery where she worked shut its doors. That's when she got the idea to launch her knitting business. "I often find myself out on a limb with a saw in my hand," she says with a laugh. "But somehow it works out.

"I always say, you can reinvent yourself any way you want." And so she has. *Yarn Soup* will be in bookstores by the time you read this, Toast is performing regularly, and her gardening projects continue to multiply.

Reinventing the Wheel

Deb Ibsen bought her first motorcycle at forty-two. Learning to ride has carried her beyond her fears to a great new joy.

Deb's Lesson: *It's easy to slip into patterns as we age. We have to challenge ourselves, explore new options.*

"THE FIRST THING people say to me is, 'So you ride a Harley,'" Deb Ibsen says. "But I hate that whole vixen, women-in-leather-and-low-cut-tops look." Deb, who at forty-nine favors tailored clothes and works for an advertising agency in San Francisco, may not be a biker babe, but she's among the growing number of women who are taking up motorcycle riding at midlife.

She's always been bewitched by speed. "I lived on my bicycle when I was a little girl, and I could never go fast enough. I loved horses." But Deb didn't take action on her dream to own a motorcycle until midlife. "I finally got tired of letting my fear get the best of me." Her first ride came on the cusp of forty when her husband took her out on his brand-new bike. "I was so frightened to see cars going sixty miles an hour four feet away, I almost threw up in my helmet," she recalls. But facing down her fear became another reason to ride. She started small and eased her way into it. "I didn't just buy a bike. I took a three-day safety course sponsored by the state of California. The first time you're actually on a bike, somebody is pushing you across a parking lot." The statistics on injuries and fatalities sobered but didn't dissuade her. "Eighty percent of the deaths involve three things: under age twenty-five, no helmet, and alcohol. I'm over twenty-five, I always wear a helmet, and I will never take a drink then get on a bike."

When she bought a motorcycle—a lightweight Suzuki GS 500—at forty-two, riding was every bit as exciting as Deb had imagined. "I just loved having this machine that could transport

me to beautiful areas—like a convertible but more seamless."
Deb also enjoyed the second glances she got when her auburn
hair tumbled out of the helmet. "Even now in the twenty-first
century, breaking barriers for women is still a big deal," she
says. "I'm very big on confounding expectations. I put a GIRLS
RULE! sticker on that first bike."

Motorcycle riding isn't intuitive for either a driver or a cyclist, and Deb found the process of relearning how to use her
body both demanding and rewarding. "The turn signal is in a
weird place, the brakes behave differently, and changing gears
is a whole new exercise." Again, she approached the project
with maturity and caution, keeping to the secondary roads until
she built up her skills and confidence. "It takes a while for con-
trolling the bike to become second nature, and during that time
you're at risk. The majority of accidents happen during the first
month of ownership." Two years after she started riding, she
upgraded to a bigger bike, a BMW R1100R, that felt more stable
at high speeds. On nice days, Deb rides it from the San Francisco suburb where she lives into the city to work.

Deb is proud that she got past what she describes as a lifetime of conditioning. "My father was an emergency room physician, and when I was in high school he said, 'If you ever get on
a motorcycle, just don't come home.'" For two years, she didn't
tell him that she'd bought a bike. Then one day he came for a
surprise visit and saw the motorcycle parked in the garage. He
didn't say anything, but Deb decided to confront him. "It was
just like the old days; all of a sudden I was ten again," she says.
"I saw his jaw clench as he asked me, 'What happens if you lose
a leg?' You never stop being your parents' kid. But if I can't decide things for myself at forty-five, when can I?" Ironically, it
was her mother's death from cancer at fifty-nine that would help
convince Deb to seize the moment and start to ride. "She
thought she'd live into her eighties. I have no idea how long I

have, and I've got a lot of things still to do." A lymphoma scare in her early forties pushed Deb over the top. The biopsy was negative, but she realized, "It would have just sucked to die of cancer without experiencing the risky things I love to do.

"It's really easy as we age to slip into patterns and not consider options," Deb continues, and this is something she's always on guard against. "My big fear now is being single, something that I never in a million years thought would happen." Six months after Deb and her husband of eighteen years split up, she is still struggling to chart a new course for herself. "I had a path all figured out, but it's been blown out of the water. Maybe that's good, but I have to re-create my future at the not-necessarily-attractive age of forty-nine." She's trying to shed old ways of thinking and adopt a new, *anything-goes* attitude. "I could move to London. I could start doing the traveling I've always dreamed of," she says. Deb is also rethinking her fundamental approach to the world. "I'm not outgoing, and I have to change that or I'll never meet anyone. I need to be able to sit in a square in Paris and look approachable."

Deb's experience on the bike has given her the courage she needs. "I think of how comfortable I am on a bike and it demonstrates that you can get used to anything if you stick with it. I'm trying to use that in other parts of my life." Meantime she's recalculating the risk of motorcycle riding, from the new perspective of being single. "A good friend of mine had a skiing accident. He's only forty, and he's paralyzed from the neck down. I spent a day with him a couple of months ago and saw what his life is like," she says. "What struck me is how dependent he is on others. It was a very sobering afternoon. Now that I no longer have a spouse, the thought of an accident is really daunting." While she sorts through the new reality, Deb is still riding, and even hoping to make a cross-country trip one day.

She's a little surprised to discover how big a role caution is playing in her life plan these days. "I would think that as you get older, you have less life to lose, so you're more likely to take risks. I'm finding out that it doesn't work that way. I know too much; I realize all the things that can happen," she says. But whatever direction the next chapter of Deb's life takes, one thing's sure: Fear will never prevent her from savoring every moment as it happens. "I've been reading books about the power of now, how we spend too much time thinking about the past or the future," Deb says. "When you're on the bike, you have to be present. You can't drift forward or back." It's a great metaphor for how she intends to live her life.

The Artist's Way

When her two girls were growing, Donna Sallee stayed home to raise them. After her twenty-five-year marriage ended, she lived many people's dream—supporting herself as a painter.

Donna's Lesson: *To transform a passion into a profession, you have to learn to value your work. It takes great self-confidence to set the right price for your creativity and vision, but if you don't your venture will fail.*

DONNA WHITESIDE SALLEE was forty-five, and she'd never supported herself. Now that was going to have to change. She was leaving her marriage of twenty-five years, determined to earn a living the way many people only dream of—by selling her art. Could she make a go of it? Only time would tell.

Donna grew up in a small town in Connecticut. "My mother raised five of us, and she was always there. I knew I would stay home with my kids," she says. Donna's mother died of breast cancer when she was in high school, and one of her brothers was killed by a lightning strike when she was twenty-five, strengthening her resolve to live her life to the fullest. "I wasn't raised to support myself," she says. "I went to art school, which was a wonderful education, but I never really thought about making a living. My ex-husband, Steve, came from a family where women didn't work." Steve got a job in Indiana, and, living in Amish farm country, Donna turned to her art to pass the long, lonely days. "I was painting and exhibiting at a couple of shows a year, making pocket money."

A year later, Steve's work took them back east, to upstate New York, where their two children, Shannon and Dana, were born. When Shannon was six, they moved again to Indiana, then a year and a half later to St. Louis, and finally to southern Florida. Donna occasionally did paintings of people's homes or wedding portraits on commission. "And I always tried to paint one thing each year for myself, mostly of the girls growing up."

Shuffle your art. Take down all your paintings and posters, and live bare-walled for a week. Then begin to rehang things, considering not so much what size painting fits the space, but which one you want to see where.

She wasn't enthusiastic about moving to Miami, but to her surprise Florida won her heart. "Being an artist in the tropics is wonderful. I love the flowers, and the shapes and shadows of the palm trees. I could sit in my yard all day long and watch the birds. I love looking out and always seeing color." In Florida, she began painting wooden bowls with images of angels and Santa Claus, and buying unusual, attractively shaped pieces of furniture at tag sales and flea markets. She'd paint them with nursery scenes or lush, brightly colored flowers on a checkerboard background. She started selling her pieces at art shows and a couple of shops in Fort Lauderdale. The work was fun, though she had no idea she was laying the foundation for a successful business.

When their younger daughter, Dana, was a senior in high school, Steve took a job in Indiana, though he commuted back to Florida for weekends whenever he could. Donna stayed to sell their house while Dana finished out the school year. "I didn't want to leave," she says. "I didn't want to lose my friends here, or my connections for selling my work." A house came on the market in a sleepy little community of 1950s-era bungalows, only a five-minute walk from the ocean near Fort Lauderdale. The two-bedroom cottage needed work, but the price was low. Donna and Steve bought the house the same day they saw it. "If I was going to move to Indiana, I figured at least I could come back here and work." In the meantime, she would use the little house as her studio. By this time, she was earning enough money to pay the mortgage.

But the bungalow by the beach led Donna toward a new way of life. While Steve was in Indiana, Donna was spreading her wings. "I was doing work I loved, everything was falling into place for me," she remembers. "I was making better money, feeling really good about myself. When Steve was away, I didn't miss him. I felt so free." She tackled various projects indoors and out in the small, palm-shaded yard, transforming the dark little house into a beautiful home. "I'd go to Home Depot to buy some brackets, and come home with two sets of French doors. It felt great making these decisions for myself." The marriage dwindled, and Steve and Donna decided to separate.

Donna, who didn't ask for alimony, now says, "If I'd thought hard about it, I would have been scared to death to leave the marriage. But some inner voice told me I could handle this." She applied herself to her work, lived frugally, and hoped for the best.

"The bowls and small pieces of furniture were time consuming to paint, and I just wasn't getting enough money for them, especially when I sold through a shop," she says. She needed to think bigger. On Florida's Atlantic coastline, new neighborhoods were being created, with houses going up all the time. Many of them were multimillion-dollar properties with owners who could afford pricey custom decor. Occasionally, Donna teamed up with an interior designer, painting murals for her clients.

Shortly after moving into the bungalow full-time, she had what seemed like a great opportunity. *Ladies' Home Journal* did a short profile of Donna, showcasing her work. The story, which went out to a readership of more than four million, did generate some phone calls, but not a single commission. "The calls weren't from prospective clients," Donna says. "They were women all over the country who wanted to paint for a living, who wanted to be just like me."

Donna had one critical business lesson to learn: Charge enough to assure herself a comfortable living. "It's hard to ask as much as you should," she admits. "You meet a young couple and feel guilty. I always become friends with my clients, and I'm bad about money. I don't even check what other artists are charging." She knew if she was going to support herself, she had to raise her rates. "I'm still under market, but I did just set a twelve-thousand-dollar fee for a wall mural," she says. "Back when I started, I remember painting an entire ceiling for two thousand."

Commissions flowed in as admiration for her work rippled through the interior design community, and happy clients showed her painting to their friends. In the affluent neighborhoods where Donna works, people love the concept of an artist in residence. "Here everybody has their housecleaner, their nanny, and their artist," she says, laughing. "Baby rooms are big. You paint one in a neighborhood, and everybody wants you." For the first time in her career, Donna finds herself telling people she's so busy that she won't be able to start a job for two or three months.

After five years on her own, she's confident of her ability to earn a living. Still, she's ridden through some rough patches. "Last summer, it got really quiet, and I worried about paying the bills," she says. She'd had an expensive medical procedure and flown to California several times to visit her daughter Shannon, who was in graduate school at Berkeley. "That was my first little panic, the only time I had to take money from my reserves." Then, out of the blue came a new client with a big commission. Since then, Donna has learned to pace her spending through the fertile and fallow seasons. "If it's a slow time, I can always paint furniture for a shop," she says. "Or I can take the opportunity to work on my own house."

She finds herself content with living alone for the first time in her life. "I really am at peace. I have family in Florida just a three-hour drive away." She starts every day with an early-morning walk through the neighborhood. At fifty, she says, "I'm more self-confident, more assertive. I'm not going to take a job I don't like. I'm simply not going to waste my time." Painting murals can be quite physical, climbing ladders, working for hours curled into an unnatural, cramp-inducing position, and Donna sometimes worries about how long she'll be able to keep it up. But then she considers her life so far. "If you had told me twenty years ago that I would be living here, doing this work, I couldn't have imagined it." So she carefully lays her plans for the next phase of her business: By hiring a professional to photograph her twelve-thousand-dollar job and putting together a brochure, she's hoping to ratchet other commissions up to five figures. Regardless of what lies ahead,

Donna remains an optimist, eager to see how the next decade of her life unfolds.

Love Match

On a whim, Beth Whelan took a few tennis lessons. To her surprise, she discovered she was good, very good. Now she plays five times a week.

Beth's Lesson: *A pastime can produce a surprising payoff— powerful intergenerational friendships with people who share your passion.*

ON AN AUGUST morning, Beth Whelan stood on a tennis court at Princeton University at age forty-seven, competing in the United States Tennis Association's North Atlantic Regional Championships for league tennis. "It's a really big deal. We call it the nationals because it's the end of the line for mixed doubles," Beth says, adding that "I felt fortunate to be a member of my tennis center's 7.0 mixed doubles team." No one was more surprised to find her there than Beth herself.

"I had never played sports as a kid. It was a standing joke that I'd be the last one picked for any team in gym," she says. "I couldn't get a ball in a hoop. Instead, I danced and did shows and plays."

As an adult, Beth continued to emphasize the performing arts over athletics, volunteering to produce and direct school plays. A registered nurse, she organized her schedule to be with her two sons, Danny and Ryan. "I was the cupcake mommy," Beth reports. "After Ryan was born, I worked nights, holidays, weekends—times when my husband would be home. I loved my work and I needed to stimulate my brain and not just watch *Sesame Street,* but I also threw myself into motherhood. I was the class parent who'd come in and help the teacher, the chaperone for field trips. I was PTA president."

For five years, she was the nurse at the Cornwall Central High School in the upstate New York town where she lives. One day, the star of the girls' tennis team came back to visit her old teachers. "Marla was in her first year at the University of Rhode Island, so I asked her about school, how she was doing on the tennis team." Catching a whiff of Marla's excitement for the game, Beth asked if Marla could teach her to play.

Beth still remembers the first time they went out on the court. "She hit the ball to me, and I was so proud that I managed to hit it back that I forgot to return it the second time." That first summer, Beth took ten lessons. By her own account, she was anything but a prodigy. "By August, it was still a challenge to hit the ball two or three times in a row."

The next summer when Marla came home from college, they hit the courts again. Beth's strokes were improving, and Marla told her she should join the local fitness club, which had indoor courts where she could play year-round. She signed up for a five-week tennis drill, and the pro invited her to play on the 2.5 doubles team. "We didn't win once. I was the poster girl for telling my opponents, 'This is my first time doing match play.' Then they'd slaughter us. Now I know you have to stick those shoulders back and look like you have all the confidence in the world."

The team's less-than-stellar showing didn't discourage Beth. Tennis was fun. The next summer, she took lessons from Marla again, and the following fall the pro asked her to be the captain of the 2.5 team. "We went from worst to first, winning our division and the regionals competition," Beth proudly reports. She moved on to become captain of the 3.0 team, and was named the club's Athlete of the Month. "When they put my picture up, my kids were astonished. They said, 'My mom—an athlete?'"

Her game progressed to the 3.5 level, and she began to play on the club's mixed doubles team. "A lot of my friends don't like mixed doubles because the name of the game is 'Hit to the woman.' The men hit hard, but I don't mind. I have a lot of drive when I'm playing." She also has the maturity of a woman at midlife. "Marla says I have the it factor. I'm very in the moment when I play. If I hit a bad ball, I shake it off. I'll say to myself, *That point is over, move on.* And I do."

Her mixed doubles team proved to be a powerhouse, triumphing first in their division, then at regionals and sectionals—putting them on the slate for the final competition in Princeton. "My partner Tim and I lost our match, but we played our best, and that felt good. It was an honor just to stand on the court—something 99 percent of USTA players never get to do." Because the other two mixed doubles pairs won, Beth's team took the trophy.

For Beth, the sweetest accomplishment is neither the championship title she now holds, nor even the delight she gets from playing four or five times a week. It's the unexpected intergenerational friendship that's bloomed. "Marla is so much more than my tennis instructor. She's my makeup and clothes shopping buddy. In my houseful of boys, she's the daughter I never had. I still call the scores in to her from every competition match."

At midlife, Beth has truly hit her stride. "What Christiane Northrup says in *The Wisdom of Menopause* is absolutely true. In my forties, I've got all this feistiness," she laughs. "Now, because of tennis, I'm healthier than I've ever been. I have more energy. My heart is so happy—figuratively and literally. I never saw myself as a competitor, and the fact that I am gives me new confidence in life. I have a scrapbook of newspaper clippings that I flip through and say 'Is that really me?'"

Beth's boys are now seventeen and twenty-one, and the

running joke is, "Will dinner be served tonight or are you playing tennis?" These days, Beth has no guilt. "Everybody's grown
up, they're nice people, I did my job." And no regrets—well,
maybe just one. "I wish I'd started playing tennis ten years
sooner."

Her Heart Will Go On

*After a double tragedy, Bonnie Luke found solace in creat-
ing an act as a celebrity look-alike and doing fund-raisers
for charity.*

Bonnie's Lesson: *A new interest that's compelling and
challenging can help you move forward from grief.*

WHILE SHE WAS in her forties, Bonnie Luke suffered more
tragedy than most of us can wrap our minds around. But in the
midst of her grief she found new meaning in her life, launching
a surprising avocation that has brought peace to her, inspiration
to others, and help to needy children around the world.

In August 1996, when this story opens, Bonnie's life was
rich and full. Originally a nurse, she had reinvented herself as a
fitness instructor when her first child, Tyler John, was born in
1981. By the time her second baby boy, Trevor Chase, came
along two years later, her studio was the largest dance-aerobics
facility in southern Utah. Her third son, Trenton Boyd, was born
in New Jersey, where the family had moved when her husband,
Boyd, landed a job selling boats. Two years later, the family
moved back to Utah, settling in the picturesque mountain-
ringed town of St. George, where Bonnie taught fitness classes
at the Green Valley Spa.

On that fateful summer day, they were taking a family vacation in the northern part of the state. "We'd just ridden ATVs
over Beaver Mountain and we decided to take a boat ride on

Bear Lake Reservoir," Bonnie recalls. Her boys had water-skied from the age of three and were strong swimmers. "They always wore life jackets, and I never worried one bit about them." But something went very wrong on this sunny afternoon. After wakeboarding for a few minutes, Trevor suddenly let go of the rope and sank into the water. When the boat circled back, he was floating facedown. Boyd jumped into the water, and Tyler, who was only fifteen, managed to pull his brother into the boat. Their efforts to revive him failed. Trevor never regained consciousness, and twenty-four hours later the family made the heart-wrenching decision to remove life support. "It was terrible," Bonnie remembers. "Trevor was the catalyst of our family, compassionate and sensitive, a peacemaker. Just a happy thirteen-year-old boy."

Shuffle your life. Rearrange the elements of your life, break the routines. If you normally work out before work, do it after work for a week. Try a new restaurant instead of your old favorite. If you're a novel fanatic, read something on the nonfiction best-seller list. Watch the morning news on a different channel. Mixing up the people you see, the information you receive, and the way you receive it can start you thinking along new lines.

Tyler took the death, which remained unexplained by an autopsy, particularly hard. "He and Trevor did everything together," Bonnie says. Two years later, almost to the day, tragedy struck again in the cruelest kind of déjà vu. Enjoying an outing with a group of friends on Gunlock Reservoir, just half an hour's drive from St. George, Tyler took a hard fall waterskiing, and when the boat swung around to pick him up he was unconscious. When one of Tyler's friends called Bonnie at home, she thought he must be playing a terrible prank. "It was a nightmare," Bonnie says. "Call it mother's intuition, but I knew Tyler wasn't going to make it."

As Bonnie grieved this unimaginable double loss, her Mormon faith gave her solace. "I knew I'd be with my family again, and that we all have purpose here on earth. Nothing just happens. My boys taught me so much from their deaths—that you have to have courage and faith." Bonnie buried a son for the second time and went right back to work. "That saved me. I punched a little harder and kicked a little higher to escape the pain," she says, adding, "My mother had always told me, 'That's life, so put a smile on your face and don't let it bring you down.' She prepared me, never knowing what I'd have to face."

Her mother's counsel helped convince Bonnie to say yes when a friend suggested that she do a Céline Dion impersonation for the Green Valley staff Christmas party that year. "People always said I looked like Céline, and I figured it would take my mind off my grief." It helped that Trevor had been a Dion fan. "We'd sing along to 'Because You Love Me' in the car, and a friend of Trevor's sang that song at his funeral."

Bonnie bought a fall the color and style of Dion's hair, a sparkling blue off-the-shoulder evening gown, and a pair of brown contact lenses. A girlfriend did her makeup. At forty-three, Bonnie was thirteen years older than Dion, but the resemblance was uncanny. The night of the party, she lip-synched "My Heart Will Go On." "My hands were shaking so badly, I couldn't even hold the microphone," she says. "I thought everybody would laugh at me." There were more than three hundred people at the party, and since Green Valley sometimes has celebrity spa guests, most of them thought it was really Dion.

As simple as that, Bonnie had a new hobby. She did six other Christmas parties that year, just for fun. "It got easier every time," she says. For an awards banquet at a local college, she learned to perform "Because You Love Me." "For two years, I just lip-synched those two songs," she says. Then an agent who handles celebrity look-alikes saw her act and told her that if she actually sang, she could make big money. Bonnie found a vocal coach and started taking lessons. "One door after another opened for me," she says. "I knew I was supposed to be doing this." She began giving motivational presentations. "I put together a program where I'd sing 'My Heart Will Go On' then talk about life and attitude and happiness. I spoke at church youth groups and clubs. Because I'd lost my two boys, people listened to me."

The gigs kept growing, first locally, then in Salt Lake City. Finally, Vegas and LA came calling. Bonnie did a private party at a small hotel on the Strip, and was booked for a photo shoot of celebrity look-alikes for a movie poster for Universal Studios of Japan. Then, two years ago, she was invited to perform at the Aladdin hotel, where she sang for eight thousand people. "I was so naive, I had no idea it would be that big. On stage, it was little old me and Cirque du Soleil. I made a thousand dollars, they paid all my expenses and put me in a wonderful suite. I thought, *This is nice.*"

Seven years after that Green Valley Christmas party, Bonnie now has agents in Las Vegas, Salt Lake, and Los Angeles as well as an assistant to handle her bookings, and she performs about four times a month. She does as many fund-raisers as she can, including some for a favorite nonprofit, Champs for Children. When Bonnie goes to Vegas, she makes a thousand to fifteen hundred dollars a night.

She hasn't given up her day job, though. At fifty, she takes the experience for what it is, enjoying the excitement and using her talent as a platform for charity work. "People get caught up in the glitz and glamour," she says. "But I'm at an age where I've learned what's important in life. These agents come in and say they'll make you famous. I worked with a Britney Spears look-alike, and that little gal had stars in her eyes. She was so young." Bonnie turned down a five-year contract one agent wanted her to sign.

Now fitness director at Green Valley, Bonnie has her life in perspective and knows she's got the best of both worlds. "If I never do another Céline gig, I'll be a happy person," she says. "I have a family, friends, my job. Balance is important." But she's grateful for the emotional growth that performing has stimulated. "I've always been confident, but the Céline act has taught me to let the ego go, stop worrying about what people think. The Céline act moved me way out of my comfort zone and led to motivational speaking, which I love. My whole life, I've wanted to inspire and uplift people, encourage them to be the best they can be." She'll always feel the pain of her two boys' absence, but she's honored them by remaking her life. "My boys taught me even more from their deaths than they did when they were alive. Spiritually, I could never be where I am today without the experience of losing them. I've learned that, yes, my heart will go on."

CHAPTER 8

⌒

Going to Extremes

I SAT IN MY little gray sports car in the paddock at Lime Rock racetrack, about to accelerate onto the long straightaway, wondering what in the world I was doing. The night before, I had fetched the car from the body shop, where it required five thousand dollars to fix the damage after a big doe bounded in front of me on a densely wooded road (no amount of money would fix the deer, but I wasn't in the mood to be sympathetic). The scenario that kept looping through my mind wasn't standing on the podium at Le Mans. It was taking the car right back to Quality Auto Body after I spun into a wall at Lime Rock.

I was participating in what's cleverly called a driver education day, but is really an opportunity to get out on a racetrack and drive as fast as you can. Newbies like me go out with an instructor. Rarely is anybody hurt, but often at least one car leaves the track on a flatbed. For most of the people who participate in DE days, which are sponsored by car owner clubs, the primary emotion is joy, as they learn to drive the proper line through the turns and floor it down the straightaways. For me, the primary emotion was fear. *Okay,* I bargained with myself. *Do this, and it will cover you for 2004.* Since I turned fifty, I had promised to do something that scared me at least once a year.

Facing Down Fear: The Once-a-Year Plan

In my late forties, I noticed I was beginning to make safer choices in life, shying away from the new and unexplored, sticking to things I already could do well rather than sticking my neck out and trying something difficult. Marrying that observation with my foolhardiness gene, I came up with a formula for meeting my fifties head-on. I call it the thrillseeker's theory for successful aging. The way I see it, you've got to fight the conservative impulse that leads you to make ever-saner, more sensible choices. If you don't turn that old phrase, *Better safe than sorry,* on its head from time to time, the circumference of your life will shrink and shrink. To keep it vital and interesting, do something that scares you at least once a year. Facing down fear reminds you that you're tough, adventurous, capable. As long as you feel that adrenaline surge of success every twelve months, you'll remember to keep living large.

For me, the challenge always involves danger—or, even better, the illusion of danger, which is the case with bungee jumping, an activity I've engaged in not once but twice. It sounds risky but actually is relatively safe. When I was fifty-one, I went rock climbing for the first time, a sport that most people are giving up, not taking up, at that age. At fifty-two, I drove my car on the Lime Rock track. At fifty-three, I went skydiving for the first—and probably last—time. These are all good exercises for an adrenaline junkie like me.

If such activities sound silly rather than spectacular, foolhardy rather than fun, there are lots of other ways to reconnect with your inner hero. Maybe it's giving a speech even though your stomach is churning and your face threatens to erupt in flop sweat like Albert Brooks in *Broadcast News.* Isn't it fascinating that public speaking tops surveys as our biggest fear, beating out even the Grim Reaper? You'd rather die than get up in front of a hundred people? If that's how you feel, imagine the thrill when you take the stage—and hear the audience laughing at your jokes and offering enthusiastic applause. For a recent divorcée, the scariest thing could be inviting that cute guy in the legal department out to lunch; the last time you were in dating mode was three decades ago, back when women did not ask men. It could be moving alone to a new city where you don't know a soul, as a friend of mine recently did. The point is to give yourself a healthy shove out of your comfort zone. Once you've stepped beyond it, survived, and even triumphed, victory is sweet. Your arena of action expands a little, making it easier to sign on for the next scary and potentially life-enriching act.

Thinking Big, Really Big

The extremists in this chapter have stepped way outside their comfort zone. I would never compare my own accomplishments to theirs—exploring and charting underwater caves, bicycling around the world, running the Hawaii Ironman triathlon, building an airplane. I'm proud just to share a generational outlook. But they can inspire the rest of us by showing how much is possible if we're willing to risk failure and try something daring.

These extremists all have the same bighearted, big-picture outlook, and they all had to conquer a basic fear—*Can I actually do this amazing thing?* One of my fellow climbers on Kilimanjaro remarked, "An adventure is an experience where you don't know the outcome." He was so right. Triumph at something you're not sure you can achieve—well, there's no greater satisfaction.

The boomer impulse toward mega-projects has spawned some interesting trends, such as the evolution of marathons from an elite athletes' sport to everyday occurrences. I have more than a dozen friends who've run a big-city marathon (every one, I might add, was over forty at their first race). When I was at *More,* people told us we were crazy to hold a marathon limited to women over forty. But twenty-six hundred women came out the first year, and it's become an annual event. Midlifers make up a solid contingent of Ironman entries, too. They're at the wheel in the majority of cars out on racetracks for driver education days across the country.

Going the Distance

The willingness to tackle a big challenge is one quality the people portrayed in this chapter share. There's another characteristic just as crucial to their success: staying power. Anybody who can suspend disbelief for the single second it takes to leap off a ledge can bungee jump. It's a thrill, not a commitment.

The really impressive thing is to keep working toward a goal even on the bleak days when nothing goes right and it feels like the universe is against you. Louis Licari broke his back when an inattentive driver ran into his bike just a month before he was slated to compete in the Hawaii Ironman. All that training, all that effort, erased in an instant. As soon as the bones had knit, he was right back to his training regimen. I have a small understanding of the resolve required to get back on the bike. Five years ago, when a dog ran into the road, I sailed over the handlebars, snapping my collarbone. Six weeks later, I was well enough to ride again, but it took another month for me to screw up my courage and do it. It was tempting to let other activities fill the blank space in my life. Louis got back on the bike and completed the Ironman just one year off schedule, at fifty-one instead of fifty.

> **Spend a day at the library.** Even small-town libraries have private collections, special programs, offbeat periodicals that you never see as you cruise in and out, just picking up the book you requested. Befriend a librarian, get a tour, explore all the nooks and crannies.

Mary Senft had to address a different kind of challenge as she constructed an airplane. What threatened to throw her off course wasn't as dramatic as an accident; it was the learning curve of a new endeavor, which can be deeply discouraging on a bad day. I have a pretty good idea of the difficulties she surmounted, because my husband also built an airplane. While the Falco took shape out in our barn, I marveled at how this impatient man I'd married just kept on truckin' when things got tough. The first section he built was the tail. (The cheapest part, it's the litmus test for answering the two universal questions of homebuilding: *Can I really do this?* and *Do I really want to?*) Steve built the tail five times before he got it right. Ever-more-inventive strings of curses wafted across the lawn from the barn, so I always knew when things weren't going smoothly, but he stuck it out. On a bright June day six years after he began building it, the Falco flew. I always told people that airplane was worth every penny of the money we spent simply for the demonstration it gave our daughter Brook—who was six when Steve started working on the tail—of what you can accomplish when you just plain refuse to give up.

Even Steve is amazed by Mary Senft's accomplishment. In eighteen months, she built what is arguably the most complex homebuilt on the market. Then she embarked on an even more mind-boggling project—constructing a vintage airplane, not from blueprints or plans, all of which have been lost, but from photographs.

The other thing that impresses me about the people in this chapter is the quiet way they went about their tasks. None of these accomplishments was a stunt. None of these people was looking for kudos or publicity (except the round-the-world bikers, because they were fund-raising for asthma research). These men and women were doing extraordinary things because it answered a need deep inside them.

And these magnificent obsessions opened up rich new areas in their lives. For Cindy Butler, cave diving has led her to new fields of study—surveying and mapping, the flora and fauna of the caverns she explores. For the Holmes-Eber family, biking around the world has ignited a passion to live outside the United States. Mary Senft has a new area of expertise that encompasses engineering, drafting, wiring, and working with a variety of materials, from aluminum to composites. For Louis Licari, becoming a competitive athlete has brought him a whole new circle of friends who know him not as a celebrity hairdresser, but as that take-no-prisoners guy on the bike.

Getting Motivated at Midlife

It's no accident that midlife is prime time for going to extremes. Opportunity plays into it: This is often the age when we have the resources—the money and time—to take on a big project. But there's more to it than that. For many people, it's the right moment psychologically. We have the confidence to attempt something huge, because we've enjoyed enough successes in life to believe in ourselves, and suffered enough failures to know they're not fatal. Furthermore, midlife is the time when we often begin asking those big, existential questions—*Why am I here? How can I make my life meaningful?* (Hence the midlife crisis, when the answers don't satisfy.) It's a fertile time for thinking big—really big.

It's no coincidence, either, that so many going-to-extremes projects rely on physical skills. Completing a marathon or climbing a mountain is an age-defying act. Knowing that our bodies are healthy and strong makes us feel more vital.

Taking a Page from the Extremists

Most of us are never going to bike around the world, build an airplane, or enter an Ironman competition. But we can all go to extremes in our own way. Maybe it's planting our first garden from scratch, with heirloom seeds, or learning to bake bread by studying the chemistry of fermentation, as a friend of mine did. It could be building a dry-stone wall or learning to play the violin, a notoriously difficult instrument at any age. The crucial things are the question you ask at the beginning, *Can I do this?*—and the answer you give at the end, *Yes, I can!*

The Life Entrepreneurs

Around the World by Bike

Paula Holmes-Eber overcame asthma to become a dedicated cyclist. When she was forty-four, she and her family biked around the world.

Paula's Lesson: *For forty years, you follow other people's rules, having a family, making a living. Then it's time to make your own.*

As an athlete, Paula Holmes-Eber was a late bloomer. Plagued with asthma so bad her doctors thought she might not see adulthood, Paula remembers spending most of sixth grade in bed watching the other kids play tag outside her window. But when more effective medication brought her condition under control in her midtwenties, she made up for lost time: "A lot of people did their sports in high school, then became couch potatoes. When my medicines got better, it was wow! Suddenly, I could camp, hike, bicycle."

She took to the outdoors the way only a woman who's been denied something her entire life can. Her college boyfriend, Lorenz Eber, grew up in Germany and had been cycling for years; they fell in love on ten-speeds. For a honeymoon, they cycled through Europe. When their two daughters were born, they just popped the girls into a trailer and towed them along. Paula says, "I tell other parents, don't wait until you think they're 'old enough.' By the time they're eight, they want iPods and X-Boxes." Anya and Yvonne both inherited the outdoors gene; they crave adventure and like nothing better than waking up in a tent.

Over the years, as the cycling trips grew in ambition, an idea was incubating to make the biggest journey of all—circling the globe. Paula remembers, "To me, once a kid who couldn't even bike down the block, this was a miracle." It seemed like an impossible dream—almost ten thousand miles and mind-boggling logistics, all tied up with miles of red tape.

"Being at midlife is partly why we went," says Paula, who was forty-four when they started the trip. "From birth to your forties, you're put in a program. You're supposed to have a good education, get married, have a house, a career, a family. When you're young, these things consume you. Then one day, you say, *Okay, I've followed the rules, now I'm going to make my own*." Midlife crisis? "That's the soul hollering, *Look up! There's more!*"

Paula and Lorenz spent three years mapping out the route—which would ultimately touch twenty-five countries—recruiting corporate sponsors, and acquiring the equipment they'd need, including two sturdy Burley tandems festooned with panniers to carry all their worldly goods. They launched their own non-profit, Bike for Breath, to benefit asthma research. Organizing the journey was a huge task, but as they chipped away at it things seemed to fall into place. "If you're on the right path, things come together. People are attracted to something exciting." A lawyer friend helped them set up their nonprofit, Paula was granted a sabbatical from her job teaching anthropology at the University of Washington, and the city of Bainbridge Island, Washington, where Lorenz works as an engineer, promised to hold his job for him.

Plant a tree and celebrate its birthday each year. If you don't have a yard, plant it in a pot. The point is to keep your life growing as fully and richly and fast.

Still, as the departure date approached, money was a concern. They'd raised seventy-five thousand dollars, but the Ebers took a hard line on where those funds should go. "That money was for asthma research, not to pay for a vacation around the world," Paula says. "If we'd been able to raise a million dollars, sure, we would have used some of it to finance the trip." So they went to Plan B: refinancing their mortgage.

They rented their house, found a sitter for their dog, and pushed off on May 7, 2003. Anya was thirteen and Yvonne, eleven. Their route began in Greece, headed north through Turkey, and circled back through Italy, Austria, Germany, Holland,

France, and England before heading west toward Poland, the Baltic states, Russia, and Mongolia to Beijing. They cheated only once, crossing the vast expanse of Siberia by train. After cycling through Taiwan, they island-hopped across the Pacific, touching down in Australia, New Zealand, and Tonga before completing the trip with a trans-America ride. By the time they clicked off their cyclometers for the very last time, it was sixteen months later and they'd logged an amazing 9,332 miles.

On a budget of about twenty-five dollars a day for each of them (airfare for four ran an additional seven thousand dollars), there weren't a lot of frills. They camped six days a week, treating themselves to a simple hotel on the seventh, when they'd do the laundry and send e-mails. At first, they didn't push too hard, happy to achieve twenty-five miles in a day; as they grew stronger, the number rose to around sixty. But on a journey like this, the physical strength needed is easily trumped by the mental strength required. At times, the world was utterly foreign, even to these savvy travelers, with no concierge to help sort it out. Far out in the countryside, with no knowledge of the local language, it could be frightening when things went bad. Cycling along Taiwan's sparsely populated east coast, they were having lunch at a palm-thatched hut when a magnitude-6.6 earthquake hit. Back on the road, Paula remembers, "We were snaking along the cliffs, aftershocks were moving the earth under our bikes, and we could see where the quake had dropped boulders the size of cars onto the road. If we hadn't been having lunch when the quake hit, we could have been under one of them."

Then on Tonga one night, Anya woke up screaming. A centipede had bitten her hand. Crouching over a guidebook by flashlight, they read the following sentence: "The bite of the molokau is not normally lethal to adults." It was terrifying. "We were not about to go to the hospital," Paula says. "It was the

kind of place you check in and never come out." With antihis-
tamine from their first-aid kit, they nursed Anya through the
night. By the next morning, they knew she would be fine.

"The trip was pretty much constant stress, constant adrenaline, until we got to Australia, New Zealand, and the US," Paula
says. "It was raining, snowing, or hailing, or it was 110 degrees,
or there were mosquitoes or horseflies—something that made
your body miserable every day." Just when they'd think they
couldn't go on, though, they'd have one of those experiences
that made the whole trip worthwhile.

Paula's most cherished day was the approach to China's
Great Wall. "Chickens were running across the road; people on
bicycles were pulling everything from mattresses to little stores.
Off on the horizon was this very faint line. All day, it grew bigger and bigger. It was overwhelming to feel the wall's immen-
sity in the midst of these snow-covered mountains, and feel the
history behind it."

Crossing the vast Gobi Desert in Mongolia was another high
point. "I've always felt the romance of nomadism," Paula says.
"Everything the Mongolians own can be put on a camel. They
don't have anything in terms of how we measure wealth, but
they have a rich spiritual life, a strong sense of community, the
freedom to live as they want." She stops to consider, then
laughs. "Of course, if I were to live in Mongolia for ten years, I
would probably not romance it in the same way."

On good days, the cycling was like a meditation—the
rhythm of the pedals, a beautiful landscape passing by, being
out in the air. On bad days, the whole family wanted a divorce.
"In the beginning, we had a lot of silly arguments," Paula says.
"You don't realize how little time an American family spends together. Suddenly we were in each other's faces 24/7." When
they hit Eastern Europe and Asia, the stress meter topped out.

At one time or another, everybody flipped and wanted to go home. Fortunately, they all picked different days.

What kept wooing them back was the exceptional experience. "On a bicycle, you become part of the place and people appreciate that you're making the effort to really see the country," Paula notes. "There was so much excitement, so much energy. You'd get to a point where you'd think this is too crazy, then the next day a teacher in Taiwan would invite you to stay at her house."

Among their two hundred pounds of baggage—clothes, tents, cooking equipment, food—hung in six panniers on the two bikes, was a small cache of textbooks, from which Lorenz and Paula homeschooled the girls every night. "Sometimes it was hard to sit down and teach after a long day on the road, but the girls were adamant. They didn't want to get left behind." And the journey itself was an education; they'd talk about Karl Marx and the ravages of communism as they cycled through the Baltic states.

It was an extraordinary year and a half. "Passing through colorful villages and gorgeous scenery, you felt like you were in heaven." And as they grew more confident of their ability to deal with whatever the world threw at them, they began to savor the difficulties, too. When people question exposing their daughters to danger, Paula says she felt safer on the back roads of Latvia then in some of the US cities they cycled through. "No one became seriously ill. No one got robbed, mugged, or attacked. The only real injury was when Yvonne broke her foot racing her sister in a youth hostel."

What they didn't realize during those challenging, amazing months on the road was that the hard part was still ahead of them: returning home. "It was a gift to have our jobs waiting for us," Paula says. "We came back to our house, our dog, our neighbors, everything the way we'd left it." The problem was, *they* weren't the same. They'd lived by their wits for a year and a half, and now normal American life seemed inconsequential, even boring.

Coach a kids' team. Whether it's the debate squad or junior varsity tennis, it'll widen your life—reconnecting you with a different generation if your own kids are grown, or giving you a better picture of the world your school-aged kids inhabit.

The trip had charted a new direction in their philosophy of life. "We lived without anything, then came back to a garage full of boxes and thought, *We didn't need all this stuff for a year and a half, why would we want it now?*" Lorenz started calling himself Lord of the Things, commenting that all he did was repair, maintain, and manage their possessions. They spent eight months getting rid of possessions, paring their lives down. The American dream felt like a nightmare. "People think if they just run a little faster on the treadmill, earn a little more money, they'll be ahead. But the new job means a longer commute, more expenses, more eating out, and they never get to the nirvana they're looking for."

Finding nirvana is what occupies the Holmes-Ebers these days. "Our ideas are all over the place, from going to Africa where Lorenz can help build communities to moving to a yurt in Mongolia. Anya wants to go to Ireland, grow vegetables, and become a Druid." Paula feels an obligation to repay some of the riches the world has shown them. Finding an adventure that works for everybody is the trick. "That was the lesson of the ride: You can't have people pulling in four directions." Right now, she and Anya are writing a book about their round-the-world trip. But they are determined not to live in the past with their pictures and memories. Paula says, "I want to have something else to talk about in six years that's just as exciting." No doubt they will.

Flight of Fancy

When she was forty-three, Mary Senft embarked on a project few men—and almost no women—ever undertake: building a high-performance airplane.

Mary's Lesson: *Stubbornness is underrated as a character trait. If you don't know you can't do something, you probably can.*

MARY SENFT TOOK her first airplane ride when she was two weeks old. Though her father quit flying when she was five, throughout her childhood Mary had a dream that she could fly, without wings. Once she took the yoke for the first time at twenty-nine, she never had that dream again. Now she was living it.

"My brother was taking flying lessons. At fourteen, he was too young to drive, so I'd drop my two girls with our mom, then drive him to the airport." Before she knew it, she was taking instruction, too. Mary, who worked as a probation officer, wasn't wealthy, but she knew her priorities. "It was either buy a new coat or fly for two hours. I could make that old coat do for another season."

When Mary earned her pilot's license, she entered a rarefied world: Fewer than 5 percent of pilots in the United States were women. Shortly after she turned forty, she took an even more extraordinary step and joined a much more exclusive club when she became an aircraft homebuilder. Again, it was a man in her life who got her to the starting gate.

"My first husband wanted me to be Susie Homemaker, and it was frustrating for me," Mary recalls. "We divorced when I was thirty." A year later she married the doctor who'd given her a flight physical. Otto, who was twenty-nine years older than Mary and also a pilot, encouraged her to pursue a career in the air. "One year, my Christmas present was to get my commercial license," Mary says. She went on to earn an instrument rating, an instructor's rating, and a rating to fly multi-engine aircraft. She even got a flight engineer's type rating for a Boeing 727. At that point, she and Otto imagined she would join a major airline.

Then came a turning point. "Otto had carotid surgery. Here's my best friend in the whole world hooked up to life support. It hit me hard, and I knew I had to get my priorities straight." He recovered, but Mary vowed that she would spend her life with Otto, not flying around the world for American or TWA. Still, she was restless at home. "We were living in Georgia, and at the time it wasn't proper for the wife of a physician to have a job," Mary remembers. "All our neighbors were going to work in the morning, and I was staying home going crazy." Otto, who had accepted a position as a flight surgeon for United Airlines, noticed his wife's restlessness.

Otto told Mary that he wanted to build a Lancair IV-P, a sophisticated 350-horsepower airplane. "I said, 'Fast airplanes kill pilots. I'm not sure I want to help you build anything that's going to kill us,'" Mary remembers. Otto had lost his medical, and couldn't fly anymore, so Mary would be pilot in command. And because of the 51 percent rule—the homebuilder-pilot must complete more than half of the work—Mary would have to get involved in the project.

Which is exactly what Otto intended.

Like most homebuilders, they started small, first journeying to the factory in Redmond, Oregon, where the Lancair kits are manufactured, then ordering the materials to build the tail. "It's the least expensive part, and if you screw it up, you can start over," Mary notes. "In the beginning, I told Otto I'd give him twenty hours a week on the airplane, but by the end of week two, I was having such a great time, I was working on it from eight to five every day."

Neither of them had ever built anything like an airplane before, and they were lucky to have a mentor, a retired mechanic named Bill whom they met through the Experimental Aircraft Association, a 170,000-member organization based in Oshkosh, Wisconsin, that supports homebuilders. "I had no basic skills," Mary says. "I was pretty good with a sewing machine and a vacuum cleaner, but an airplane? I figured, I'm a college-educated person, I should be able to learn this."

She was right. Mary discovered she had a real talent for the exacting work of composite construction, carefully shaping and forming layers of epoxy-soaked fiberglass cloth. And whatever she didn't know, Bill could teach her. "It was such fun to learn to use all these new tools," she says, "and to realize there was a real function for all that geometry and trigonometry I studied way back in high school and college."

It's an extraordinarily complex process, involving a whole host of disciplines from woodworking to electrical wiring. But the building went pretty smoothly. Otto worked on the Lancair on his days off, but Mary was clearly in charge. "I'm a perfectionist, and when we were laying up fiberglass, I came in the next morning and found three huge bubbles in it," she says, then adds, laughing, "I told Otto, no more glasswork for you!" After that, Otto spent his time sanding the fiberglass to prepare the airplane for painting.

Mary was forty-three when she started building the Lancair. Eighteen months later it was finished, an amazingly short completion time for any homebuilt, let alone a high-performance design capable of nearly the speed and altitude of a propjet airliner.

One of the dangers of homebuilding is that the pilot-builder gets so wrapped up in the construction process that she doesn't fly while the airplane is coming together. Then, eager to make the first flight, she takes off in a brand-new type of airplane, with deplorably rusty skills. Mary sidestepped that risk by hiring a professional test pilot to make the first flight. "I chose someone who was also a flight instructor, so I could get checked out in my own airplane."

In any case, she wanted the experience of seeing her creation take off. "It was the most awesome experience—better even than having a child," she says. "For eighteen months, we'd physically lifted every piece of that airplane. When I saw it go down the runway and lift off under its own power—there aren't words to describe the feeling."

When her airplane had been flying for six months, Mary embarked on another project that made the Lancair seem like child's play. She began to build a historic 1929 airplane, and this time there was no kit to buy, nor even any plans to work from. She only had photographs. The Alexander Eaglerock "Bullet" was the first aircraft to combine a single, low wing with retractable landing gear and a closed cockpit. Only eleven were built, none of which still exists today, and the plans were destroyed in a fire at the Smithsonian. Aviation pioneer Edith Foltz flew a Bullet to win second place in the first Powder Puff Derby, a famous women's air race. "My friend Bill had a piece of an original Bullet wing, and when people would visit the shop and ask about it, he'd tell them about the airplane. I heard that story fifty times and loved it."

This time it was Mary who approached Otto. "You need another project," she told him. He laughed and said, "Honey, what do you want to build?" Nine years later, the Bullet replica is still coming together. Mary hopes it will make its first flight in four months. She worked with an aeronautical engineer to analyze photographs of the plane. For the Lancair, Mary had to learn how to read blueprints; for the Bullet, she had to learn how to draw them.

"When it's finished, I'm going to fly it to air shows to tell two stories: the historical significance of the airplane and its importance for women," Mary says. "I also want to show people what you can do if you have a little tenacity."

Hire a personal shopper. Many big department stores, like Macy's, offer free consultants to help women and men find clothes that fit and flatter. Sign on for an introductory session, with a specific budget and mission in mind. Remember, you don't have to buy everything that's recommended, but you'll be surprised to see how good clothes you didn't pick look.

She's amused to realize how naive she was at the start of both projects. "I didn't know what I was getting into with either airplane. The second time, I figured if I could build the most sophisticated kit airplane on the market in eighteen months, surely I could build an airplane from photographs in three years. I was so stubborn, I wasn't going to quit."

While the Bullet was being born, Otto was dying. He had Alzheimer's, but as his world faded and dimmed, Mary kept him in her life. She'd send him to day care for half a day, then bring him to the shop to be with her while she worked for the other half. "One afternoon, the day-care group came out in their wheelchairs and walkers, and I gave a little talk," she remembers. "It was a good day for Otto, and he was so pleased." When he died two years ago, Mary had no regrets. "I do not begrudge the shortness of the time we had together," she says. "I'd do it all over again."

But she couldn't keep the airplane they'd dreamed up together. "After Otto died, I couldn't get back in the Lancair." She sold it to a test pilot, who's currently upgrading the plane with a turbine engine.

Today, at fifty-four, Mary is on the brink of completing the second project, and has never felt better. "At this age, we're like fine wine. At my flight physical six months ago, the doctor told me I was in really good shape," Mary says. "I'm not an athlete, but I have ten times as much energy as most people.

"My father died of Lou Gehrig's disease two days after his thirty-ninth birthday. I was twelve, and I realized that life is short and if I was going to do anything, I needed to get busy."

I checked in with Mary as the book was going to press. The Bullet hadn't flown yet, largely because building it had brought another exciting reinvention to her life: She was flying to Maui for a Valentine's Day wedding on the beach. The lucky groom? Bob Hanson, the engineer on the Bullet project.

First Ironman at Fifty-one

Celebrity hairdresser Louis Licari has another life, far from his luxurious hair salons. He's a triathlete.

Louis's Lesson: *Life is a big race: It's all about preparation and planning. If you do that right, success is a foregone conclusion.*

THE WORST THING about the accident was knowing it was about to happen, and not being able to do a thing about it. Louis Licari was seventy-five miles into a hundred-mile triathlon training ride when a landscaping truck pulled out of a gas station in Nyack, New York, and broadsided his bicycle. "I got slammed," he says. "I was in shock." The gas station owner ran out, saw the scene, and knew not to move the fallen rider. It was sprinkling rain, so he threw a tarp over Louis's chest while they waited for the ambulance. Meantime, Louis's trainer, who'd been riding a little ahead, circled back, saw the tarp, and thought Louis was dead. "I could hear Mike, and he was hysterical," Louis remembers. "I figured I was finished." Several hours later, in the emergency room of the local hospital, still strapped to a backboard, Louis could only look straight up. As he was wheeled in and out for MRIs and X-rays, he says, "I could see from Mike's eyes that the news wasn't good. I wiggled my toes and told myself, *At least I'm not paralyzed.*"

As it turned out, Louis was lucky. While three vertebrae in his neck were broken, there was no nerve damage. Fourteen weeks in a neck brace allowed the fractured bones to knit. But what couldn't be mended was Louis's plan to celebrate turning fifty by competing in the mother of all triathlons, the Hawaii Ironman. On the day of the crash, the race was just a month away. For ten years, Louis had focused his life on this goal, working out twenty-five hours a week, honing his swimming, running, and biking skills, entering shorter races. Now his dreams lay ruined, all because of a driver's momentary inattention.

Once Louis's injury had healed, it was frightening to think about getting back on the bike. It would have been very easy to walk away from the challenge he'd set himself. Louis already had a full life. One of the top hair colorists in the country, he runs a bicoastal business, employing 120 people in salons in New York and Beverly Hills. When Susan Sarandon, Jodie Foster, and Ellen Barkin need a touch-up, they come to him, and Louis appears regularly on the *Today* show, as a beauty and style correspondent.

Louis could have rejected the dangerous pursuit of road biking and returned to his first love, painting. But he didn't. As soon as the neck brace was removed, Louis was back to his Herculean training schedule. Not giving up on his goal was that important to him. "I truly believe that as we get older, our lives become smaller. We become so involved in work, we end up talking to the same ten people every day," he says. "Training and competing is the one thing that takes me completely away from my life and opens me up to a new set of people." He also loves his anonymity within the triathlon pack. "When I'm on the road, in bike shorts, with my helmet and sunglasses on, I am not Louis Licari, colorist to the stars. I'm just Louis, and it feels great."

> **Become an expert.** Pick a subject that's always intrigued you and learn all about it. Whether it's pirates or petunias, approach it from all angles—Google it, read books, rent DVDs. It could lead to a new passion; for sure, it'll make you smarter.

When he came to Manhattan from a small town in upstate New York, with a freshly minted fine arts degree from Syracuse University and an ambition to be a painter, he couldn't have imagined athletics taking center stage in his life. "I was a child of the 1960s," he says. "When other kids were playing sports, I went to Woodstock." His career as an athlete began casually and grew slowly. "I was married in my twenties, and my wife and I would run in Central Park." Divorced at thirty, Louis began entering races and discovered he had a real talent for running. Then he got a bike and did a few AIDS fund-raiser rides. He was two-thirds of the way toward a triathlon. When he was in his forties, someone introduced him to Mike Gostigian, a three-time Olympic pentathlete, and Louis auditioned to become one of Mike's personal training clients. "Mike watched me run and said, 'Wow.' We did a bike ride and he was less impressed. When we got in the pool, I saw him turn white. I was a horrible swimmer." Luckily, Mike loves a challenge; Louis was in.

At the same time Louis was discovering his athleticism, he was forging a new career. "I didn't have the worldliness or ability to sell myself you need to be a painter." Louis was nearing thirty, still waiting tables to support his art. "That was just not acceptable." He began to consider other careers, eventually enrolling in beauty school. "My hairdressing abilities were nil," he says. "Everything I did looked like a cake that flopped." He got a job as a shampoo boy at Pierre Michel, where he discovered there was a specialty tailor-made for him: hair colorist. "What I knew and loved was color. I had the eye, I just needed to understand hair dye rather than paint." He became well-known salon owner Robert Renn's assistant. One day, when *Vogue* cover model Rosie Vela arrived late for an appointment, Louis got to color her hair. She loved it, and word spread. "Models started coming to me. Then I turned Robert De Niro gray for *Once Upon a Time in America*." At thirty-seven, Louis opened his own salon.

As Louis's business flourished, so did his passion for athletics. When he started entering mini triathlons around age forty, he knew about the Hawaii Ironman but never thought he'd be equal to the world-famous race, which combines a 2.4-mile ocean swim, a 112-mile bike ride, and a 26.2-mile run. "Honestly, I don't know where the chutzpah came from," he recalls, "but one day, I just said, 'I'm going to do it.'" He entered longer and tougher races, enrolled in Ironman training camps, got up before dawn and drilled with Mike six mornings a week. "The thing about me is, I don't give up. No matter what, I show up and finish," Louis says. "If I have to crawl across the finish line, I will. Ironman was my mantra."

Finally, after the healing and the physical therapy, a rigorous training routine that built his body back from the accident, the day arrived for which Louis had waited a decade plus a year: the Hawaii Ironman. "I was frightened like you would not believe until the race started," Louis says. It was a foggy day, and the ocean was rougher than it'd been for the Ironman in years. Competitors swim out to a sailboat, keeping the mast in sight above the crests of the waves, and swim back. The rollers were so high and the fog so thick, Louis couldn't see his target. "When one of the lifeguards on surfboards paddled by, I'd shout, 'Which way?'" Louis figures he put in 3 miles trying to complete the 2.4-mile swim. "Talk about scary. If you don't finish the swim in a certain time, you're disqualified. Once I got through the swim, I knew I'd finish."

The Ironman, Louis notes, is uniquely geared to the midlife competitor, the seasoned athlete. "It's a matter of pacing yourself, holding on to your energy, eating right, and having the right discipline, all of which demand maturity." One of the best moments Louis remembers was spotting the age—a decade older than Louis's—inked on the calf of another competitor who ran past effortlessly. "It's so great to think *That's who I want to be,*" Louis says. "I really believe in mentors, following those who have what you want. You don't have to be a genius to do this, you just have to copy behavior."

He says he doesn't even remember the time for his first Ironman, or the second one, which he did the following year. "They weren't brilliant" is all he'll say. But he is competitive enough to be looking forward to turning fifty-five next year: "Then I'll be the baby of the next five-year age bracket. After the Ironman, you're high as a kite," Louis says. "The only thing you can think about is, *I can do better. I can do better.*"

When we talk, Louis is training for his third Ironman, four months away. Right now, he's nursing a stress fracture in his right ankle, which he casually tells me "is breaking from the inside out." It doesn't stop him from competing in the Hudson Valley's first mini triathlon of the season. He trusts his gurus—his doctors, his trainer, Mike, and his physical therapist, Dr.

Lorenzo Gonzales, who works with him three times a week. "He's gotten me through every injury, and I've had more than a few," Louis says. Louis has just bought a place on the beach in Los Angeles so he can swim in the ocean when he's working in the Beverly Hills salon. He hasn't had time to paint in years, and that's okay. "Frankly, I don't have time to miss it."

Louis is convinced that the Ironman is a lot like life: "The hardest part is getting to the starting line." It's all about preparation and planning; if you do that smartly, succeeding at the actual event is a foregone conclusion. How long will he be able to keep competing? "I have no idea," he says. "I've seen guys do it in their eighties. I don't know if that will be me, but I will always be a triathlete at some level."

Cave Woman

A small inheritance allowed Cindy Butler to join a very exclusive community of divers—those who swim deep into underwater caves.

Cindy's Lesson: *What's the best way to spend an inheritance? By investing in yourself.*

WHEN CINDY BUTLER graduated from nursing school at twenty-five, she figured she was finished with formal education and had embarked on a career that would suit her throughout life. Her skills were marketable just about anywhere, and nursing offered enough variations, from home health care to a hospital ICU, to keep her interested. She was right: Her work never stopped being rewarding, but as she approached midlife, she began to crave something more.

Opportunity knocked at forty-one when Cindy received a small inheritance from her stepmother. She didn't want for the basics. Divorced with no children, she owned a home in a central Florida community. The windfall presented a chance to season her life with a dash of adventure. The only question in Cindy's mind was whether to go up or down: Should she learn to fly or scuba dive? "I was in my forties and felt it was time to do something different with my life, get out of the rut." In the end, the decision came down to dollars. "Scuba diving looked inexpensive," Cindy says, adding, "Boy, was I wrong. Eight years later, I probably have twenty thousand dollars in gear." Nevertheless, it's money well spent. Becoming a diver has opened the door to a new activity that gives her both a mission and a passion.

> **Talk to a stranger.** Vow to start up a conversation with one person you don't know every day—waiting in the checkout line at Home Depot, at the post office, dropping the kids off at school. Most days, this will just help pass the time. But eventually, you'll click with somebody. Too often, by midlife we stop adding friends. Consider this the interview phase to new friendships.

Cindy signed up for a weekend certification course near her home in Haines City, Florida, adding course after course. "I went directly from open-water diving to advanced open water, then took a wreck diving course in the Keys," she says. After posting a request for a dive buddy at an online group for wreck divers, she met the guy who changed her life. "Bill took me into my first cave, at Manatee Springs. It was amazing," she says. "I was a *Star Trek* fan, and as a kid I wanted to be an astronaut. When he turned out the light, being weightless surrounded by black water was like being in space. I was hooked." Open-water diving seemed too tame after this experience. Cindy knew she wanted more. But her second experience wasn't so magical: She got disoriented when the water silted out and visibility closed down. As she made her way out of the cave, she re-members, "I was close to panicked." Cindy understood that she had to learn this potentially lethal sport right. "The guy who ran the shop where I was training was a complete cave man. The next day, I got in front of him, stomped my foot, and said, 'You have got to teach me how to cave dive or I'm going to get killed.'"

Since that day, Cindy has not stopped learning. First, she took a full year of cave diving instruction. "I had only done fourteen open-water dives when I started caving, and my in-structor knew his job was to slow me down." By that time, she'd discovered she wanted to do more than simply dive for fun. She yearned to find new caves. "Some people cave dive for the thrill, like a roller-coaster ride. Then there are people like me, who do it because it's a passion."

While Cindy was learning to dive, her sister was losing a battle with breast cancer. "She had one round of chemo while I was doing the open-water training. She started another round when I began cave diving, and only lived three months." Cindy was devastated. "She was only fifty. That was a real eye-opener to me," Cindy says. "I decided to stop making the four-hour trip up to Gainesville every weekend to dive. I found a job and moved there."

Cindy's second home in her adopted city of Gainesville is Suwannee River State Park, where she co-leads a volunteer dive team that is mapping a network of underwater caves. She spends all day Saturday and Sunday lowering herself into sink-holes that might lead to caves, exploring a watery underground realm. Her team has discovered two new caverns. "It's about the only primary exploration you can do on the planet anymore," Cindy says. Her work at Suwannee has earned her the National Association for Cave Diving's conservation award. As a serious cave diver, she's one of a very elite group. "Among hard-core explorers, there are probably only four or five women in Florida. It sounds romantic, but it's hard work—writing reports, putting maps together, tallying survey data, giving lectures for the Park Service. Most women have other things going on in their lives—kids and grandkids and husbands."

One caving activity leads to another. At a cave system where she guides evening dives during the week, she met Tom Morris, one of the leading experts on cave animals, which include albino crayfish, blind shrimp, and other crustaceans. "I started helping him collect specimens, and it got me interested." Since then, she's taken courses, read books, and attended state park workshops to learn more about the creatures. Collecting water samples to check for nitrate levels from nearby dairy farms has sparked an interest in water quality. "That got me into the whole ecology thing. Once I learn something, it takes me to a new subject."

Last year, Cindy fulfilled her dream to visit the largest cave system in the world, on Mexico's Yucatán Peninsula. "It was a blast," she reports. "My area of expertise is dark water and small caves. I guess I wound up with that reputation because if there's water in it, I'll go anywhere." Using satellite maps, her team zeroed in on sites that looked like cave entrances. Then, locating the sites with a GPS, they hacked through the jungle to find them. Cindy and her friend Donna discovered a new cave in Mexico, which she named Little Fishes. "It's awesome to be the first person into a place, and very humbling. You realize how big the world is," she says. "Sump diving, where you go through water and then come up into a dry cave, is like finding another world. Nobody has ever breathed that air or walked on that land. No insects, no sounds. It's very eerie."

The only injury Cindy has had is a broken hand. "I snapped a bone climbing into a sinkhole in Mexico. I wouldn't let them cast it because I wanted to dive the rest of the week." She's extremely mindful of the safety precautions divers should take, such as always having a line that can lead you back to the cave entrance. "I try to avoid harrowing experiences," she says. "You don't just get injured cave diving. If it's too harrowing, you're dead."

Over eight years of diving, Cindy's enthusiasm has never flagged. "We're always looking for a pattern in the sinkholes, trying to connect the caves. When you do, it's a mystery solved."

Slowly but surely, diving has taken over Cindy's life: She's moved and switched jobs to have more time in the caves, and new people have come into her life via a shared passion for caving. "All my buddies are divers now. Pretty much every weekend, somebody is staying at my house, and when I travel to dive I always have a place to stay. I have friends all over the world." Cindy recently landed a new job as a hospice nurse. "I drive around doing home visits all day. I love being outdoors, and when I'm on the road, I'm always looking for clumps of trees in a farmer's field that suggest a sinkhole." Her nine-to-five hours leave weekends free for cave exploration at Suwannee. When she turns fifty in a month, she'll celebrate with a group of friends on a caving trip to Tennessee.

Right now, cave diving is keeping her young, but Cindy knows that eventually she'll age out of the sport. "People can open-water dive until they die, but doing exploration work in the jungle, climbing in and out of sinkholes, wearing gear that weighs as much as I do . . . I won't be able to do that forever," she says. "I do notice it's harder to stay in shape than it was ten years ago, and to keep the weight off. When we do a tough trip—twelve to fourteen hours in a cave—I'm wiped out. It makes me feel better when the younger people are exhausted, too." But, she also finds it a great motivation to stay fit. "I'm usually the oldest person on a caving trip, and being with younger people energizes me." Her dive buddy is sixty-one, the oldest cave explorer she knows. Meantime there's no shortage of worlds to conquer. "Australia has great caves that I'd really love to see. And Mexico is practically hollow. I could go down there and dive the rest of my life."

Learn to drive a stick. Come on, it's not as hard as you think, and you don't have to be sixteen with a newly minted license to learn. It's one of life's little accomplishments that makes you feel street-smart—a stepping-stone to learning other new skills.

But best of all, Cindy's embarked on a never-ending course of study. "Before I started diving, I didn't know anything about surveying or how to make a map," she says. "Now I'm studying biology, ecology, the cave critters. What's really wonderful is not just the experiences I've had, but all that I've learned." Currently she's setting up a cave diving museum and reference library. "There's no central location for information about cave exploration. One time, we found out a cave we'd carefully surveyed had already been mapped. It was a total waste of time." She and her partners are planning a climate-controlled mobile office to house the collection of documents and dive gear, as well as a Web site. "That's the new mission," she says. "Like I said, this is a hobby that just keeps expanding."

CHAPTER 9

Finding Your
Heart's Desire

I WOULDN'T SUGGEST THAT anybody change their lives the way we did," Karen Masell tells me with a laugh. Then she reconsiders. "Well, maybe once in your life, you need to act impulsively." Burned out by many years at the same jobs—she is an elementary school teacher, he as a contractor—Karen and her husband, Dick, relocated to Colorado without a game plan, when she was fifty-six and he was sixty. Their house in Naples, Florida, sold within weeks of being listed, forcing them to sort through more than two decades of memorabilia and possessions in just two months. "We didn't even know where we were going to live," Karen remembers. The Masells rented a condo in Breckenridge and only then began to figure out their new lives. The first time I talked to Karen, it was a year and a half later. They'd moved closer to Denver, and they knew the location was right—they loved the craggy grandeur of the Rockies—but were dismayed to find that despite months of searching, neither of them had found a job. Both yearned for

work that would challenge their intellect and spark their enthusiasm. Tired of putting up trophy houses in a wealthy Gulf
Coast city, Dick dreamed of building log homes. Karen wanted
to set her educational credentials to work in a new way, perhaps by working for a textbook publisher. But, she says, their
ages seemed to defeat their efforts. "We'd apply for jobs for
which we're well qualified, and get no response."

Karen and Dick were at the tenderest point of life reinvention, when the brave, new future is still fuzzy, and what you've
given up can loom much larger than what you hope to gain.
Karen's spirit was still upbeat, but she was quick to critique the
rashness with which they'd made the change and second-guess
some of their decisions. "I wish we'd bought right away instead
of renting," she says. "We talked about redoing a house and
then selling it." That would have provided a sense of purpose
and a revenue stream, as well as rooting them in their new
town. "I should have started volunteering right away, to get involved in the community," she adds, speculating that she could
have made contacts that would have led to a new job. She was
anxious about their future, hoping they could make a new life
against the rugged landscape that so moved them.

Things worked out for Dick and Karen. Six months later, she
was teaching in the afternoons and using the mornings to flex
her creative spirit by writing about child development and
launching a small business to sell custom-made bulletin boards.
Dick had found a job at a building company based in Denver.
During those difficult months when they couldn't even land an
interview, much less a job, it would have been easy for the
Masells to turn tail and move back to Naples, where they had
friends and business contacts. Now, on the far side of that scary,
unsettling time, they were glad they'd honored their dream and
stayed put. They had made it past the toughest, most discouraging period of reinvention.

The Reinvention Crazies: When the Dream Feels Like a Nightmare

Almost everyone I talked to in researching this book experienced a time of uncertainty on their way to a satisfying future. As they described their doubts and fears, I recognized the symptoms because I'd suffered them myself—living to a backbeat of worry that could escalate to panic on a bad day.

For me, the crazies struck as soon as I left my job. For the first few weeks, I sat at my computer terror-stricken, wondering if I'd just made an enormous mistake. All the confidence I'd felt executing major decisions involving millions of dollars as editor in chief of a magazine had evaporated. Suddenly, I had less self-assurance than an eighth-grader at the first school dance. I questioned whether I'd be a success as a freelance writer. Would people offer me interesting work? Would I be able to deliver the kind of smart, insightful stories that would invite encore assignments? In those first few weeks, the future seemed less than rosy. How could I write a competent article when I couldn't even get my e-mail to work?

When people asked me how the new life was going, I flashed a big, phony smile. "Couldn't be better," I'd say, feeling like an imposter. Even Steve never suspected that I was one bad day away from running back to New York to take a job, any job. It was probably a mixture of self-preservation and pride that kept my game face firmly in place—I thought if I expressed any doubts, that would whip them up into a self-fulfilling prophecy. If I admitted the possibility of failure, I would fail.

I was lucky. For me, the crazies only lasted about a month. By then, I'd figured out how to run my computer (after an early-morning phone tutorial with my old IT director, a kind and generous man) and was happily at work on my first assignments. I missed the camaraderie of having a staff around me every day, but I loved my new office, a little building behind our house with a view of the barn and the parade of wildlife—turkeys, deer, groundhogs, and the occasional black bear—commuting across the yard. Doing errands was a novel and appealing enterprise when Steve and I headed out together. And when my articles were well received, I had a growing sense of pride in successfully deploying a new skill.

> **Take a pottery class.** Get your hands dirty and get in touch with your creativity. Working with clay is a great metaphor for remodeling your life, and it's a much more forgiving medium for the artistically challenged than watercolors or oils.

When I'd run into other people who were reinventing their lives, like me, they always concentrated on the good stuff—the rewards of the new city, the new job, the new baby, the new mate. Like me, they never mentioned the reinvention crazies. Maybe it's a natural reflex. When somebody asks you how you are, they expect to hear a quick and breezy "Fine, thanks," not a catalog of complaints. But I also think we stick to the Pollyanna version of our reinvention stories because we suspect we're alone in suffering sleepless nights worrying whether we've made the right choice. The minute I mentioned my own dark days, the floodgates would open, and my fellow reinventers would cop to them, too. Mostly the crazies boiled down to one primal fear: *Can I make this new life work?*

What finally dawns on us is that change is hard and negative thoughts are natural; everybody has them. The crazies may be an epidemic among reinventers, but it's not a fatal disease. It can be tough surviving the crazies, though, when you think everybody else is gliding blissfully into a bright new future. It's a relief to know you're normal, that the crazies are the head cold of reinvention—everybody suffers from time to time.

We need to demystify the process, talk about the fears, so that reinventers don't have to go it alone. When Betty Rollin wrote about being treated for breast cancer in the early 1970s, it started a conversation about a disease that until then had dared not speak its name. Before you knew it, there were support groups to help women through the frightening days of diagnosis and treatment. The women didn't just swap life experiences; they brainstormed ways to combat the disease on a much grander scale. Fund-raising drives were launched; supporters biked, ran, and walked their way to hundreds of millions of dollars of research money. We should take a lesson from the courage and resolve of these women, who showed that you can triumph over a much bigger problem than a wobbling reinvention.

The Power of Sharing Our Stories

We Life Entrepreneurs are still at the whispering stage. We need to talk about the scary stuff, so that when the crazies strike, nobody assumes his idea is bad and he's destined to fail. It's starting to happen. With so many boomers remaking their lives, chatty Web sites are springing up to encourage the conversation, like Aginghipsters.com or Boomerwomenspeak.com. Then there's the burgeoning field of life coaches, launched to assist in solving work and relationship quandaries. In the United States today, there are more than fifteen thousand of these self-help professionals, who will provide motivation and strategic thinking for men and women contemplating life changes.

Laura Berman Fortgang, a life coach I interviewed during my own period of angst, is the author of *Now What? 90 Days to a New Life Direction*. She advises using that time frame as an assessment period during which you will not worry about, or even measure, success. For ninety days, you do your best to make intelligent decisions and execute your new life plan. Then, at the end of three months, you sit down and see where you are. It's a good way to postpone the crazies until a time when, if you're lucky, they no longer make sense. Another life coach I spoke with pointed out that what's crazy is *not* experiencing doubts and fears when you're taking such a big step. Sometimes the worries are constructive, pointing toward weak points in your life plan.

> **Rent *Flight of the Phoenix*.** After crashing in the desert, a small band of passengers craft a crude flying wing out of the wreckage and save their own lives. I prefer the original 1965 version, with Jimmy Stewart, to the jumbled 2004 remake, but either conveys the message that anything is possible.

Of course, the bigger the change, the scarier it can be. Taking up a new pastime, whether it's woodworking or playing golf, can be frustrating at times, but it's not worrisome. Change your work life or your family situation, though, and you're reengineering the underpinnings of your life. The ultimate remedy is to listen to your heart. If you can reach past the doubts and fears, deep into the core of your being, you'll know whether the crazies are telling you something—that you're on the wrong path—or whether you're suffering normal psychological growing pains. All of the successful Life Entrepreneurs I've talked with had one thing in common: They shared a strongly held conviction that their new path was right. Beyond the panic du jour, this confidence burned steadily like a pilot flame, despite troubles that might reduce them to tears or leave them tossing and turning in the wee hours—negative cash flow in a new business, the first big fight in a fledgling marriage, a disappointing grade in a new degree program. If they could feel the encouraging warmth of that little flame, they could put their fears aside and concentrate on making the reinvention work.

Taking Care of Your Number One Asset: You

You have to guard that flame by taking care of yourself. The crazies don't just prey on your mind, but can affect your health as well. No matter how all-consuming your reinvented life may be, be sure to make time for whatever nourishes you. Maybe it's a spiritual practice like meditation or yoga or Pilates or prayer. Maybe it's a soothing pastime such as gardening or baking. Whatever gentles your mind deserves at least an hour of your day, every day, no matter how busy you are.

The wise reinventer exercises and eats better than ever before. This is a critical time to nourish both body and soul. Think of yourself as being in training. A big life change can be the psychological equivalent of a marathon; be sure you're keeping your body and mind in top form to complete it.

I hadn't been sick in years, but after I quit my job I went down with three colds, one after the other. I asked Pamela Peeke, MD—one of the nation's leading stress gurus and the author of a number of books on how to stay fit and healthy after forty—about this. She told me that my experience was typical for anybody living through a period of magnified life stress. "The immune system has a refractory period. You can smack it around, and it fights and fights to keep you in balance," she said. "But eventually too much of the stress hormone cortisol floating around in your system takes its toll, usually two to four weeks after the initial insult." She was right on the money. I got sick two weeks after leaving my job. Once my mind settled down, though, my body did, too, and after that I cruised through a bitter winter with nary a sniffle.

Charlie Paddock is a seasoned Life Entrepreneur with some good strategies for handling fears and doubts, developed during a lifetime of reinventions. In his late twenties, after serving in Vietnam, he left a career in the air force and returned to college to earn a PhD in computer information systems, working four part-time jobs to support his wife and two daughters. A decade later, he reinvented himself again, after suffering a tragic life-altering year during which both of his parents died and his wife asked for a divorce. "My life fell apart," Charlie recalls. "I couldn't write, I couldn't even think." He took a deep breath and reformulated his life by moving to Las Vegas—"I didn't want to stay in Phoenix and watch my wife date"—where he taught at a local university. Then, at forty-one, he took a flier, leaving a faculty position to become an actor. "I'd always wanted to do it, and I figured now, when I was single, was the time." He found enough work, mostly in commercials, to support himself. In 1994, he remarried and moved to Salt Lake City, where his new wife worked as a textbook sales rep. Shazam, another life change. For a decade, Charlie became Mr. Mom to their three children. Now, at fifty-seven, father of five and grandfather of twelve, he's ready to return to teaching. To prepare himself, he hit the books and learned a new programming language so he'd be up to speed on computers and technology. The first time we talked, he'd landed only one interview. Six months later, he's teaching part-time and working at Starbucks. "Having been out of the workforce makes it hard. There's suspicion about why I left and why I now want back in," he says. "And they're looking at new PhDs who are cheaper to hire and, as they see it, more pliable." Charlie may be navigating the crazies, but he's far from discouraged. His ever-changing life has taught him a valuable lesson. "When I advise students, I always tell them to worry less about your life and try to make yourself a good person." He adds, "I never believed I'd be doing one thing for the rest of my life." Charlie hopes to write a book about his experience as Mr. Mom. "As I look back, the greatest thing I've done is putting good kids in the world."

What If You Can't Answer the Fundamental Question: *What's Next?*

There's another group of Life Entrepreneur wannabes for whom the crazies would be a dream come true, because it would mean they were embarked on a new life plan. These are people who are dissatisfied with their lives but can't envision the change that will reward them. They are the men and women of the traditional midlife crisis. They feel the need for change—often acutely—but don't have a script for the next chapter of their lives.

Instead, they find themselves replaying that postcollege cliché—only now it's not our parents but our children who shake their heads and say, "Poor Dad, he just hasn't found himself yet." One friend who was having difficulty envisioning a new path that would revitalize his life described it as being in the Doldrums, a windless area of the South Pacific so named by sailors for the way their spirits sagged as their ships sat becalmed in the hot, muggy air. It's a perfect metaphor for someone in full-blown midlife crisis: *I need a new direction for my life, but I'm not going anywhere.*

There are a number of reasons why it can be surprisingly tough to figure out the next step, even for a seasoned midlifer. Often it's a career move that stymies a potential Life Entrepreneur. He knows he isn't happy at his current job—maybe it never satisfied, but with the obligations of a growing family, he's never had the option of changing it before. And he's been so shuttered into it, putting his head down and getting the work done year in and year out, that he's never allowed himself to think about what really makes him tick. Or maybe, as with so many people these days, the reinvention is being forced on her: She's been downsized out of a job, possibly a job she liked quite a lot, in a shrinking industry that doesn't hold the promise of a similar position at another company. Forced out of an appealing job, it's hard to move past mourning your bad luck to envisioning even more pleasing work.

The Examined Life: Road Map to a Better Future

This is a time to think deeply about what moves and motivates you. How can you combine your aspirations and your skills to find a job that makes you happy to go to work in the morning?

A friend of mine, Jeri Sedlar, wrote a book about how to retool your career at midlife that addresses this very issue. Owners of an executive search and transition coaching firm, Jeri and her husband, Rick Miners, encourage clients to think about their "drivers"—the elements of their personality that must be satisfied in order to make a job rewarding to them. Their book, *Don't Retire, Rewire!* lists eighty-five different drivers, from the pleasure of accomplishment to the need for recognition to a thirst for adventure. Think about what is most meaningful to you. Is it how much money you earn? How creative your job is? Whether the work you do helps others? When you've begun to identify what really motivates you, you're ready to tackle the task of figuring out what kind of work matches your aspirations.

Here's a list of questions to ask yourself. (And bear in mind, this is a short list, just designed to prime the pump. Part of the exercise is figuring out a personal list of questions that defines what's important to you.)

- Is it important for me to keep learning at my job?
- Am I fulfilled by working for an organization that helps others?
- Is it critical that I call my own shots?
- Do I prefer working with other people, or am I happiest when completing a project on my own?
- Which is more important to me: the comfort of a secure position or the thrill of taking risks?
- Is making a certain amount of money critical?

Keep your answers honest—what you really feel, as opposed to what you think you should feel—and let each answer lead to more questions. Before you know it, you'll have a map of your personality against which you can measure various jobs.

I've used the example of work, because it's at the heart of the majority of balky reinventions I've encountered. But you can use the same analysis to contemplate other changes, too. The key to arriving at the right answer is posing the right questions.

It's Now or Never: The Flash Point

You can ponder a reinvention, analyze it, plan it down to the last detail. But none of that counts unless you push the start button. Dreaming about an exciting new life is pleasurable, no-risk, so seductive that if you're not careful it can become an end in itself. You can literally think a life reinvention to death. Imagining how great it would be to move to Montana, plant a grove of fruit trees, or open a B&B can draw you into Someday Syndrome—staking your satisfaction on a virtual future that somehow never quite takes shape.

Amid the distraction and bustle of day-to-day life, it's easy to endlessly postpone taking action. What makes the difference for most successful Life Entrepreneurs is an aha! moment—an instant of epiphany or a telling experience that motivates them to launch a big life change. I call it the flash point. Just as we all remember where we were when we heard that President Kennedy had been shot, or when we watched Neil Armstrong take that first bounding step onto the moon, many Life Entrepreneurs forever recall the moment they decided to go for it.

> **Buy a bike.** There's nothing like sailing through the air much faster than you could walk or even run to bring out the kid in you. It's great exercise for body and mind. Wear a helmet.

My own flash point came one winter morning when I was having breakfast with a colleague. Over yogurt and granola at a favorite cafe near our offices, she told me that her husband had just suffered a recurrence of prostate cancer. They hoped a new round of treatment would keep the disease at bay for a good many years. My husband, Steve, had had a prostatectomy seven years earlier and was cancer-free. But we both knew there are no guarantees. *What if he gets sick? Or what if something happens to me?* I suddenly found myself thinking. I didn't want to look back with regret at the way we'd led our lives. At the time, I was deep into Someday Syndrome: I'd been talking about my big life plan—to quit commuting and try writing instead of editing—for years. I told friends I was going to do it when our daughter finished college, after that last big tuition check had been written and cashed. But once she graduated, I just kept reporting to work. I needed an event to break the strong gravitational pull of a comfortable job, a steady income, a secure health plan. That breakfast was my wake-up call. At the end of the week, I resigned.

Sometimes the flash point isn't of your own doing: A number

of reinventers have told me that getting fired turned out to be the best day of their career. Tossed into the deep end of the pool, they swam to an exciting new life. For those of us who have to create our own flash point, it can be tough. If you're stuck at the starting gate, it can help to talk to successful Life Entrepreneurs. Call up a friend who's just made a big life change and invite him to lunch. Ask your book group to read Anne Tyler's *Back When We Were Grownups,* in which a fifty-three-year-old woman questions the choices she's made in her life. Or cruise blogs by other fledgling Life Entrepreneurs. Type "midlife reinvention" into Google's blog search, and you'll find quite a few. Whatever route you choose, the point is to get your reinvention to the talking stage, to test-drive it with family and friends, make it feel real.

Choice: An Embarrassment of Riches

Choice itself can be unsettling, even immobilizing. When there are so many possibilities, it becomes impossible to settle on just one. One Life Entrepreneur I talked to told me about a postdivorce experience that's a wonderful metaphor for the issue of choice. "I walked into Target shortly after my separation to buy some towels. I wasn't going to make a big deal out of it, just pick up some towels and go home," he says. "Suddenly I faced this *wall* of towels—all different colors and patterns. It was overwhelming. I couldn't deal with the choices and I just left the store."

Often, casting off from the known—whether it's a job or a relationship—can carry you into a sea of choices so vast, their sheer number can threaten to swamp your reinvention. And this is one place where all the experience that precedes midlife doesn't do us any favors. As we proceed through life, every choice we make narrows the succeeding options. We pick a major at college, and that suggests a type of career. We accept a job offer and begin building an area of expertise. By the time we're forty or fifty, our lives are defined by the choices we've been making for the past twenty or thirty years. We're so used to considering only the "sensible" choices—those that lie within the ever-narrowing field that's defined by a cascade of decisions we've already made—that we've gotten out of practice at taking a broader view. When we were eighteen or twenty, we had to decide what to do with our lives. At that time, the horizon seemed almost infinite. Now, with an identifiable set of skills and proclivities, and a track record of experiences and successes, we're tempted to think only of "logical" next steps.

But the best thing about a reinvention is often the way it surprises and delights you. As one woman told me, "I never imagined I could run a triathlon; I never even thought of myself as an athlete." There's something invigorating about pursuing an unexpected new path, whether it's taking up painting or writing, adopting a child, or marrying after four decades as a singleton. It can make you feel invigorated, revitalized . . . young. The trick is to make sure it's a surprise that satisfies, not one that is simply a stunt.

But how do you close the chasm between not knowing what you want and crafting a new life plan? One method is to work with a life coach. Many of them counsel their clients over the phone, and some offer workshops on how to make successful changes. If you do decide to hire a professional, choose your coach with care. It's a rapidly growing field, one that isn't regulated by law. The International Coach Federation credentials coaches, and the organization's Web site is a good starting place for your search. Once you've zeroed in on a coach (many of them have Web sites, which can give you a sense of their accomplishments and whether they sound sympatico), ask to talk to some of the clients he or she has counseled.

For self-starters who prefer to go it alone, there are a growing number of organizations that can help, such as The Transition Network, which offers lectures and workshops for women
over fifty who are contemplating life changes. You can simulate
some of the exercises you'd complete with a coach or in a
workshop. One interesting way is to adopt an idea from Bill
Gates. For more than twenty years, Gates has been going on
solo retreats twice a year that he calls "Think Week." He spends
the time holed away in a waterfront cottage in the Pacific Northwest, reading briefing papers on various aspects of Microsoft's
business and trends in the computer field. Think Week ensures
that in the day-to-day running of Microsoft, Gates doesn't lose
sight of the bigger picture. The product of his intense reading
week is hundreds of e-mails he dispatches to colleagues, plus a
Think Week summary and reading list that he distributes to his
senior staff. Imagine devoting that same time and attention to
your own future.

> **Step away from the screen.** Unplug the TV for a month, but don't
> just go cold turkey; plan how you'll spend your time. Sign up for dance
> lessons, get a stack of novels you've been meaning to read, dust off the
> Trivial Pursuit board, map out new daily walks. Make sure at least one
> evening a week features a brand-new activity. When you plug the TV
> back in, you'll have a host of pastimes competing for your attention.

Your retreat could be solo, or you could put together a small
group of friends who all want to change their lives. If you can't
afford to be away for a week, try a weekend. The key to success is using the retreat to clear your head of all the static of
everyday life—the demands on your time, the needs of your
loved ones. Start with a clean page and begin to think about
what's important to you. Dream big. Craft an ideal life plan—

what you'd do if money, time, education, family obligations were not a factor. Once you have a dream plan, you can measure it against the realities of life, then fine-tune it to be doable. It's like a sculpture. If you start big, you can always carve it down to size. But if you begin with too small a piece of marble, your sculpture is doomed to failure.

Your required reading can be a lot more exciting than Bill Gates's stack of briefing papers. Take along the biographies of your favorite players in history—from Marie Curie to Katharine Graham, from the Dalai Lama to Lance Armstrong. Reading about other people's lives will inspire you in reinventing yours—the obstacles they encountered, how they kept their faith in themselves.

As you put your plan into action, remember this motto: *Think big, start small.* Once you've figured out the kind of change you want to make, there may be a way to test-drive it before committing fully to the course. Often volunteer work can offer a window into a new professional life, for example. Say you're considering a second career as a teacher. Tutoring in an English as a second language program could reveal whether teaching will be as rewarding as you imagine. If you're thinking about having a child, you could babysit for a relative or friend's children, or volunteer in the child care at your synagogue or church.

Remember, too, that you don't have to have the picture of your new life perfectly formed in your mind when you begin. There's nothing wrong with a few blurry edges. As you move forward, it's important to be open to options, mindful that you'll have to make adjustments, rework your plan. Once you become comfortable with change, it can become a wonderfully creative force.

Finally, avoid the kind of "blinders thinking" that limits our vision with empty but discouraging phrases like "Oh, I could never do that" or "That would never work" that keep us from finding our heart's desire. When things seem tough, it's easy to descend into hopelessness. Resist that. One of the characters in Dan Brown's novel *Angels and Demons* uses the trick when solving puzzles of "remembering the answer," which assumes she knows it, rather than "finding the answer," which suggests she might not.

And on a bad day, consider that your right to reinvent is written into the foundation of our government by one of our country's foremost Life Entrepreneurs, Thomas Jefferson: The pursuit of happiness is an inalienable right. Make it your declaration of independence, too.

Keep in Contact with *Tomorrow*'s Life Entrepreneurs. For more about the lives and works of the forty-five women and men profiled in this book—Web addresses for their businesses and nonprofits, updates on their doings—visit susancrandell.com.

APPENDIX

Sources and Resources

Here's a list of organizations, books, Web sites, and other resources that have given me smart information, something new to think about, or maybe just a good laugh. It's a starting point for your own bibliography of reinvention. When you look up a title on Amazon.com, be alert to what customer reviewers say, and what other books the company also thinks are right for you. Likewise, explore the links from the sites I've named. Only you know which ones will ring your chimes. But they're all worth checking out.

GENERAL REFERENCES

AARP Okay, let's acknowledge right now that we're all way too young to join AARP, a nonprofit that provides services including insurance and investment products to Americans over fifty. Get over it, and send the group a check. The magazine and newsletter have interesting news and tips, and every year of membership,

I've saved more on rental cars and hotel rooms than I pay to belong (aarp.com).

The Baby Boomer Generation The big paisley letters announcing this blog say it all: Attitude is central to the discussion groups and reporting on pop culture for our generation (aginghipsters.com).

The Boomer Initiative This nonprofit, modeled after AARP, promotes the interests of the baby boom generation. Best bet: Click on your birth year for a "what happened when" list (babyboomers.com).

Boomernet Funky and nostalgic, subtitled "The Baby Boomers' Surfing Center," this site, more than ten years old, is a pioneer. There's a useful list of links to other boomer-friendly sites (boomernet.com).

Boomer Women Speak Women contribute stories from their lives, participate in forums (boomerwomenspeak.com). A sister site, National Association of Baby Boomer Women (from the same founder), offers info and discounts for a pricey membership fee (nabbw.com).

The Breaking Point: How Female Midlife Crisis Is Transforming Today's Women The *Wall Street Journal*'s "Work & Family" columnist Sue Shellenbarger interviewed women who've made stressful transitions at midlife.

The Complete Idiot's Guide to Reinventing Yourself You know life change is a revolution when it's become a title in this mega-series. The author is Jeff Davidson.

International Coach Federation This nonprofit certifies life coaches, making it a good starting point for finding a competent professional (coachfederation.com).

Inventing the Rest of Our Lives Suzanne Braun Levine, a former editor in chief at *Ms.* and a *More* contributing editor, gives smart advice to midlife women looking for adventure and satisfaction.

Life 2.0: How People Across America Are Transforming Their Lives by Finding the Where of Their Happiness *Forbes* magazine writer Rich Karlgaard examines the pluses and minuses of making a geographic move.

"Midlife in the United States" In one of the most important pieces of research on our generation, the MacArthur Foundation has funded a long-term big-picture study on what middle age is really all about (midmac.med.harvard.edu).

***More* Magazine** A general-interest magazine covering beauty, fashion, food, health, relationships, and news, it's the only one out there for boomer women. You can subscribe, and enter the annual over-forty model search or the over-forty marathon, on the Web site (more.com).

My Life in the Middle Ages Magazine writer James Atlas offers a series of insightful—though decidedly downbeat—essays about issues that arise in midlife.

Red Hat Society Founded in 1998 to challenge society's expectations about women over fifty, this group has grown to more than a million members in hundreds of chapters all over the United States, who wear brightly colored chapeaux and kick up their heels (redhatsociety.com).

Rules for Aging Award-winning *Time* writer Roger Rosenblatt gives us fifty-eight hilarious—and largely true—guidelines. Two examples: "Never do it for the money," and "Never work for anyone more insecure than yourself."

ThirdAge This Web site (thirdage.com) for men and women forty to sixty with sections on health, beauty, money, and work runs personals ads for midlifers in conjunction with eHarmony.com.

2Young2Retire A spunky site by a couple who reinvented their lives in their sixties, and now advocate finding new projects and passions. Check out the life reinvention stories in the section titled "Unretirement" (2young2retire.com).

WORK

Don't Retire, Rewire! Jeri Sedlar and Rick Miners, who own an executive search and transition coaching firm, lay out simple rules for finding satisfying work.

Now What? 90 Days to a New Life Direction by Laura Berman Fortgang. A life coach plots out a step-by-step game plan for reinvention.

The Reinvention of Work: A New Vision of Livelihood for Our Time Matthew Fox, an Episcopal priest, examines what makes a job spiritually meaningful.

Time Off for Good Behavior: How Hardworking Women Can Take a Break and Change Their Lives Mary Lou Quinlan took a sabbatical from her job running a major ad agency, and it changed her life. She profiles thirty-seven women who've made similar work reinventions. Men can benefit from the advice here, too.

The Transition Network Offering meetings, seminars, and an e-mail newsletter, this New York–based nonprofit helps women over fifty make life changes (thetransitionnetwork.org).

What Should I Do with My Life? Po Bronson conducted revealing interviews with men and women of all ages who've made significant life changes. Their stories made this book a best seller and a reinvention classic.

ADDING MEANING

BBB Wise Giving Alliance Charities that meet twenty standards set by the Better Business Bureau are listed here (give.org). You can also check out the worthiness of charities on Charitynavigator.org.

Ethical Wills: Putting Your Values on Paper Barry K. Baines, MD, offers tips on how to hand down your principles as well as your principal (ethicalwill.com).

Network for Good You can search for a specific nonprofit in your area, or fill out a quick profile and ask the Web site to suggest organizations where you can volunteer (networkforgood.org/volunteer).

Rockefeller Philanthropy Advisors This nonprofit offers research and counsel on making your charitable contributions count (rockpa.org).

EDUCATION

Association for Non-Traditional Students in Higher Education The Web site of this nonprofit, which advocates adult education, has a number of useful links to other organizations and institutions (antshe.org).

Back to College The Web site has a helpful Q&A and resources for returning college students, including sources of scholarships (back2college.com).

Languages Abroad The Web site is a solid introduction to the world of learning a language where it's spoken (languagesabroad.com).

National Registration Center for Study Abroad This non-profit places students in college in forty-two countries worldwide (studyabroad.nrcsa.com).

The Scholarship Book, 11th Edition: The Complete Guide to Private-Sector Scholarships, Fellowships, Grants, and Loans for the Undergraduate This classic remains the top resource for tracking down scholarships.

FAMILY

Adoption.com The leading resource for adoption information offers a reunion registration service where birth parents and kids can search for each other, and links to private investigators who can help.

Ancestry.com This commercial site can get you started tracing your family tree.

Classmates.com For a fee, this blast-from-the-past company will reconnect you with high school chums.

***Conceive* Magazine** Advice and information for couples confronting fertility issues (conceivemagazine.com).

Foundation for Grandparenting This nonprofit sponsors education, research, networking, and grandparents' rights (grandparenting.org).

Grandparents Magazine There's no print publication, just a lively online site with activities, resources, message boards, gift suggestions, and product reviews (grandparentsmagazine.net).

Grandparents Today Part of the iParenting Media Network's group of Web sites and publications, it encourages grandparents to have active relationships with their grandchildren (grandparentstoday.com).

Match.com Along with eHarmony.com, this is a major player in the online romance game.

Mothers Over 40 This UK-based site translates very well, with interesting info for and commentary by midlife parents (mothersover40.com).

My Boyfriend's Back After divorcing New York City Mayor Rudy Giuliani, Donna Hanover married her high school beau. Her book interviews other midlifers who've reunited with old flames.

Plum **Magazine** The American College of Obstetricians and Gynecologists publishes this glossy for pregnant women over thirty-five (plummagazine.com).

HEALTH

Fight Fat After Forty This is just one of several titles by marathoner Pamela Peeke, MD, who brings a refreshingly sensible perspective to weight maintenance at midlife.

Healthy Aging Harvard-trained MD and alternative medicine acolyte Andrew Weil creates a game plan for spiritual and physical well-being.

The RealAge Makeover Dr. Michael F. Roizen's angle on staying fit and youthful is calculating your "real age," predicated on how healthy your body is, which you can do on his Web site, Realage.com. He and fellow TV doc Mehmet Oz have collaborated on a latter-day *Our Bodies, Ourselves* called *YOU: The Owner's Manual.*

Sex and the Seasoned Woman Some reviewers have criticized Gail Sheehy for depicting midlife women as oversexed. But isn't that exactly what we need to correct the conventional wisdom that ardor dies at fifty?

The Wisdom of Menopause This classic from gynecologist Christiane Northrup—spiritual guru to a generation of women—demystified menopause when it was published in 2001. It is still the gold standard.

Younger Next Year The title might be oversell, but this book by Chris Crowley and Henry S. Lodge, MD, contains solid tips for living a healthy life. *Younger Next Year for Women* highlights gender-based guidelines.

Your Long Erotic Weekend Husband-and-wife sex therapists Lana Holstein and David Taylor, both MDs, run workshops at the Miraval spa. Midlifers themselves, they have smart advice for rekindling romance at any age.

TRAVEL

Abercrombie & Kent Here your adventure comes with a sizable splash of luxury. I did their spectacular gorilla-tracking trip in Uganda (abercrombiekent.com).

Condé Nast Traveler Magazine Best of the big American travel magazines (I ought to know; my daughter's an editor there), *Traveler* has a smart, sophisticated news section including an ombudsman service. Check out the Green List for winning ecotourism destinations, the Hot List for the best new hotels and resorts, and the Readers' Choice Awards winners for favorite places worldwide.

Destination Wedding Travel The Web site of a Boston-based travel agency that packages destination weddings around the world is a good starting place to shop for a ceremony (destinationweddings.com).

Elderhostel Trace Lewis and Clark's path, learn to paint on Nantucket, cycle through Germany and France . . . this nonprofit, which has been offering educational trips to an over-fifty-five audience for three decades, is catering these days to the lower end of its age group—us (elderhostel.org).

The Expert Expatriate: Your Guide to Successful Relocation Abroad Though aimed at people moving abroad for work, Melissa Brayer Hess and Patricia Linderman's book has practical information on settling into a new culture plus snapshots of expats' experiences.

Mountain Travel/Sobek I kayaked in Baja with this leading adventure travel outfitter, a trip notable as the only vacation where my husband ever slept in a tent (mtsobek.com).

Under the Tuscan Sun American food writer Frances Mayes restores a house in a picturesque town in Tuscany.

Wilderness Travel I used this well-respected outfitter, which offers soft-adventure trips worldwide, to climb Kilimanjaro (wildernesstravel.com).

A Year in Provence Peter Mayle's first book about moving to southern France is his best, a rollicking account of expat life.

PASSIONS, GOING TO EXTREMES

Experimental Aircraft Association This nonprofit (eaa.org) promotes aircraft homebuilding, publishes the magazine *Sport Pilot,* and sponsors one of the world's biggest air shows every summer, in Oshkosh, Wisconsin.

The Outdoor Life Network Inspiration for the adrenaline-inclined, the fast-growing cable channel OLN televises National Hockey League games, the Tour de France, the America's Cup, and the Boston Marathon (olntv.com).

Last Minute Flight Circle-Pacific tickets and other last-minute long-haul bargains (cirpac.com).

Thrill Planet Purveyor of a dozen adrenaline activities from rock climbing to bull riding (thrillplanet.com).

Acknowledgments

THIS BOOK COULDN'T have happened without the generous help of friends and colleagues across the country who answered my e-mails and calls seeking reinventers. I am grateful to everyone who introduced me to a Life Entrepreneur, and especially to the men and women who took time out of their exciting new lives to share their stories with me. They are the stars of this book, and I am humbled and delighted to be their casting director.

Thanks to my agent, Lisa DiMona, the matchmaker who brought together an idea that was percolating in my brain and a publisher who was seeking an author for the very book I wanted to write. Not only did she dispatch the e-mail that got this project rolling; she and her partners at Lark Productions made me keep redoing the proposal until I finally got it right. Thanks to my editor, Leslie Pockell, and the rest of the team at Warner Books, for creating a cover that I loved immediately (everybody thinks that exuberant woman riding shotgun is me) and shepherding my words from manuscript to print. The editors at *More* and *AARP* magazines helped move my thinking along by assigning me articles that dovetailed with the topics in this book.

Finally, thanks to my first reader and toughest editor, my daughter, Brook. It was a busman's holiday from her day job as

281

an editor at *Conde Nast Traveler* to spend evenings and week-ends making sure her mother doesn't look foolish—well, not *too* foolish—in print. We've done so much together—bungee jumping, skydiving, rock-climbing, white-water rafting—I'm glad she's had a central role in this adrenaline rush, too.

Index

283